Edward C. Downs

Four Years a Scout and Spy

Edward C. Downs

Four Years a Scout and Spy

ISBN/EAN: 9783337087494

Printed in Europe, USA, Canada, Australia, Japan

Cover: Foto ©ninafisch / pixelio.de

More available books at **www.hansebooks.com**

FOUR YEARS
A SCOUT AND SPY.

"GENERAL BUNKER,"

ONE OF LIEUT. GENERAL GRANT'S MOST DARING AND SUCCESSFUL SCOUTS.

BEING A NARRATIVE OF THE THRILLING ADVENTURES, NARROW ESCAPES,
NOBLE DARING, AND AMUSING INCIDENTS IN THE EXPERIENCE
OF CORPORAL RUGGLES DURING FOUR YEARS' SERVICE
AS A SCOUT AND SPY FOR THE FEDERAL ARMY;

EMBRACING HIS SERVICES FOR
TWELVE OF THE MOST DISTINGUISHED GENERALS IN THE U. S. ARMY

By E. C. DOWNS,
MAJOR OF THE TWENTIETH OHIO VETERAN VOLUNTEER INFANTRY.

Illustrated.

ZANESVILLE, OHIO:
PUBLISHED BY HUGH DUNNE,
NORTH FOURTH STREET, ADJOINING COURT HOUSE.
1866.

Entered according to Act of Congress, in the year 1866, by

E. C. DOWNS,

In the Clerk's Office of the United States District Court, for the Southern District of Ohio.

STEREOTYPED AT THE
FRANKLIN TYPE FOUNDRY,
CINCINNATI, O.

TO

LIEUTENANT-GENERAL U. S. GRANT,

*Whose undaunted energy, heroic valor, superior generalship,
and devotion to his country,
have proved him*

"THE RIGHT MAN IN THE RIGHT PLACE,"

And won for him

A WORLD-WIDE FAME;

*And to the gallant Officers and Soldiers
who have nobly assisted in sustaining our glorious nationality
by crushing the great rebellion,*

THIS VOLUME IS RESPECTFULLY DEDICATED.

1

PREFACE.

It was with much difficulty that I was induced to give to the public a narrative of my experience as a scout and spy. It was the intense interest with which the people have listened to my narratives, whenever I have related them, and their earnest entreaties to have them published, that have prevailed upon me to do so.

I entered the army from purely patriotic motives. I had no vain ambition to gratify, but simply a desire to sustain and perpetuate the noble institutions that had been purchased by the blood of our fathers. I valued the cause of liberty as well worth all the sacrifice that it might cost to save it. I saw at once that the conflict was to be one involving great principles, and that in the end Truth and Justice *must prevail*.

The part that I have borne in putting down the great rebellion is the one that naturally fell to me by the force of circumstances, and entirely unsolicited. My relation in the affairs of life seems to have been such as to have just adapted me to that part that fell to my lot to act.

I have, without doubt, been indiscreet at times. Who has not? But the reader must remember that he who goes from the peaceful pursuits of life, for the first time, to engage in the art of war, does so with a lack of experience. Soldiering was not my trade. War is demoralizing in its tendency. This fact, I trust, will very much lessen any feelings of prejudice that may arise, in the course of these narratives, from passages clothed with the rough-and-tumble of army life.

Rough language and blunt manners are characteristics of war, because its tendency is to destroy the finer feelings of our natures. Some of the language used is of that character, and it would fail to be a truthful representation of the reality if rendered less so. The incidents that I have narrated are all of them facts that have occurred in my experience, and, without further apology, I submit them to an indulgent public.

LORAIN RUGGLES.

CONTENTS.

CHAPTER I.

Parentage—Early discipline—Childhood incidents—Subsequent occupations—Driven from Mississippi—Works on rebel fortifications—Escape to Illinois—Enlists as a soldier—Supposed to have deserted—How he got his name—Examination by the Surgeon—Roster of the Regiment...................... 11

CHAPTER II.

Moves to Cincinnati—Detailed to guard the forts—Meets a secesh lady—First scout—Unexpected visit of the Colonel—The drill—Bad report—The mischief investigated—Attempts to discover the rogues—Innocent man accused—The accusers skedaddle—Who got the chickens....................... 22

CHAPTER III.

"Marching orders"—Arrives at Fort Donelson—The surrender—Goes North with prisoners—Meets an old friend as a rebel Captain—The Captain attempts to bribe him—Expedition up the Tennessee River—Touching incident—Battle of Shiloh—Captures an Enfield—Recommended as a scout.... 30

CHAPTER IV

Rumored attack upon Grand Junction—"General Bunker" sent out as spy—Passes himself as a rebel soldier—Falls in with rebel cavalry—Visits a rebel camp—Attempts to deprive him of his revolver—Discovers a Yankee forage party—Undertakes to return—Captured by Yankees, and robbed of his revolver and money—Passes as a rebel spy—Sent to the Provost-marshal—Sent to General Hurlbut—Returned to Grand Junction... 38

CHAPTER V.

Fired at by a citizen—The sick overseer—How he was cured—Pickets fired on—Trip to White Church—Visits General Van Dorn—Meets a rebel spy—Reports to General Leggett—Grand Junction evacuated—Again sees the rebel spy—Attempt to arrest him—Drinks wine with the rebel General Jackson—Discovers a hole in the fence.................................... 53

CHAPTER VI.

The value of the Oath—Attempt to take "Bunker's" life—Sent to Grand Junction—The hazardous ride—Shoots the picket—The chase—Unfortunate occurrence—The chase abandoned—Meets with guerrillas—They invite him to drink—Renewed vigilance—The battle of Middleburg.................... 69

CHAPTER VII.

Attempts to visit the enemy's camp—Learns the strength and position of the enemy—Return intercepted—Perilous situation—Loses his mule—Frightened by men of his own regiment—The plan to capture the enemy—The negro's report—The forces discovered—Disposes of a rebel picket—Reports his discovery... 76

CHAPTER VIII.

Sent to find the enemy's pickets—Suspicious circumstance—Sick child—Captures three citizens standing picket—Releases them—Falls asleep—Perilous situation—Fortunate turn of affairs—Attack on the pickets—A very pious man—He proves a rebel spy... 85

CHAPTER IX.

Sent to Somerville—Finds himself a prisoner—Taken to Cold Water—Meets with old acquaintances—Is paroled—Runs with the 2d Arkansas Cavalry—Goes to Lumpkins' Mills—Interview with General Price—Stays all night with his brother, the rebel General—Return to Bolivar—Reports to General Ross—"Steals the Colonel's horse," and returns to the enemy—Runs away from the enemy....................................... 93

CHAPTER X.

Sent to Grand Junction to capture guerrillas—Suspicious incident—Strategy to get out the guerrillas—Orders disobeyed—The rebel flag—The very kind secesh lady—The mistake—Out of the frying-pan into the fire—Guerrillas watching for them—The attack—The prisoner—Result of the trip............ 103

CHAPTER XI.

Sent to Lagrange—Observes two cavalrymen—Arrival at Lagrange—Waits for the cavalry—Accompanies them out—Takes his departure—Is pursued—Evades the pursuit—Finds himself cornered—Crosses the Cypress Swamp—Robbed by outlaws—Disloyal citizen—The fate of the robbers............... 115

CHAPTER XII.

Starts to find General Bragg's forces—"Wools" the secesh farmer—Receives a bottle of rum—Guerrillas washing stockings—Finds Bragg's advance—Recognized as a Yankee spy—Ordered off his mule to be shot—The clamor of the crowd—Recognized as a Confederate spy—Rebel Surgeon vouches for him—Is released—Gray-headed rebel brought to justice—The Sutler of the 2d Arkansas Cavalry a prisoner—What became of the guerrillas that were washing stockings.................... 127

CHAPTER XIII.

Reconnoiters Hickory Flats with a squad of seven men—Shoots at the mark—Orders to march with two days' rations—Cause of the alarm—Reconnoiter beyond Whitesville—Major Mudd's trap—"Bunker" entices the rebs into it—Rides into the trap behind a rebel Captain—Sent out beyond Pocahontas—Passes as a rebel artillerist—Secesh citizen stands guard for him—The very kind secesh lady—The anxious wife—Discovers guerrillas burning a human being..................... 139

CHAPTER XIV.

Starts on a trip for General Lauman—His instructions—A Confederate widow—Discovers a squad of rebel soldiers—Captures part of their arms—Learns the whereabouts of guerrillas—Attempt to capture them—Guerrillas escape—Captures a prisoner—Cause of guerrillas' escape—The "General" and squad get arrested—The charges and specifications................ 157

CHAPTER XV.

Unfortunate state of affairs—Informality of charge and specifications—Assistance of friends—Fails to get a trial—Gloomy prospects—Evidence accumulates—Guard-house incident—The "General" concludes to help himself—Narrow escape from guerrillas—The capture—Reaches his regiment—Himself and squad released.. 169

CHAPTER XVI.

Starts for Grenada—Instructions—Is captured—Returns to Water Valley—Starts again—Arrives at Grenada—Condition of Price's army—He returns—Again sent to Grenada—Proposes some fun—Plan of strategy—Plan unnecessary—Returns with rebel cavalry—Bivouac at Big Springs—The attack—More fun than bargained for—The result............................. 182

CHAPTER XVII.

The forage party—Runaways—Daring scout—Narrow escape—The line of battle—Safe return—Scout reports—Assumes the character of a rebel prisoner—Finds a friend—How he introduced himself—Where he belongs—The burning of Holly Springs—The heroine—What she captured—Shows partiality—Offers assistance—Rebel doctor executed........................ 192

CHAPTER XVIII.

Arrival in Memphis—Daring robbery—Detailed by the Provost-marshal General—Assumes the character of a rebel Major—Secesh acquaintances—Captures a rebel mail—A jollification—A rebel trader—Plan to run the pickets—The escape of the outlaws.. 204

CHAPTER XIX.

Reports to Major-General McPherson—Instructions—Disguise—Starts for Vicksburg—Changes his route—Reports to General Denver—Acquaintance with a cotton-buyer—Plan to make money—Visits guerrilla Sol. Street—The arrangement consummated—Visit to General Price—Arrival at Jackson—Robbed of his field-glasses—Introduction to President Davis—Visit to Vicksburg—Visit to Edwards' Station—Meets his bear-hunting comrades—Visits Black River bridge—Robbed

of his horse—The return—Reports to General McPherson—
Reports to General Grant............................ 217

CHAPTER XX.

Return to Mississippi—Instructions—Visit to Troy—Movement of cavalry—Reports to General Denver—Is arrested—Federal cavalry driven back—Is released—Visits Greenwood—Journey to the Mississippi River—The perilous crossing—Again arrested—Interview with Gen. Prentiss—Takes the oath of allegiance—Meets a friend—Makes his escape—Reports to Gen. Grant.. 233

CHAPTER XXI.

Return to the regiment—The Henry rifle—The march from Milliken's Bend—The tug of war—The army crosses the Mississippi—Capture of Port Gibson—Battle of Raymond—Amusing Capture—The charge on Jackson—Battle of Champion Hills—The rebel courier—Sharp-shooting—The gallant charge—The march to Vicksburg—The place besieged............... 245

CHAPTER XXII.

First sharp-shooting at Vicksburg—Silences two guns—The riflepit—Shoots a Carolinian—The Carolinian's comrade—Outshoots a squad of sixteen—The defiant rebel—Shoots for Gens. McPherson and Logan—Beats the Parrot rifles—Joke on the Adjutant-General—Visit to Admiral Porter—The French spy—The disclosures—Capture of a rebel dispatch—The fate of the spy.. 259

CHAPTER XXIII.

Sent for by General Grant—Instructions—Crosses Black River—Is captured by rebel cavalry—Sent to General DeVieu—The interview—Passes as Johnston's spy—The attempt to escape—The pursuit—Fired at by Federal pickets—Again fired at by the enemy—The pursuers driven back—Again fired at by Federal pickets—The alarm—Reports to General Osterhaus—Reports to General Grant............................ 275

CHAPTER XXIV.

Visit to Chickasaw Landing—Surrender of Vicksburg—Visit to the city—The paroled Major—The Yankee trick—Returns to Vicksburg—Made detective—Is sent to Yazoo City—Attends a guerrilla organization—Makes them a speech—Returns to Vicksburg. 286

CHAPTER XXV.

Taken sick with the ague—Encounters his Satanic Majesty—The Devil afraid of General Grant—Expedition to Bogue Chitto Creek—Captures a rebel Colonel—Enlists as a veteran—Makes a speech to the soldiers............................. 295

CHAPTER XXVI.

Frightened by a dead Colonel—Burns Confederate corn in face of the enemy—Gets into a tight place—A frightened Major—Captures information—A headstrong Captain gobbled up—Captures a rebel Provost-marshal General—Encounter with General Ross' cavalry—A strange adventure—Races with a rebel Colonel—A hard-hearted woman.................. 305

CHAPTER XXVII.

Starts home on veteran furlough—Trouble at the table—Bluffs the Captain—Suspected of being a rebel spy—Commissioned officer serves him at the table—Kind attentions at home—Silences an old maid—Returns to the front—Shot at twenty-one times—The remedy—A Union lady—The dwarf weaver—The weaver beheaded—Goes into Marietta as a spy—Confederate side of the lines—Escape from the rebs—General McPherson's death—Hard fighting............................... 331

CHAPTER XXVIII.

Goes to Ohio to recruit—Raises twenty-one men—Difficulty with the Governor—Visits Lieutenant-General Grant—Order from the War Department—Again in difficulty—Runs away from the Governor—Reports to General Sherman—Georgia raid—An amusing coincident—Reports to General Granger, at Mobile—Reports to General Grierson, in Texas—Makes a trip to the Upper Colorado—Incident at General Grant's head-quarters—The war over................................. 358

CHAPTER XXIX.

Ludicrous effect of fear—A Corporal outflanks a Captain—A good Union man—A touching appeal—A scene among the wounded—An old Secesh discovers his mistake—Suggestions from experience—Concluding thoughts........................... 390

INTRODUCTION.

LORAIN RUGGLES was enlisted by me in December, 1861, at Columbus, Ohio. The name of "General Bunker" was given to him by the men in his company, and it was by that name that he was most generally known in the army, and very many knew him by no other name.

Mr. Ruggles is a man possessed of great presence of mind, a strong memory, and not a little of native wit, and great power of physical endurance. These, with his knowledge of the Southern people and country, admirably fitted him for the duties of a scout.

The narratives here related are of facts that actually occurred in his experience, and very many of them are as well authenticated as any facts in history can be. There has been no aim at making this a work of general history, but simply a narrative of personal experience, coupled with only so much of the general history of the war as is necessary to explain the cause of the events that transpired in his experience. Many of these are incidents of daring that are without parallel in the scout service. The following testimonials of the value of his services and the truthfulness of his reports will be read with interest:

"HEAD-QUARTERS 1ST BRIGADE, 3D DIVISION,
"17TH ARMY CORPS, December, 11, 1863.

"*Captain E. C. Downs, 20th Ohio:*

"CAPTAIN—I have known Mr. Ruggles since December, 1861, when your company was first mustered. I remember very well his first expedition as a spy, in June, 1862, when the 20th was at Grand Junction, then an exposed outpost, under command of General Leggett.

"Since that time he has been continually employed on such duty, often on expeditions of extreme hazard. He has shown as much address as daring. Many a camp-fire has been enlivened with stories of his adventures while commanding officers have set high value upon his reports.

"I remember Mr. Ruggles as one of our best sharp-shooters in the war. His skill as a sharp-shooter, as well as scout, often got him leave to go out from the line on somewhat independent duty. At Champion Hills I gave him leave to go out with company A, which was sent out as skirmishers to open the way for an advance, on account of his skill.

"At the siege of Vicksburg, he had a special permanent permission to be among the sharp-shooters on the advanced lines. On the day of the general but unsuccessful charge in May, he was mainly instrumental in driving away the artillerists from two of the enemy's guns on the right of the Jackson road.

"His Henry rifle, given to him by General Grant, was one of the marked pieces among the sharp-shooters of the 17th Corps at that siege.

"Very respectfully, your ob't serv't,

"M. F. FORCE,

"*Brig.-Gen'l Vols., late Colonel 20th Ohio.*"

"HEAD-QUARTERS 3D DIV., 17TH ARMY CORPS,
"VICKSBURG, MISS., December 7, 1863.

"*Captain E. C. Downs:*

"DEAR SIR—Mr. Ruggles (or 'General Bunker,' as he is better known) has acted as scout and spy for me on very many occasions since the early part of June, 1862, and is now acting in that capacity. In this character he has been remarkably successful, seldom ever failing to satisfactorily accomplish the mission on which he was sent.

"Many scenes of his life as a spy are intensely interesting. It has been my fortune to meet in life very few persons who could so successfully act an assumed character.

"At some future time, I shall probably be at liberty to relate a few incidents of considerable interest in his career, of which he himself is as yet ignorant.

"Very respectfully,

"M. D. LEGGETT,

"*Brigadier-General.*

"MEMPHIS, TENN., November 28, 1863.

"*Captain E. C. Downs:*

"DEAR SIR—You wrote me sometime since, inquiring as to the services of Mr. Ruggles as a scout and spy for the Union army. In reply I would state that Mr. Ruggles was a superior man for the work assigned him, and the information obtained through him of the movements of the enemy was always reliable.

"In the discharge of his duties, he was active, energetic, and heroically brave. His gallantry in the service deserves honorable mention in the work of which you speak.

'I am truly yours, etc.,

"LEEMAN F. ROSS."

"HEAD-QUARTERS 17TH ARMY CORPS,
"DEPARTMENT OF THE TENNESSEE,
"VICKSBURG, MISS., December 15, 1863.

"*To whom it may concern:*

"This is to certify that Mr. Ruggles has been employed by me at various times during the past year, and I have always found him brave, adventurous, and truthful.

"His services as a scout have been very important, and he deserves well of the military authorities.

"JAS. B. MCPHERSON,
"*Major-General.*"

"ZANESVILLE, O., July 31, 1866.
"*Major E. C. Downs:*

"DEAR SIR—It affords me pleasure to state that I am personally acquainted with Mr. Lorain Ruggles, known in the army as 'General Bunker.' He belonged to my command, and I know he was regarded as one of the most intrepid scouts in the 17th Army Corps. He was in high favor with all our general officers, and I think rendered more efficient service in the capacity of scout and spy than any man with whom I am acquainted. He certainly deserves well of his country.

"I never knew him to give false intelligence, and in his forthcoming work should recommend it as a truthful narrative of his personal adventures, many of which I am known to.

"G. F. WILES,
"*Late Colonel 78th O. V. V. I., and Brevet Brig.-General.*"

"CARROLLTON, OHIO, June 27, 1866.

"*Major E. C. Downs, Zanesville, Ohio:*

"MAJOR—I am glad to add my testimony to the reputation of 'Bunker' as a scout and spy. I believe him to have been the most reliable and successful scout in the Western army.

"'Bunker' had the confidence of Lieut.-General Grant and Major-Generals McPherson and Logan, which he earned by skillful labor during the campaign which resulted in the capture of Vicksburg and its garrison. 'Bunker' deserves well of his country. Yours truly,

"B. F. POTTS,
"*Late Brevet Major-General U. S. Vols.*"

"CARBONDALE, ILL., July 1, 1866.

"*Major Downs:*

"DEAR SIR—I am well acquainted with Mr. Ruggles, or, as we called him in the army, 'General Bunker.' He was certainly a very excellent scout, and performed great service in that branch of duties. He served as scout for me, as well as for many others, and at all times performed his part well, ran great risks; was not only a good scout, but one of the best sharp-shooters perhaps in the army.

"Yours truly,

"JOHN A. LOGAN."

"WASHINGTON, D. C., July 9, 1865.

"*Major E. C. Downs:*

"DEAR SIR—In the work of which you speak, you are at liberty to refer to me concerning the value of the services rendered by Mr. Ruggles as a scout and spy. His reports were always reliable, and were held in high estimation by me.

"Yours truly,

"U. S. GRANT,
"*Lieutenant-General U. S. A.*"

Such testimonials as the foregoing give the narratives contained in the following pages a reputation of reliability that can not be doubted. Whenever a mission of great danger was to be executed, Mr. Ruggles was the man that was usually chosen to perform it. His quick comprehension and heroic daring enabled him to address himself to the work, which he rarely ever failed to accomplish. Often the boldness of his designs proved to be the reason of his success. Very few have equaled, while none have excelled, him in that line of duty. Many of the incidents in his experience are so wonderful that in them the "truth seems stranger than fiction."

THE AUTHOR.

FOUR YEARS A SCOUT AND SPY.

CHAPTER I.

Parentage—Early discipline—Childhood incidents—Subsequent occupations—Driven from Mississippi—Works on rebel fortifications—Escape to Illinois—Enlists as a soldier—Supposed to have deserted—How he got his name—Examination by the Surgeon—Roster of the Regiment.

I WAS born in the town of Copley, in what is now known as Summit County, Ohio, on the 17th day of June, 1823, and at the time that I entered the army I was thirty-nine years of age. My father's name was Alfred Ruggles. At the time of his death he was living with his second wife. His family numbered twelve sons and seven daughters. I am the youngest of seven children by my father's second wife.

My father was a blacksmith by trade, and all of his sons, except myself, were learned the trade, under his personal instruction. Lorenzo Ruggles, my father's second son by his first wife, after having finished his trade, was sent to college and educated. He is the General Ruggles of the Confederate army.

When I was ten years of age my father died, leaving a large farm disposed of by a will. The children went to law, and spent the entire property in breaking the will and settling the estate. In consequence of that I was thrown upon my own labor for my support at a very early age.

My father was an old-fashioned strict disciplinarian; in the government of his family "he ruled with an iron hand." His government was not only rigid but chilling. The deviation of a hair from the paternal command was usually followed by a whipping, and sometimes one was administered without proper investigation.

People often ask me, "What is the essential qualification of a good spy?" My answer is, "It requires an *accomplished liar*." I mean by that, a man that can *successfully practice deception*. I do not mean by that that a man must be an *habitual liar*. There is nothing that I despise more than a man whose word can not be relied upon. Whether deception, as I have practiced it in the discharge of my duty as a spy, is a moral wrong, I shall not here attempt to argue. Of this much I am sure: it has many times saved my life, and perhaps the lives of thousands of others, besides saving immense sums of money to the Government.

Whatever of the art of deception I possess has been somewhat shaped by the chilling discipline administered to me by my father. An incident or two from my early life will serve to show what that discipline was, and what effect it may have had in my after career.

In my childhood days I was noted as "a mischievous boy." I suppose that means that I was constantly devising or hunting some sort of diversion. My father usually kept wrought nails of his own manufacture to sell to his customers. These I used to get and drive into the fence, firewood, shade-trees, or any thing else that came in my way. This my father had forbidden me to do, but sometimes the impulse of the moment would cause me to break over, and as often I would be whipped for my disobedience.

One day, as my father was going away from home he charged me particularly not to go into the shop during his absence. While he was gone I became so much interested in play that I never thought of going to the shop. Near the close of the day my father returned, and it so happened that he needed a few wrought nails to use the first thing after his arrival. On going to the shop after some, he found his nail-box empty. His last impression, on leaving, had been that I *would* get them, and now his first impression was that I *had* got them. Consequently, I was immediately summoned to give an account of them.

"My son, what made you go into the shop during my absence?" inquired my father.

"Father, I did not go into the shop," I replied.

"Somebody has been there and carried off my nails. Nobody else was here but you; you *must be* the one that got them."

"I did not get them, father; neither did I go to the shop. I certainly did not."

My father knew that I had been in the habit of getting them, and, though he had never known me to tell him a willful lie, nevertheless, he thought that I had carried off his nails. I had not only disobeyed, but had lied about it. It was too aggravated an offense to let pass without punishment. Taking a hickory gun-wiper that stood in a corner of the shop, he gave me a severe whipping, and then said, "Lorain, what did you do with the nails?" Again I denied getting them, and again he whipped me, which was repeated several times. At length "forbearance ceased to be a virtue"—at least, my poor back *felt so*—and I said to him, "Father, if you won't whip me any more, I'll tell you what I did with them."

"Well, what did you do with them?"

"*I drove them into the grind-stone block.*"

After having talked to me about the wickedness of telling a lie, he sent me into the house, little thinking that he had been *forcing me to tell one*.

The next morning, as I was standing by, a customer entered the shop for some nails. He had called the day before, and finding nobody present, and needing them for immediate use, took all that he could find, weighed them, and returned home. "There, father," said I, "I told you that I did not get your nails!" His heart smote him for the whipping that he had given me, and he wept like a child. The incident, however, had its effect, and not many days passed until I was again placed on trial.

Myself and sister Electa attended the district school. Our nearest neighbor, Mr. Moss, had a daughter about the age of my sister, who used to attend the same school; her name was Cordelia. She was a very proud-spirited girl, and improved every opportunity to show off. Her mother bought her a new work-pocket; this she would frequently display, and say to my sister, in a proud, haughty way, "You haint got no new work-pocket bought out of the store." It displeased me considerably to have her assume to be any better than my sister; so I resolved to stop it at the first opportunity.

One day, as we were returning from school we espied a squirrel that had taken refuge in a small tree by the roadside. Cordelia laid her work-pocket at the roots of the tree, and she and my sister mounted the fence, and commenced to climb the tree to catch it. Discovering the work-pocket, I picked it up unperceived, and started on. Coming to a bank of loose earth, where a tree had been recently uprooted by the wind, I buried it, and then returned toward my companions and called to them to come along. The girls had started to overtake me, when Cordelia, missing her work-pocket, returned to get it. She searched for it a long time, but without success. Failing to find it, she accused me of getting it, which I stoutly denied. At last, complaint was made to my father. Both of the girls had seen it lying near the tree, but neither of them had seen me have it. My father asked me what I had done with it; but I denied having seen it. "You *must* have taken it," said the old man, "for nobody else was there that could have taken it."

"I *must* have got the nails too," I replied. This outflanked him; he remembered having whipped me once wrongfully, and feared a repetition of the same thing. The result was I evaded punishment, and my father never found out what I had done with the work-pocket.

The next summer, after my father's death, I hired out on board of one of the packet-boats running on the Ohio Canal, as cabin-boy. I continued for three summers to follow the canal in that capacity, and for four summers following I was a canal driver. The last three seasons I drove the same team, and at the end of the third season I received from the Transportation Company a prize of ten dollars for having kept my team in the best order.

The winter following, my seventh season on the canal, I went down the Mississippi River to Arkansas, and spent the season chopping steamboat wood. While thus employed on Island Twenty-eight, I had the fortune to kill a very large black bear, which I sold to a steamboat captain for what seemed to me at that time a great price. The incident turned my attention to trapping and bear-hunting. I spent several successive winters in hunting and trapping in the wilds of Arkansas. In the winter of 1851 and 1852 I was employed in hunting wild hogs in the Yazoo bottoms for a man in Vicksburg, Miss. I was thus engaged at the same time that the fourteen French hunters were killed by wild hogs in the Yazoo bottoms. I spent one year as an overseer for Mr. James Ford, of Memphis, Tenn., on the French palace plantation, near the fort of Island No. 60. My summers were usually spent on the Mississippi and its tributaries. In the summer of 1859 I went to

Pike's Peak, and thence to Salt Lake. The winter of 1860 and 1861 I was at work on White River, Ark., and had several hands at work with me, filling a contract for shingles for a man by the name of Hanner, in Bolivar County, Mississippi.

In the spring, I commenced to deliver the shingles, but Mr. Hanner refused to receive them, on the ground that the country was engaged in war. His refusal to receive them provoked me, and I said to him, "All you need is a good thrashing, and then you'll behave yourself and not talk so." That enraged him, and he turned and left me, muttering vengeance as he went. An hour later he returned with a party of men, threatening to hang me if he should catch me, but I was not to be found. Mr. Hanner did not accuse me of being an abolitionist or a Northern man. He was soon after made Colonel of the 17th Mississippi Zouaves. Knowing that my life was in danger there, I made my way to Memphis, Tenn.

At Memphis, Tenn., I found the secession element decidedly too hot for me. I saw no other way for me to do but "aid and comfort" the secession movement or leave the country.

Lying at the levee was a steamboat just getting up steam, destined, it was said, for St. Louis, Mo. She had on board a cargo of picks, spades, wheelbarrows, and whisky. I took passage in her and went to Columbus, Ky., and there she stopped and commenced to discharge her cargo. I soon learned that she was going no further.

At that place I came across Mr. James Ford, for

whom I had been an overseer on the French palace plantation. He gave me a warm greeting, and said that he was glad that I had come. He was at that time in command of the post, and engaged in fortifying the place. He persuaded me to take charge of a gang of negroes and work on the forts, which I did, to kill all suspicion until an opportunity occurred for me to escape. When I had been there engaged for five days, the steamboat Amelia came up the river and landed, on her way to Cairo, Ill. I happened to know the pilot, and told him that I was in a tight place, and by his assistance I secreted myself on board the boat and went to Cairo. It was the last steamer that was allowed to pass by Columbus, Ky., until the place was captured by the Federal army.

From Cairo I went to Toledo, O. Recruiting for the Federal army was going on rapidly all over the North. In the fall of 1861 I visited the principal cities in Ohio, in search of a company of sharpshooters, in which to enlist. I found several such organizations, but none of them were officered by men that suited me. In the month of December, while at Columbus, Ohio, I met Lieutenant Downs, of the 20th Ohio Volunteer Infantry, with a squad of ten men, on his way to Trumbull County to recruit. Liking his appearance and that of his men, I enlisted, on condition that he would furnish me with an Enfield rifle.

From Columbus we took the first train of cars to Cleveland; it was late in the evening when we arrived. Passing a boot and shoe store that was yet open, I obtained leave of the Lieutenant to stop and purchase a pair of boots before going to our place of lodging. The Lieutenant and party did not stop, but continued on to the hotel where we were to stop. After having purchased a pair of boots, I got into an interesting conversation with the shopkeeper, and remained somewhat longer than was necessary. I had been intrusted to the care of Corporal Grinnell by the Lieutenant, and my long absence had created a suspicion in the mind of the Corporal that I had deserted. He had also heard Lieutenant Bostwick, while in Columbus, advise Lieutenant Downs not to enlist me, for fear I would run away. At last he started out with three men in search of me, and found me still at the shop. I have since had many a joke with Lieutenant Bostwick and Corporal Grinnell about their suspecting that I would desert. They have been among my warmest friends in the army. The next morning, at eleven o'clock, we reached Warren. At that place the party dispersed to their homes, and I was furnished boarding at the Eagle House, where I remained for ten days.

On Monday, January 8, 1862, we met to go to the regiment, then at Camp King, near Covington, Ky. The squad had increased by accession of recruits to twenty men. Our journey passed off pleasantly, and in two days' time we reached our regiment. The party that went home with the Lieutenant had carried their knapsacks with them; not knowing at that time the name for them, I asked the Lieutenant if he had a "Bunker Hill" for me to wear on my back. From that I received the name of "Bunker," and have been more generally known by that name in the army than any other.

The next morning after our arrival in camp, we were marched over to the Surgeon's quarters for examination. From a list of names that the Lieutenant had handed him, the Surgeon called "Lorain Ruggles!"

"Here I am, Doctor," I answered; "what do you want of me?"

"I want to examine you, and see if you are sound."

"Oh, that's it, is it. You need not be to that trouble, I'm *sound* enough."

"Well, but I must *see* whether you are sound or not; hold out your hands; work your fingers; touch your hands over your head."

Going through the motions, I added, "*Oh, I tell you that I am all right.*"

"Are you ruptured," he continued.

"*Ruptured!* what is that?"

"Are you bursted?"

"No, I ain't *quite* busted yet; I've a couple of dollars left."

"You don't understand me, Mr. Ruggles," continued the surgeon, placing his hands on my abdomen. "Are your *bowels* all right?"

"*Oh, I understand you now! They are a little thin; the rations don't relish well yet.*"

The doctor succeeded at last in making me understand, and having finished his examination, we were accepted as a soldier in the United States army.

Like all other recruits, as soon as mustered in I was placed under drill. To me the "steps" and "facings," "times" and "motions," were perfectly incomprehensible. I formed a dislike to them that I could never get over. I was expert in the forest at handling my piece, and I did not see why the same times and motions that would kill a bear would not kill a "reb."

The following is a list of the commissioned officers that were in the 20th Ohio Volunteer Infantry at the time that I entered it:

CHARLES WHITTLESY, Colonel,
M. F. FORCE, Lt. Colonel,
J. N. McELROY, Major,
E. L. HILL, Surgeon,
J. G. PURPLE, Asst. Surgeon,
E. N. OWEN, Adjutant,
P. M. HITCHCOCK, Qr.-Master,
JAMES KNAPP, Chaplain.

Elisha Hiatt,	Captain	Co.	A.	W. W. Updegraff,	Captain	Co.	F.
William Rogers,	1st Lt.	"	"	D. R. Hume,	1st Lt.	"	"
L. N. Ayres,	2d Lt.	"	"	W. D. Neal,	2d Lt.	"	"
John C. Fry,	Captain	"	B.	J. N. Cassel,	Captain	"	G.
A. J. Edwards,	1st Lt.	"	"	G. L. Melick,	1st Lt.	"	"
R. M. Colby,	2d Lt.	"	"	Nathan Bostwick,	2d Lt.	"	"
J. M. McCoy,	Captain	"	C.	James Powers,	Captain	"	H.
Z. P. Atkins,	1st Lt.	"	"	E. C. Downs,	1st Lt.	"	"
Conrad Garris,	2d Lt.	"	"	H. M. Davis,	2d Lt.	"	"
C. H. McElroy,	Captain	"	D.	F. M. Shaklee,	Captain	"	I.
V. T. Hills,	1st Lt.	"	"	Harrison Wilson,	1st Lt.	"	"
Henry Sherman,	2d Lt.	"	"	W. L. Waddell,	2d Lt.	"	"
George Rogers,	Captain	"	E.	Abraham Kaga,	Captain	"	K.
B. A. F. Greer,	1st Lt.	"	"	David Rhinehart,	1st Lt.	"	"
W. H. Jacobs,	2d Lt.	"	"	Seneca Hale,	2d Lt.	"	"

CHAPTER II.

Moves to Cincinnati—Detailed to guard the forts—Meets a secesh lady—First scout—Unexpected visit of the Colonel—The drill—Bad report—The mischief investigated—Attempts to discover the rogues—Innocent man accused—The accusers skedaddle—Who got the chickens.

SHORTLY after I joined the regiment it moved to the city barracks in Cincinnati, Ohio. It was the duty of the regiment at that time to guard the fortifications that had been built to protect the cities of Cincinnati, Covington, and Newport. Not long after we arrived at the barracks, company "H," to which I belonged, was detailed for a three days' tour at guarding the line of defenses. Lieutenant Downs, with a squad consisting of three sergeants and twenty-seven men, were sent to guard that part of the defenses known as the Three-mile Batteries. I was one of the squad.

These batteries formed a chain of defenses running eastward from the Licking River at a distance of two miles and a half south of the city of Newport. Beginning near the Licking River, was situated Fort Shaler; a mile and a half east was Fort Stuart, and a mile and a half east of that was Beechwoods Battery.

The detail was divided into three squads, of a

sergeant and nine men each, for each of the three forts. I was one of the squad that went to Fort Stuart. That fort being between the other two, was made head-quarters of the officer commanding the detail.

We crossed the Ohio River on a ferry-boat to Newport, and then marched out. When we had gone about half-way to the forts, we were met by a lady in a carriage, who, as we passed, called out, "Hurrah for Jeff. Davis!" We took it as a downright insult, but passed along without making any disturbance. We soon overtook a young man, who told us where the lady lived, who she was, and also that she was secesh, and that her sentiments were well known in the neighborhood. She was a widow.

The next morning I asked Lieutenant Downs for the privilege of taking three men with me to scout the neighborhood for information concerning the secesh woman's disloyalty. He granted the request, with the condition that we report back promptly by 2 o'clock in the afternoon. We were allowed to take our arms with us.

We visited all the neighbors living in the immediate vicinity of the lady's residence, and they all confirmed what we had heard of her disloyalty. We then went to her house, but found that she was absent. The members of her family said that she was not disloyal, but very strongly sympathized with the secession movement. Her negroes said she was secesh. We were treated courteously by the family, and urged to stay to dinner, which we did. While the dinner was being prepared, we enlivened the time by narrating our camp stories, very much to their amusement. When we were about to take our departure, we were invited to come the next day and bring our Lieutenant. The invitation was pressed so hard that we promised to come.

At the hour specified, we reported to our Lieutenant, and gave him all the information that we had gathered concerning the woman's disloyalty and the feeling that existed against her among her neighbors. It was determined, in consequence of the insult that we had received, and her known sympathy with the enemy, to lay the matter before the Colonel on our return to the regiment.

The next day was very rainy, so we did not repeat our visit as we had promised to do. About the middle of the afternoon we were very much surprised by the appearance at the fort of Colonel Force. Had he come in the night it would not have surprised us, because he had become proverbial for "making the rounds," especially in bad weather. At the time of his arrival the Lieutenant was absent, inspecting the other forts.

The manner of the Colonel seemed strange. He was very inquisitive about our rations—whether they held out and whether we had had any other than Government rations; he also inquired whether any of us had been absent from the fort at any time. I then told him of our trip the day before. He then inquired if we had any of us been there since, and we answered in the negative. He then inspected our ration-boxes, and the grounds all about the fort, examining carefully the wood-pile, fence-corners, and bushes, evidently looking for something on the ground. After having finished his search he did not seem satisfied, but acted as if he was disappointed in something. We were all satisfied that "something was up."

Having finished his inspection, he told me to get my gun and he would drill me in the manual while he was waiting for the return of the Lieutenant. I got along finely in all the movements until he gave the command, "Charge—bayonet."

It being the most natural for me, I brought my piece down to my left side, with a half-face to the left instead of to the right, as I ought to have done.

"Not so, not so—the other way; there—fix it so," said the Colonel, fixing it in its proper position.

"I can never charge bayonet that way."

"Hold it fast; let me try it," said he, putting his hand against the muzzle of the piece.

"I will if I can." He pushed, and over I went to the ground. Springing up and resuming my old position of half-face to the left, "You can't do that again; now try."

The Colonel did try, but could not budge me. He then told me to put up my gun. I had become extremely anxious to know what had brought him over, and I resolved to give him a hint to that effect; so I said to him, "Colonel, you must like the military profession *pretty well.*"

"Why so? what makes you think that?"

"Because you came all the way over here from Cincinnati *just to drill me.*"

The Colonel smiled, but said nothing. By this

time the Lieutenant made his appearance. The Colonel took him out to one side and had some private conversation, and then left. We learned from the Lieutenant that complaint had been made at head-quarters that a squad of men from the forts had been to Mrs. ———'s house the night before and taken possession with fixed bayonets, and demanded meat, butter, chickens, and potatoes, and threatened, if the articles demanded were not given them, they would help themselves. The lady remonstrated, and finally begged of them not to disturb her property, but all to no purpose. They then helped themselves to such articles as they wanted, including about thirty chickens.

The Lieutenant seemed surprised and grieved to hear such reports about his men. He questioned us closely, as the Colonel had done, but all to no purpose; every man denied knowing any thing about the outrage. He searched the premises for any traces of chickens, such as offal, bones, or feathers, but none could be found.

The lady had represented to the Colonel that the soldiers that committed the outrage wore dark-blue blouses, and carried muskets with bayonets. The soldiers of no other regiment about there wore that kind of uniform or carried that kind of arms. When the Colonel left Fort Stuart, he went over to the Beechwoods Battery, and there the same investigation was made, but with no better result. Five of the men that accompanied me to the lady's house were taken over to see if they would be identified as having been there in the night, but the members of the family said they were not among the number. It was then arranged that the members of the family should go over to the barracks the day that we would return, and see if they could identify the men that did the mischief, on dress parade.

During the balance of our stay at the forts, the Lieutenant was very strict with us, and watched narrowly every movement that we made, but discovered no evidence of guilt. On our way back to the barracks, as we passed through the streets of Newport and Cincinnati, we seemed to be observed with more than usual interest, on account of the notoriety given us by the report. Dress parade came, and with it two members of the family, one a son of the lady, to point out the guilty soldiers. When parade was over the companies were all dismissed but company "H." The two persons then passed along the line, and succeeded in pointing out *one man*. He was a man of unexceptional character, and the very last man in the company that would have been guilty of such a thing; and besides he had been on duty at the fort next to the river, which was more than three miles distant from the lady's house.

Whatever suspicions the officers of the company might have had of men in the company, they were then well convinced that an innocent man had been wrongfully accused. The Colonel still believed that some of the men in the company had done it. It was then arranged that the son should return the next day and bring another member of the family— a young man that was teaching there—and see if he would have any better success.

Passes were prohibited us for ten days. Each one of the men on detail at the forts was examined separately, and I was called in for examination several times. After he had questioned me over and over again about it, I said to him, "Look here, Colonel, that would be a right smart trick for new recruits to do, wouldn't it? Besides, they tell me, Colonel, that you are like a comet; that you come when no man knoweth it. Supposing that you had "made the rounds" that night, and found Lieutenant Downs' men all gone. He would have been in a *pretty* fix! By and by the guard would call out, 'Halt! who comes there?' 'Chicken thieves!' would have been the reply. *That would have been nice!* You would have sent *every man* of us home in disgrace! I tell you, Colonel, Lieutenant Downs aint so big a fool as to let his men get disgraced in that way! He aint, indeed he aint."

The Colonel then walked his room back and forth, as if in a deep study, and then stopped, and facing me, said: "Is this the first time you were ever caught in a scrape of that kind?"

"You haven't caught me in *that yet*," I replied.

"That will do," said he; "you are either *innocent* or *very well drilled!* You can go to your quarters."

The next afternoon the two young men came over. When they arrived, the battalion was on drill, except the new recruits. While watching the drill, the son of the lady undertook to point out to the man that had accompanied him the person that he had previously pointed out. That, I thought, was not fair. I told the new recruits what was being done, and they all began to gather around the two young men to frighten them off. Some would cackle like hens; some crow like roosters; some pinned paper on their coat-tails; others would slip pork rinds into their coat pockets, and then accuse them of *stealing soap-grease from the poor soldiers!*

It was a rougher reception than they had bargained for, and, as soon as the crowd opened, they broke for the street and never came back again.

The "chicken scrape" is among the incidents of the past. Several of the men of the detachment that were on the forts at that time have nobly sacrificed their lives, and others their health, in the cause of their country; and, however well they loved chickens, they have all since proved themselves brave, heroic soldiers. In a future reckoning, the depredations committed that night will vanish when weighed by the "hurrahs for Jeff. Davis" by the lady in the carriage.

I leave the reader to draw his own conclusions, but I am inclined to think that *somebody got the chickens.*

CHAPTER III.

"Marching orders"—Arrives at Fort Donelson—The surrender—Goes North with prisoners—Meets an old friend as a rebel Captain—The Captain attempts to bribe him—Expedition up the Tennessee River—Touching incident—Battle of Shiloh—Captures an Enfield—Recommended as a scout.

On the 9th day of February, 1862, the regiment received "marching orders." It was a day of hurry and excitement. The order was received with delight by the men, for they had become tired with the dull monotony of guard duty, and were eager for a change.

It was a wet day, and the streets were filled with mud and slush from the rain and melting snow, and our feet dragged heavily as we marched to the levee, but, nevertheless, our hearts were light and cheerful. Little did we realize the hardships, the privations, and the sufferings that were in store for us, or think of the change that would take place ere we returned to the soil of our own loved State.

Two transports—the Emma Duncan and the Dr. Kane—were ready for us at the levee, and we embarked on board of them, and were soon under way. At Warsaw, Ky., we took on board two companies that had been doing duty there, and then proceeded on our way. We had an abundance of room—

which added much to our comfort—and a pleasant trip all the way to Paducah, Ky., where we reported for orders on the 13th of February.

We were immediately ordered to report to General U. S. Grant, near Fort Donelson, without delay, and in a few hours we were under way. We reached our destination Friday afternoon, February 14th. The fighting had commenced, and at the time of our arrival our gun-boats were engaged with the rebel batteries in sight of where we landed.

The regiment was ordered to report to Colonel— since Brigadier-General—McArthur, commanding a brigade on the extreme right of the Federal lines. To reach our position we had to make a march of ten miles. The weather was cold, and the ground covered with several inches of snow. We started very early on the morning of the 15th to take our position. Being unused to marching with heavy knapsacks, the march was fatiguing to us in the extreme. We succeeded, however, in getting our position in line of battle by 10 o'clock, A. M.

At the time we took our position the battle was raging with intense fury. The roar of musketry, the crash of artillery, the scream of shells, the whiz of bullets, and the sight of the dead and wounded were not calculated to fill the minds of inexperienced soldiers with very pleasant sensations; nevertheless, every man of the regiment exhibited a coolness and firmness that would do honor to veterans in battle.

Toward night the enemy withdrew within his

fortifications. That night we slept on our arms, in line of battle, on the snow-covered ground, expecting to renew the battle in the morning. The next morning—Sunday—about nine o'clock, the news came that Fort Donelson had surrendered.

Such shouts as went up from that army had never been heard before. From one end of the line to the other, cheer after cheer went up, until it seemed as if the trees of the forest were repeating the shouts. It was a glorious victory! It exceeded by far any victory previously achieved since the commencement of the rebellion. Over 14,000 prisoners were captured, besides an immense amount of artillery and small arms.

The 20th Ohio was one of the regiments that was detailed to guard the prisoners to the North. Companies A and H were assigned to the steamer Empress, and were intrusted with the guarding of 2,300 prisoners. Soon after daylight on Monday morning we were on our way down the Cumberland River.

Nothing of unusual interest occurred until we arrived at Bloody Island, opposite St. Louis, Mo., where we were to land the prisoners and embark them on board the cars, for Chicago, Ill. It was in the evening when we arrived there, and the prisoners remained on board until the next day.

I was on guard that night, and my post was at the gangway, with instructions to prevent, at all hazards, any attempt of prisoners to go ashore. About 1 o'clock at night a rebel Captain stepped up to me, and addressing me by name, said, "How are you?"

I recognized in him an old acquaintance by the name of Captain Brown, with whom I had formed an acquaintance at Island No. Twenty-eight, in the summer of 1852. At that time he was the owner and captain of the Memphis and Nashville packet steamer Sligo. When the rebellion broke out he raised a company at Nashville, and was made a captain in the —th Tennessee Infantry. At one time, while in difficulty in Memphis, Captain Brown had rendered me valuable assistance.

"How are *you*?" said I, as soon as I discovered who it was. "What are you doing *here*?"

"I'm a prisoner, and my old friend is guarding me."

"Yes, I *see!* Quite a change since you and I last met."

"Yes, something of a change! I hardly expected to meet you in arms against me! You have lived a long time in the South. Do you think that you are doing exactly right to take up arms against us?"

"The old government and the old flag are good enough for me," I replied, "and I mean to stick by them so long as I live."

"Do you expect to pin the States together again with bayonets?" he asked.

"I don't know whether we shall *pin* the States together again or not; but I *do know one thing;* we'll have the *soil back again*, whether we have the people or not."

"See here!" said he. "Do you remember of my assisting you one time in Memphis, when you was in trouble?"

"Certainly I do! And you had my gratitude for it."

"Well, I am in trouble. Can you render me any assistance?"

"I will if I can."

"Well, you can."

"How?"

"By letting me cross your beat and go ashore."

"I *can't do that.*"

"Why not? I helped you; why not help me?"

"Because I am no traitor to my country! I never asked you to raise your hand against your country to assist me."

"Here, take this watch; perhaps I can buy you," said he, offering me a splendid gold watch.

"Not *much* you can't buy me! I think too much of the stars and stripes for that."

"Take it," said he, "and let me cross your beat, and I'll give you a hundred dollars in gold besides."

"*I can't do it,*" said I; "*don't you ask me again.*"

Captain Brown went away quite chop-fallen, satisfied, I presume, that gold was not at par with genuine patriotism.

We guarded the prisoners to Camp Douglas, near Chicago, Ill., where we remained nine days, and then returned to Bloody Island, where we arrived on the 6th day of March. That night the regiment embarked on board the steamer Continental, for Paducah, Ky., which place we reached in time to join in the grand expedition up the Tennessee River.

At Paducah, General Sherman and staff came on board the Continental, and made it his head-quarters;

and that boat, preceded by the gun-boats, led the fleet.

When under way, that vast fleet of steamers, loaded down with troops, as they moved along, one after another, at nearly equal distances apart, presented a grand and imposing appearance. The weather was mild and pleasant, which added much to the interest of the trip. The banks of the river often presented crowds of people that had gathered to witness the grand display of force that was penetrating the territory of the rebellion. Sometimes we were cheered by the crowds that lined the banks, indicating their loyalty, and at other times a sullen silence told plainly that we were not welcome.

One little incident occurred that I shall never forget. We had on board a citizen of Tennessee, who owned a large plantation on the left bank of the Tennessee River, about eight miles below Savanna. He was an exile from home on account of his devotion to the Union. An attempt was made by his neighbors to capture and hang him, but he succeeded in making his escape, and in getting through to Paducah, Ky., after having suffered a great deal from hunger and exposure, incident to traveling by night, through forests and swamps, to evade discovery. The last that his family had heard from him was that his disloyal neighbors were in pursuit of him, determined to hang him, and they did not know whether he was alive or not.

As we neared his plantation, a group of persons was observed standing on the bank of the river not far from his residence. He requested the captain of the boat, as we passed, to run the boat near the shore, so that he might recognize his wife and children, if they were there. The crowd on the deck of the steamer moved back, to give him a large clear space, that his family might more readily recognize him. As the boat neared the shore the group proved to be his wife, children, and servants, gazing with intense interest at the passing fleet. It was a touching scene, when that exile from home recognized his loved ones.

"I am alive! It is me!" he shouted, swinging his hat. "I am coming home! Glory to God! The Union forever! Hallelujah! Glory! Glory!" etc. He jumped and shouted as if in ecstasies of delight.

Such manifestations of love for home and country are unmistakable evidences of patriotism and loyalty. The incident is but one of thousands that have been witnessed in the prosecution of the war.

From that time on, nothing of special interest occurred in my experience until the battle of Shiloh, or Pittsburg Landing. The battle was fought on the 6th and 7th of April, 1862. I acted my part in that bloody conflict, but the details of the battle I must leave to the pen of the historian. At that battle I succeeded in capturing an Enfield rifle. My "handspike" was turned over, and with it dissipated the disgust with which I had carried it.

The next day after the battle of Shiloh, a circular was sent to the company commanders, from brigade head-quarters, requesting them to send in the names of such men as were trustworthy and suitable for scouts. Captain Downs (formerly Lieutenant Downs) sent in my name as one, which opened the way for the experiences that I shall narrate in the following chapters.

Early in June, soon after the evacuation of Corinth, the 20th Ohio Regiment moved to Bolivar, and soon after to Grand Junction, Tenn.

CHAPTER IV.

Rumored attack upon Grand Junction—"General Bunker" sent out as spy—Passes himself as a rebel soldier—Falls in with rebel cavalry—Visits a rebel camp—Attempts to deprive him of his revolver—Discovers a Yankee forage party—Undertakes to return—Captured by Yankees, and robbed of his revolver and money—Passes as a rebel spy—Sent to the Provost Marshal—Sent to General Hurlbut—Returned to Grand Junction.

Soon after the evacuation of Corinth by the forces under General Beauregard, a part of General Grant's army was distributed along the Ohio and Mississippi and the Mississippi Central, and also the Memphis and Charleston Railroads, to garrison the principal towns and open up communication for supplies by railroad instead of by the Tennessee River, which was becoming so low as to be an uncertain route for supplies.

At the time I speak of, Grand Junction was garrisoned by a small brigade of infantry and a battery of artillery, under command of Brigadier-General M. D. Leggett. Grand Junction is situated on the Mississippi Central Railroad at its junction with the Memphis and Charleston Railroad, and was an exposed outpost.

A rumor had become current among the citizens

that a large force of the enemy's cavalry was in the vicinity, preparing to capture the brigade garrisoning the post. General Grant, who was still at Corinth, informed General Leggett by telegraph that his command was in danger; that an attempt would be made to capture his force; that he would be attacked on his right by cavalry and on his left by infantry, and advised him to vacate the place and fall back to Bolivar, twenty miles north of Grand Junction, where the Mississippi Central Railroad crosses the Hatchee River. The enemy's force was represented to be 900 cavalry at Davis' Mills, and three brigades of cavalry at what is known as the White Church, on Wolf River, the former nine and the latter twelve miles from Grand Junction, in a south-west direction. An additional force of a division of infantry were said to be at Salem, seventeen miles south-east of Grand Junction.

General Leggett had some doubts about the rebels having very much force near the place, and the large quantities of cotton that were being brought in, and the abundance of corn for forage, made it an object to hold the place as long as prudence would admit, and he resolved to ascertain whether there was any cause for alarm before vacating it.

General Leggett sent for me and told me what he wanted, and asked me if I was willing to undertake the job. It was the first opportunity that I had ever had of working as a spy, and I had for a long time been anxious to try my hand at it, and I felt certain that I could do the Government more good in that way than in any other. It was my time to strike, and I determined to improve it. I told General Leggett that I was willing to try, and would do the best that I could, and if I got back safe, "all right;" if not, my fate would be no worse than that of others before me.

I returned to my quarters and made the necessary arrangements, and the next morning, at daylight, I started out on the road to Salem, disguised as a Confederate soldier belonging to infantry.

The day was clear and pleasant, and a recent shower had laid the dust and cooled the air, and made it much pleasanter traveling than is apt to be the case in that country in the month of July. I was on foot, and the coolness of the atmosphere very much facilitated my progress. I was not interrupted in my progress until I had gone about eight miles, when I observed, as I approached a planter's house, a negro woman in the yard, engaged in churning. Being somewhat fond of buttermilk, I resolved to pay the inmates of the house a visit. As I approached the house, a lady came to the door, and, observing my Confederate uniform, seemed pleased to see me, and asked me to walk in and be seated, to which I complied.

"Where have you been?" she inquired.

"I have been out to the Yankee pickets, and I had a fight with them last night and killed three of the d——d Yankees. They killed my horse for me in the fight, and I am going back to Salem to get another that I left there. I have walked until I am tired. Seeing the woman churning in the yard, I thought I would stop and rest myself, and see if you would have the kindness to give me a drink of buttermilk."

"I am glad you did. You shall have all the buttermilk you want. You are not a-gwine to *walk* to Salem, are you?"

"Yes. I've got another horse there, and I do n't like to trouble any body for the use of one."

"Well, now, you are not a-gwine to walk down thar; we've got heaps o' horses and mules, and you shall have one to ride. Bob! Bob!" calling to a darky in the yard, "you run right quick to the cotton-gin and fetch your master."

While Bob went on a double-quick for his master, the lady ordered me some buttermilk and wheat biscuit. While I was eating, the planter came in.

"Lord bless you, John!" exclaimed the lady, as her husband entered, "here is one of *our soldiers*, and he has had a fight with the Yankee pickets and has killed three of them! He says he's gwine to walk to Salem after another hoss. I tell him that he's not a-gwine to walk when we've got heaps o' mules! I think any of our soldiers that has killed *three Yankees* is entitled to a mule to ride!"

"You can have a mule in welcome; there's no occasion for you to walk," said the planter.

"Thank you!" said I, "I am under very great obligations to you for your kindness, but it may not be possible for me to return this way. I will not take a mule, but I am a thousand times obliged to you."

With many blessings from them, and an urgent invitation to call if I returned, I took my departure. When about twelve miles from Grand Junction, I was overtaken by a squad of thirteen rebel cavalry, including one Sergeant, under command of a Lieutenant.

"How are you, boys?" said I, as they came up.

"Fine!" said the Lieutenant. "How do you do?"

"I'm getting *pretty near well*, I thank you."

"Where do you belong?" he inquired.

"To the 13th Tennessee Infantry, Col. Vaughn's regiment."

"Ah—yes, yes; he's all right. I remember of seeing him in Corinth last spring," said the Sergeant; "I have a cousin in the same regiment."

"Where do *you* belong?" I inquired.

"To Jackson's First Battalion of Cavalry," answered the Lieutenant. "Where are you gwine?"

"I am gwine down to my regiment," said I. "I have been sick, and have been home in Osceola, Mississippi County, Arkansas, and I am gwine down to Salem to report myself to the nearest head-quarters. I have heard that there is some of our forces there, and I want to find out where my regiment is."

"You are mistaken," said the Lieutenant; "there is none of our forces there. And besides, it is not necessary for you to report at any head-quarters. Your regiment is at Tupelo, where you will have no difficulty in getting to it. We have some spare horses here; get on one of them and ride."

I mounted one of the horses and rode along with them. I learned, from conversation with them, that their regiment was stationed at Tupelo, Miss., and that they were detailed to traverse the country and visit all the planters, and tell them to haul their cotton, corn, and bacon to a place known as the Double Block-house, where it would be guarded to prevent the Yankees from stealing it.

We only went about a mile after I mounted the horse before we turned to the right, and a half a mile more brought us to the double log-house. At that place three regiments of infantry were camped, and their principal object appeared to be to guard the stuff that the planters were hauling in for protection. Several thousand bushels of corn and large quantities of bacon had already been hauled there.

We dismounted and remained in the camp about an hour. While there the Lieutenant told me that I had better not be in a hurry about going to Tupelo; "for," he said, "the times are rather tough for a man just recovering from sickness, and the rations are not such as a sick man can relish." He told me that he was going round on to the lower Tupelo road in a day or two, and that I had better run with with them till that time, and he would put me on to a road where I would find clever people and plenty to eat. It all seemed very good advice, and favorable to my purpose, and so I accepted it.

The balance of the day was spent in visiting every plantation on the roads to the west and north of the block-house, and when we halted for the night we were within three miles of Davis' Mills.

There I was like to have a little difficulty with the Sergeant. I had with me a very nice navy revolver that I had borrowed of Colonel Force preparatory to starting out. The Sergeant discovered that I had it, and was going to take it away from me.

"What business has an infantry soldier with such a revolver as that?" said the Sergeant. "Infantry soldiers don't need them, and cavalry soldiers do. It will never do you any good if you keep it; so give it to me."

"Sergeant," said I, "you are superior to me in rank, and if you insist I shall have to obey; but if you take that revolver away from me I'll report you to Billy Jackson! I will indeed!"

"Sergeant," said the Lieutenant, who heard our words, "if Colonel Vaughn is willing that his men should carry such things, it is none of our business. Let the soldier keep his revolver!"

"Thank you, Lieutenant," said I. "I prize that revolver very highly. I bought it in Memphis, about the time the war commenced, to kill the Yankee sons of b—hes with, and when I enlisted Colonel Vaughn told me I might carry it, and I mean to do it."

"That's right!" said the Lieutenant. "Turn up as many of the d—d Yankees' heels with it as you can! Soldier, what road did you come in on this morning?"

"I came down on the Somerville road, across the Hickory flats, by the old man Pruett's, and then over on to the Salem and Grand Junction road."

"You came a very good route, indeed."

"I am aware of that, I replied. "I know this here country all through in here. Lieutenant, where did you boys stay last night?"

"At Davis' Mills."

"Haven't we got a cavalry force there?"

"No. There was only us fourteen there last night."

"The old man Pruett told me yesterday that there was, that we had three brigades of cavalry at the White Church on Wolf River."

"The old man was mistaken. There is none of our forces nearer than Tupelo, except the three regiments that you saw to-day, and a few of the same company that I belong to, that are scattered about the country on the same business that we are on."

In the morning our operations of notifying the planters was renewed, and our route lay along the bottoms of Davis Creek, toward the head-waters of the creek. About noon we very unexpectedly found a Yankee forage party.

"There is some of the Yankee sons of b——hes now!" said the Lieutenant.

"Where?" said I.

"There, up on top of the hill to the left," said he, pointing toward them.

I looked, and sure enough there they were. There was about thirty of the Yankees, and eight teams. They had halted to feed, and had stacked arms. They did not see us. We moved along a little further to a cow-path that led to the right up a ridge of ground parallel to the one occupied by the Yankees. The hollow that intervened was filled with a growth of bushes extending to the path which we were in, which screened us from view and enabled us to approach within fifty yards of the Yankees without being seen.

I now recognized the detachment as belonging to my own regiment, and one of the men was *my own bunk-mate!*

The Lieutenant told us to be quiet and not to speak a word, and if the Yankees ventured away from their arms, we would make a dash upon them and capture their arms and mules, and burn the wagons. Little did they mistrust the relation that I bore to these Yankees. I determined, if a dash was attempted, to do what execution I could upon my butternut companions with my revolver, hoping to dispose of four or five of them before my *true relation* was discovered. It was a moment of fearful suspense as we watched those Federal soldiers; but my butternut companions were too deeply interested in the watch to observe any feelings that my actions might have betrayed.

For about twenty minutes we watched them, but they did not move away from their arms. The Lieutenant, fearing his own safety might be endangered by too long a stay, silently withdrew his men, and made his way back toward Davis' Mills by another route. That night we stayed at a planter's house, ten miles from Grand Junction.

At three o'clock the next morning we were again on the move, and a two hours' ride brought us to four corners in the road somewhere south-west of Lagrange, and three or four miles distant from that place. There we halted, and the Lieutenant told me that one of the roads was the one that I wanted to take to go to Tupelo. He gave me the names of several planters that lived on the road, and advised me to stop two or three days at a place and recruit my health all I could on the way to my regiment, and assured me that the planters he had named were clever people, and that I would be welcome with any of them. I thanked him and bade him a good morning, and started on the road that he had pointed out, not caring whether it led to Tupelo or not, if I could get away from him and his squad.

As soon as the cavalry was out of sight, I made a detour through a large cotton-field to my left, and continued on until I came into a road that I supposed led direct to Grand Junction; while in company with the cavalry, we had zigzagged through the country so much that I had become somewhat confused, and I was not sure where the road did lead to. I took it, however, and moved along very fast to get, as soon as possible, as far away from the vicinity where we parted, lest, by some chance or other, I might be found going toward Grand Junction instead of Tupelo. I kept, as I supposed, a sharp look-out as I moved along, and had gone, as near as I could judge, three miles, when I was very unexpectedly interrupted in my course by a challenge of "Halt! halt! you son of a b—h!"

I was considerably alarmed, for I supposed that I must have encountered a rebel picket. On looking to see where the challenge came from, I found that it emanated from a Federal picket. A clump of bushes had prevented me from seeing him until I was close on to him. My position was clear enough now. I had taken a road to Lagrange, instead of Grand Junction, and had encountered General Hurlbut's pickets.

"Ha! ha! my butternut soldier!" exclaimed the guard, as I halted; "you got caught rather unexpectedly."

"I reckon I did," I replied.

"Where do you belong?"

"To the 13th Tennessee."

"You've got tired soldiering on short rations, I suppose?"

"I reckon I a'n't starved yet."

One of the pickets then took me to the Captain in command, at the reserve. There I was subjected to a rigid questioning and search, but I was determined to carry out my disguise until I could report to some commanding officer. My revolver and money, and other articles, were taken from me by the Captain, and then I was ordered to stand up by a tree until further orders. I remonstrated with the Captain about depriving me of my revolver and private property, and told him that "*we* always respected a prisoner's right to his side arms and personal effects." The Captain replied that I might be d—d glad to get off so, and if he had his way about it, he would shoot every rebel in the Southern Confederacy.

While standing at the tree, I observed a plantation house that stood within less than a hundred yards from me, and that it was occupied. My early start and the distance I had traveled gave me a ravenous appetite, so I asked the Captain if he would be so kind as to allow me to go to the house and get some breakfast.

"Yes," said he, "you may go; but, G—d d—n you, if you undertake to get away, I'll have you shot!"

"I won't run away," I replied; "I didn't come in here to run away. I'll come right back as soon as I get my breakfast."

When I got to the house, I met the man of the house at the door. He had evidently seen me coming, and my uniform attracted his attention.

"Good morning!" said I, as he came out.

"Good morning; won't you come in?"

"Yes, I don't care if I do; and I should like right well to get some breakfast here, if you please, for I am mighty hungry."

"Walk in; you shall have all the breakfast you want. Where do you belong?"

"To Col. Vaughn's regiment, the 13th Tennessee."

"You do?"

"Yes."

"Well, I belong to Colonel Strawl's regiment, the 4th Tennessee. I am a surgeon in that regiment; my name is Biggs. What is your name?"

"My name is *Ruggles*. I am a brother to General Ruggles."

"Is it possible! I know the General very well. What are you doing up here?"

"I am going through the d—d Yankee lines to-day, if I can."

"You are? A'n't you afraid they'll *get you*?"

"No; I expect they'll get me into the guard-house, but I'll soon manage to get out."

"Well, do the best that you can. If they *do* get you into the guard-house, you sh'an't want for anything to eat. I'll see to that myself."

Breakfast was announced as ready for me, and I

sat up to the table. They had got me fried ham, baked sweet potatoes, warm biscuit with butter and honey, and coffee with sugar and cream. I think the condition of my appetite enabled me to do that meal ample justice. When I had finished, I asked the doctor how much I should pay him.

"Oh, Lord! not a cent! Do you think I'd charge one of our soldiers for a meal of victuals! I feel thankful that I have it to give you!" Then turning, and pointing toward the pickets, he said, "But them d—d Yankee thieves down there I make pay me fifty cents for a meal of nothing but bread and meat!"

"You've got them rightly named, doctor," said I; "for they took my revolver and my money, and every thing else I had, away from me this morning."

"You need n't be surprised at such treatment as that," said he; "for there are officers down there that would steal the Lord's supper, and men that would steal the table-cloths!"

"You are about right, doctor; but I see they are looking as if uneasy about me, and I must go back."

"Well, said he, "if you get into trouble, I'll do all I can for you. I have got things fixed pretty smooth between me and the pickets, and I think I can help you carry out your plans."

"Havn't you taken the *oath*, doctor?"

"Oh, yes! I had to do that in order to get along smoothly."

"Well, you be careful and not get yourself into any scrape by it. I would advise you to say nothing, and if I get into the guard-house, you see that I get plenty to eat, and I'll wriggle out some way.

I then bid him good-by, and returned to my position by the tree. When the new pickets came out to relieve the old ones, two of the old guards took me in to the Provost-marshal. As I entered his office, I was saluted by, "Well, old hoss, who are you?"

"I am an Arkansas school-master," I replied.

"What do you want?"

"I want to see General Hurlbut."

"What do you want of General Hurlbut?"

"I want to see him. I've heard that he's a very red-faced man, and I want to see for myself how he looks!"

"*Yes, you want to see him!* You'll go to the guard-house!"

"No I won't!"

"Who are you?" he demanded.

"You give me those two guards and send me to General Hurlbut, and find out who I am!"

"Guards," said he, "take him off; take him down to General Hurlbut's. I don't know who the h—l he is!"

The guards took me to the General's quarters, and one of them went in and told the General that they had got a fellow that they had captured at the picket-line, and that he was dressed like a rebel soldier, and that the Provost-marshal could not find out who he was, and had sent him there. The General came out of the tent, and, seeing who it was, said:

"Ah, yes! I know him! Guards you can go to your quarters."

"Hold on, General," said I; "the Captain that had command of those guards took a revolver away from me that belongs to Colonel Force, and took my pocket-book, and every thing else I had in my pockets."

"What kind of d—d thieving and robbing will take place next! Guards, go and tell that Captain to march his men up here!"

In a few minutes, the Captain marched his men into the yard and formed them in a line; when that was done, "Captain," said the General, "give that man the things that you robbed him of!"

The Captain handed out the articles, one after another, and last of all he handed me *an old fine-tooth comb!* That was too much for the equanimity of the officers and men that were looking on, and they burst into a roar of laughter. The poor Captain looked as if he would sink into the earth. "That will do," said the General, when he had handed me all; "you can dismiss your men."

I told General Hurlbut the result of my trip, and he complimented me very highly upon my success, and then gave me a "little smile" of brandy and loaf sugar, and a pass to Grand Junction.

The pass saved me any further annoyance by the Federal pickets, and Dr. Biggs from the trouble of visiting the guard-house with "commissary supplies."

I reported my trip to General Leggett, and, for some reason, the brigade did not vacate the place for more than two weeks after.

CHAPTER V.

Fired at by a citizen—The sick overseer—How he was cured—Pickets fired on—Trip to White Church—Visits General Van Dorn—Meets a rebel spy—Reports to General Leggett—Grand Junction evacuated—Again sees the rebel spy—Attempt to arrest him—Drinks wine with the rebel General Jackson—Discovers a hole in the fence.

It was my duty, while the brigade remained at Grand Junction, to watch for any demonstrations of General Van Dorn's, Wheeler's, or Jackson's cavalry. For that purpose I used to ride out on a road running east and west, that lay three miles to the south of Grand Junction. I used to scout that road for about ten miles regularly every day. One morning, before going out, I called upon Captain Jacobs, Provost-marshal of the post, on business. While I was there, an overseer that I had frequently seen in my scouts came in, and requested a renewal of his pass, and a permit to carry out certain articles that he wished to purchase. He had with him the oath of allegiance. As soon as my business was completed, I started out on my scout, as usual, leaving the overseer there. I made the trip out, and had returned to within a few yards of the overseer's house, when he stepped out from a fence-corner, with a squirrel-rifle in his hands, and said to me, "Are you a Yankee soldier?"

"No, sir, I'm not a Yankee soldier, I'm a Federal soldier."

"What are you doing out here?"

"I'm watching for rebel cavalry."

"I'll soon stop your watching Confederate cavalry."

"Are you going to shoot me?"

He said nothing, but the click of his gun, as he cocked it, said "Yes." As he was bringing it to his face, I put the spurs to my horse, and as I passed, he fired, but missed me. I went in and reported to General Leggett, who replied, "You had better look out, or some of those *good Union men will kill you.*" He issued no order to have the man arrested; and perhaps it would have done no good if he had, for such characters, with their oily tongues, are as slippery as eels. As a general thing, they manage to evade justice, and get released from the Federal authorities. I well knew that if the overseer was allowed to live undisturbed my own life was in jeopardy, so I telegraphed to General Grant, then at Jackson, Tennessee, to know what to do with such a man. His reply was, "If you are a scout for the Government, you *ought to know yourself.*"

That night I went to the 20th Ohio Infantry and got two Sergeants, whose real names I shall not give, but designate them as the "big Sergeant" and the "little Sergeant"—both of them belonged to company H—to assist me in bringing the overseer to justice. Knowing that if we accomplished our purpose there would be complaints entered at head-quarters the next day, I resolved to proceed as noiselessly about it as possible. Instead of getting the countersign, and thus letting it be known that we were going out, we stole through the picket line, and nobody knew that we had left camp.

It was about four miles to the overseer's house; thither we proceeded. When we came to his yard, myself and the little Sergeant went at once to the house, and the big Sergeant went to the negro quarters. The overseer and his family had retired for the night. Our rap for admittance was answered by "Who is there?" My reply was, "Federal soldiers; get up and open the door." The summons was obeyed by the overseer's wife. As we entered we heard the groans of a man as if in distress, proceeding from an adjoining room. On going into the room I found the overseer in bed, and feigning to be laboring under severe pain. Approaching the bedside, I said to him: "You are sick, are you, old hoss?"

With great difficulty, seemingly, he answered, "Yes—I'm—very sick."

"How long have you been sick?"

"It's—going on—two weeks—now."

"You lying whelp," said the little Sergeant, unable to contain himself; "I saw you in Grand Junction this morning."

"Get up, old fellow," said I, "you need a little exercise; it will do you good to move about."

"I can't—gentlemen,—I tell you—I'm sick," (still groaning, and letting on to be in great distress.)

"Yes, that wolfish-looking face of yours *looks sick!* Get out of that!" He commenced to rise, trembling all over as if with nervous fear. "Your nerves a'n't so steady as they were this morning," I added.

"Indeed—I *am*—sick—gentlemen."

"I should think your conscience would make you tremble."

"Are you—gwine to—kill me?" he asked, getting more and more agitated with alarm.

"No, we won't kill you, but we'll give you a furlough to a warmer climate. I think it will improve your health."

"You will give—a body—time—to pray—won't you?"

"Praying won't do you any good; you will go to the warm climate, anyhow; so, hurry on them clothes and come along with us." We then walked him out of the house; we found that he could travel as strong as we could.

The wife took on dreadfully, wringing her hands and crying out, "*Have mercy! have mercy!* Don't kill him!"

"Yes, *traitors are pretty objects of mercy.* You stay where you are." She was too much frightened to follow. As we passed out into the yard, we met the big Sergeant, accompanied by a nigger who had an iron collar on his neck, with a chain fastened to it, with the other end fastened around his waist.

"Here, Bunker," said the Sergeant, "see what I have found."

"That chain is just exactly what I want. Bring your nigger around here," said I, as I led my prisoner around to the rear of the house, and out to the stable. There we found two crotches standing upright, and a pole laid from one to the other. A large box was rolled out from the stable and placed under the pole, and the overseer made to get on to the box. The nigger had been sent to the rebel fortifications to work, and had run away. The overseer had captured him, and had punished him by putting him in irons, as described. In the morning he would chain him to the plow, and at night release him and make the chain fast around his body. On searching the pockets of the overseer, I found the key that unlocked the chain. I then unlocked the chain from the negro, and placed it upon the overseer's neck, and made the other end fast to the pole overhead; and having fastened the overseer's hands behind him, I said to the negro, "This man has been your overseer for a long time—you may change about now, and be his overseer awhile."

"Lor' bress you, massa!" he exclaimed. "Thank de Lord fur dat; he's dun druv dis nigga long enuf."

"Well, you *drive* him now."

"Shall I drive him thar?"

"Yes, drive him where you please."

"I reckon he won't do dat box no good standin' there," and suiting the action to the word, he jerked the box from under him, leaving him suspended by the neck; adding, "Now, I specs he'll drive hisself. I'se more important business to 'tend to."

The overseer being in a fair way to have his "furlough approved," we returned to camp by the same way that we went out. The next morning, early, the wife came in with a complaint to the Provost-marshal that a party of Federal soldiers had been to her house the night before, and had taken her sick husband out of bed and had hung him, and begged for protection from further outrage.

The Provost-marshal said to her, "I don't believe a word of it; for no soldiers have been permitted to go out through our lines during the night. Perhaps you had a husband and perhaps not. I advise you to go back about your business and not be in here blaming Federal soldiers with that which they have never done."

During the day a forage party, on its return to camp, visited the plantation and brought away sixty contrabands, and among them was the one that we had liberated from his chains. The overseer was dead, but had been taken down and carried into the house. On his arrival in camp, the negro reported that the Yankees had made him hang his master. Outside of the lines it was generally believed that the Yankees had done it, but the soldiers generally believed that the negroes on the plantation had done it. It was never suspected that I had had a hand in it. "My personal safety as a scout demanded that he should be disposed of," is all the excuse that I have to offer. I continued to scout the road for several days after, but met with no further interruption.

Early in the month of July, the first train of cars that was to run through from Memphis to Grand Junction started out, and, when only a short distance from Memphis, was captured, and the railroad badly destroyed.

Owing to the difficulty of protecting the road from the raids of the enemy, the opening of it was abandoned for a time, and the roads from Columbus, Ky., to Grand Junction and Corinth were relied upon for the transportation of supplies. When the opening of the road was abandoned, the forces at Lagrange, under command of General Hurlbut, moved to Memphis, which left the small brigade at Grand Junction without any troops for support nearer than Bolivar, a distance of twenty miles. The exposed position of so small a force undoubtedly emboldened the enemy in their plans for capturing the post. As I have explained in the preceding chapter, the abundance of cotton and forage was an object to hold the place as long as the safety of the force would admit.

After General Hurlbut's forces left Lagrange, our pickets were frequently fired upon, and small squads of cavalry were seen, indicating a boldness on the part of the enemy indicative of a strong force not far off.

It was under that state of affairs that General Leggett requested me to go out as a spy, and learn the position and force of the enemy.

On this occasion I rode out on a mule, disguised as a rebel soldier, taking the road that led to the White Church. I saw several squads of rebel cavalry, but at some distance from me, soon after passing our own pickets, but none of them interrupted me. Just after I had crossed Wolf River, I discovered the rebel pickets; how I was to pass them was more than I knew. I resolved, however, to go on and try the effect of a bold front. With as much unconcern and freedom as though I was one of their number, and perfectly at home, I rode up, and without halting or letting on that I expected to be halted, I said, "Good morning, boys! have *our forces all got up yet?*"

"Yes," said one; "where have you been?"

"Out to the Yankee lines by the old cotton-gin near Grand Junction," I replied, still riding along.

By this time I had got clear by, without any attempt being made to stop me. At the White Church I came to the rebel camp; there I dismounted and inquired of a soldier for head-quarters.

"Whose—General Van Dorn's?" was asked.

"Yes," I replied.

He then showed me General Van Dorn's tent. I had supposed that if I found much of a force it would be that of General Van Dorn. I proceeded to the tent that had been pointed out. In front of it was the usual head-quarters guard. Saluting him, I inquired if General Van Dorn was in, and was answered in the affirmative. The moment I entered, I saw two Generals. One I instantly recognized as the Confederate General Wheeler; I had known him in Memphis before the war. Without speaking to him, I turned to the other and addressed him; I said, "General, I wish to get a pass, if you please, to go outside of the lines."

"Who are you?" the General inquired.

"My name is Ruggles."

"General Van Dorn," said General Wheeler, "don't you know him? He is a brother of General Ruggles, and belongs to the 2d Arkansas Cavalry."

"Ah! Indeed!"

"Yes, and I want to go out to the Yankee lines and see what they are doing out there."

"I wish you would, Ruggles," said Van Dorn, "and see if the Yankees have obstructed the Grand Junction and Salem road with timber. That's the road that I want to take a part of my forces in on in the morning."

General Van Dorn instructed his Adjutant to write me a pass, which I received, and then went out and mounted my mule. *"That's the road I want to take a part of my forces in on in the morning!"* was something that needed my immediate attention. I rode leisurely through the camp. Every thing was bustle and activity preparatory to a move, and confirmed what I had heard at head-quarters. As near as I could judge, the camp contained 9,000 or 10,000 men.

Having satisfied myself of the probable force of the enemy, I started back on the road I came in on. I stopped at the pickets and showed my pass, and then went on. After I had crossed Wolf River, I made a detour across the country to the right, in order to get on to the Grand Junction and Salem road, as General Van Dorn had directed me, so that if by any mishap I should be captured and sent to head-quarters, I could show that I was captured right where I had been sent.

About five miles from the White Church, I dismounted at a large, beautiful spring of water, to drink and rest myself. While there, a cavalryman rode up and halted for the same purpose; I immediately recognized him as having been one of the squad I had fallen in with and accompanied so far in my former trip. He rode a Texan pony, with a peculiarly constructed saddle, that I could not mistake as having seen before.

"Where have you been?" I inquired, as he stopped.

"I've been up to the Yankee lines."

"You must be a scout, then."

"Yes, I am a spy; where do you belong?"

"I *belong to the Yankees!*" I replied, placing my hand on my revolver, as if to draw it.

My movements agitated him. Raising his hands in a supplicating attitude, as if he thought I meant to kill him, he said, "D—do n't shoot! hold—hold on! do n't lets you and I quarrel; let us help each other, since we are both in the same business."

"Very well! just as you say about that."

"You played off the spy pretty well the other day when you was with us," he continued, somewhat composed.

"Yes, I did well enough for that time; but I am in a hurry this time, so you and I must make short visits."

At that, we both mounted and started in opposite directions, eyeing each other, with revolvers drawn, until out of sight. I might have shot him at the time he thought I intended to do it, but I did not think my own safety would admit of it.

At 5 o'clock that afternoon I arrived at General Leggett's head-quarters, and reported what I had learned, and before daylight the next morning the brigade was on its way to Bolivar, and it had not been gone an hour until General Van Dorn's forces were in possession of the place.

The movement on the part of General Leggett was a masterly one, and was conducted with such skill that, though pursued by a force chagrined with disappointment, which several times outnumbered his entire command, his brigade reached Bolivar without the loss of a single man or a dollar's worth of stores.

Shortly after our arrival at Bolivar, I was in town, accompanied by Sergeant Wonders, of the 20th Ohio. Hitched in front of one of the stores was the same little Texan pony and peculiar saddle that I had seen twice before. I knew that I could not be mistaken in them. I did not like the idea of his running at large. An encounter with him in the enemy's camp would prove fatal, so I resolved to find him and have him arrested. After searching for some time, without success, I returned to where I had seen the pony, and found that it was gone. From a soldier I learned that somebody had ridden the pony out toward the depot. I followed after, and when about half way to the depot, I saw the pony coming. I sent the Sergeant back and told him to see where the man went, and I would join him after awhile. Just before we met, he halted and commenced to fasten his pony. Stepping up to him and speaking very low, I said, "Hallo, old fellow! are you in here?"

"Yes, h—h—how d—do you do?" he said, trembling from head to foot.

"Never mind, you need n't be afraid. *It's all right*," I added in a confidential way, "you need not be afraid of me; I am in a great hurry this morning, so you must excuse me." Without further words I walked on rapidly, as though I cared nothing about him. As soon as out of sight, I made my way around to the office of the Provost-marshal. There I was joined by the Sergeant, who remained outside to watch.

On entering his office, I found him asleep on a cot. I woke him up and told him the circumstances about the spy, and that I wanted some guards to capture him. By the time I had finished telling him, he was fast asleep. I again woke him up, and commenced to tell what I wanted, when he said:

"Do—you—know—the—man?"

"Yes! I know the man!"

"Do—you—know—the—hoss?"

"Yes! I know the horse and I know the saddle."

"W-a-l—a-l-l—r-i-g-h-t!"

By this time he was again fast asleep. I tried again to wake him, but with no better success. I do not say that he was drunk, but I *do* say that he acted just as I do when I am drunk. The result was, the spy escaped, and I have never seen him since.

As we were passing along by Adams & Brother's store, a few hours after, the door chanced to be open, and we observed that the room was occupied by many citizens, engaged in a spirited conversation, and so we dropped in to see what was going on. One of the persons present I knew to be Brigadier-General Neely, of the Confederate army, who had been captured by the Federal troops when they first took possession of the place, and he was on parole of honor within the limits of the town.

When we first entered, the conversation stopped, but it was soon gradually resumed. A great deal was said about the Yankees stealing corn, cotton, and niggers, and they complained that it was ruining many of the planters. I listened a few minutes, and then, addressing myself to General Neely, said: "Gentlemen, so far as I am concerned, I have never yet stolen a cent's worth of property since I have been in the Federal army, and if I had known that a United States soldier had got to steal corn, cotton, and niggers from the citizens of the South, I would never have enlisted."

"Nor I either," said the Sergeant, "I didn't think when I enlisted that this was going to be made a nigger war!"

"For my part," I continued, "I'm getting tired of fighting for *niggers*, and if I wasn't afraid they would hang me for a spy, I'd go and join Billy Jackson's cavalry."

"And so would I," said the Sergeant; "I think I'd like the Southern people very much. I have often heard "Bunker" talk about them; he used to live in the South."

"Yes, I did, indeed! and I'm almost ashamed to be fighting against them. I used to live in Mississippi, and I have spent several years in Arkansas and Tennessee. I am well acquainted in Memphis. General, do you know Jim Ford and Charlie Ford, of Memphis?"

"Yes, I know them very well; they are wholesale dealers in produce. I get my supply of pork from them every year."

He then motioned to me and the Sergeant and one of the citizens in the room, who had been listening with a good deal of interest to our conversation, to accompany him into a back room, which we did. He then called for two bottles of wine, and asked us to drink with him, which we were not in the least backward about doing.

The citizen then said that he had not time to stay longer, and, shaking hands with us, bade us good-by, and went out.

"General," said I, when the citizen had gone, "do you know where Billy Jackson is?"

"Yes! He's not far off; if you want to join his cavalry you would have no trouble in getting to him."

"If I wa'n't afraid General Jackson would get me and hang me for a spy, I'd run away, and so would this Sergeant, and we'd join his cavalry."

"There is no danger of that," said the General, for *that was General Jackson that drank the wine with us*, and has just left. He heard all you said about joining his cavalry. If you want to go, boys, you will have no trouble in doing so."

"Well, General," said I, "since you are acquainted with General Jackson, can't you give us a pass that will make us all safe after we get out of the Yankee lines?"

"I'm on parole of honor," he replied, "and I have no right to do that."

"There would be no harm in it; the Yankees would never find it out." Pulling out my wallet, I said, "General, how much did you pay for that wine? We must have another bottle—not at your expense, but mine. It's my treat this time."

"Oh, no! no, no!" said the General, "I'll pay for the wine! Mr. Adams, bring us another bottle. Boys, you come over to-morrow and I'll have your passes fixed out for you!"

I assured him that we would, and, having drank the wine, we left and returned to camp, considerably elated with our adventure.

Unfortunately, Billy Jackson and the spy both got away. The only good that I could then do was to find the "hole in the fence" where they had gone out, and prevent a repetition of it.

I knew that Mrs. Dr. Coleman was a daughter of General Neely, and I thought that she, probably, knew where Jackson and his spy went out through our lines. I had been there a number of times, and had become considerably acquainted, and Mrs. Coleman had not yet found out that I belonged to the Federal army. Doctor Coleman was a practicing physician, and was absent from home the most of the time, visiting his patients.

The next morning I went over to see her. After we had conversed awhile, I said to her, "'Melia, did you see Billy Jackson in town yesterday?"

"Yes, did you?"

"Yes, I saw him, but I was wondering how in the world he managed to get out; the Yankees are getting mighty particular who they pass out."

"Why, I can tell you; he went right through our corn-field, and out at the water-gulch under the fence."

"Yes, yes; I do remember that place now; that's

a good place to go out. By the way, how does the doctor like the Yankees being so strict?"

"He do n't like it at all; he had to go and take the oath before they would give him a pass to visit his patients."

"Did he?"

"Yes; and I never felt so bad about any thing in my life as I did about that. The nasty, dirty thieves! I perfectly hate the sight of them. I assure you the doctor do n't consider himself bound by it; no, indeed he do n't."

She was very indignant to think that her husband had been compelled to take the oath. From there I went to see her father, General Neely, who gave me the pass that he had promised me the day before. Thus prepared, I went to head-quarters and reported.

That day Doctor Coleman's corn was all cut down, so that the pickets had a fair view of the ground without changing the line, and General Neely was sent North for a violation of his parole.

CHAPTER VI.

The value of the Oath—Attempt to take "Bunker's" life—Sent to Grand Junction—The hazardous ride—Shoots the picket—The chase—Unfortunate occurrence—The chase abandoned—Meets with guerrillas—They invite him to drink—Renewed vigilance—The battle of Middleburg.

THE troops stationed at Bolivar, Tennessee, at the time of the evacuation of Grand Junction, were under the command of Brigadier-General L. F. Ross, and my next labors in the secret service of the United States was under his orders and instructions. I made frequent expeditions from Bolivar, but many of them were so similar in the incidents experienced that I shall not undertake to give a narrative of all of them. These expeditions elicited the fact, however, that nearly all of the citizens of that part of Tennessee, in the face of the military occupation of the country, professed loyalty to the Federal Government, and to give their pretensions the color of reality, and secure the privilege to be obtained from the military authorities, took the oath of allegiance.

Every trip that I made in the disguise of a Confederate soldier revealed to me Confederate wolves clad in Union garments. On one occasion, I had been sent for, and was in the act of receiving my instructions from the Adjutant in regard to a trip that I was required to make, when an old gray-headed citizen called in to procure some military favor. The Adjutant, not supposing the little he had yet to communicate to me would give the citizen any clue to the plans I was about to carry out, finished his instructions in his presence. I observed that the old man paid more than usual attention to what was said, and, from the expression of his countenance, I suspected that he comprehended the move that I was about to make. I became so impressed with the idea that the old man meant me evil, that after I had left and the old man had taken his departure, I went back and obtained permission to take a squad of men with me.

I made the trip in the night. My route was on a road that passed the old man's house. I came upon two men by the roadside, evidently watching for somebody to pass. As soon as they discovered that a *squad* of men, instead of a *single man*, was approaching, they fled without waiting for me to come up. Had the old man succeeded, it would have been my last scout. I ascertained from the colored people on the place that the two men were the old man and his son, and that they were watching to kill a Yankee spy that they expected would pass that night.

When General Van Dorn gave up the pursuit after General Leggett's brigade, he fell back with his command to Coldwater and Holly Springs, Mississippi, and for a few weeks every thing remained quiet.

Toward the latter part of August rumor became prevalent that an attack was intended against the forces garrisoning Bolivar, which rendered it necessary to watch closely. On the night of August 27th, General Ross told me that he had heard that a force of the enemy had again got as far north as Grand Junction, and that he wanted I should ride down that night and find the enemy's pickets if they were north of the Junction; if not, to go on to the Junction and then return.

I started at 9 o'clock. The weather was warm, but the night was extremely dark, which rendered the undertaking unpleasant and hazardous. It was impossible to distinguish objects at a distance, and it would require the utmost precaution to prevent running into the pickets before I was aware of their presence.

After having arrived within three miles of Grand Junction, the ride became more dangerous than before. Knowing that my safety required increased vigilance, I slackened my pace to a very slow walk, peering forward into the dark distance with all the powers of my vision, hoping if there was any pickets I might be able to see them in time to escape.

In that manner I felt my way along in suspense, until within three-quarters of a mile of Grand Junction. Here a single sentry stepped out in the midnight darkness, not more than six feet ahead of my mule, and challenged:

"Halt! who comes there?"

I had got too close to venture an escape by running, and I resolved to make the best use of my position that the circumstances would permit, and take my chance for the result.

"A friend, with the countersign," I replied, at the same time drawing my revolver and hanging it down by my side.

"Advance one, with the countersign!" said the sentry.

"There a'n't but one here," said I; "my mule is so ugly that I don't like to dismount, and so skittish that I don't know as I can advance;" and at the same time I pretended to urge my mule forward to the sentry, who stood with his piece at "arms port." "Bring your piece to an 'order,' said I, "if you please, so that I can get my mule up without dismounting." He brought his piece to an order, and as the mule moved forward, he stepped one foot forward and leaned toward me to receive the countersign. I leaned forward, and, thrusting my revolver to his breast, *gave him my countersign!* The heavy *thug*, as he dropped, told *me* that the "*countersign was correct!*"

I did not wait to observe the effect of the report of my revolver upon his sleeping companions, but, putting spurs to my mule, I dashed back toward Bolivar. On did I press my mule at the top of his speed, fairly *flying* over the ground until I reached Van Buren. As I was passing old Billy Moore's house, his dogs sprang at my mule, from the side of the road, with an infernal yelp, and the next instant I lay sprawling in the road—stunned from the shock of the fall. How long I lay there I do not know—probably not long—but as soon as I came to consciousness, I was alarmed for my safety, and made an effort to get up. My mule had stopped when I fell, and stood facing me, only a few feet from where I lay. I managed, however, to get on my mule and go on.

A short distance from Van Buren I came to a cross-road that led to another road that came out into the one that I was on. There I halted, thinking that, perhaps, the same dogs that had done me an evil turn, by barking at me, would do me a good one by barking at my pursuers, if any there were. I had waited but a few minutes when they commenced to bark, and in an instant more I could hear the tramp of horses approaching.

I again dashed ahead down the cross-road into the other one and on to Spring Creek bottoms. Where each of the roads crosses the bottoms the water spreads out over the roads to the width of a hundred yards. I crossed to the opposite side and there halted, and listened for the splash of the water as my pursuers came up, but none came. At the cross-road, not knowing which I had taken, they abandoned the pursuit. Feeling satisfied of this, I moved on leisurely toward Bolivar.

At daylight I reached Mr. Dicken's plantation, which is within five miles of Bolivar. I had called there several times, and had become considerably acquainted with the family. Being sore from my bruises, and much fatigued and hungry from my night's ride, I concluded to give them a call. As I rode up I observed three strange horses feeding in one of the out-sheds. My rap at the door was responded to by Mrs. Dickens, who received me with a hearty welcome; and Mr. Dickens was equally glad to see me. I had, on a former occasion, introduced myself as a citizen of Tennessee, living in Memphis. My mule was cared for by one of the servants, and in a few minutes we were engaged in a free and easy conversation about the news from *our* army; and likewise we congratulated each other upon the future success of the Confederate cause. The Lincoln tyranny also came in for its share of discussion. While thus engaged, three strangers entered, without rapping, to whom I was introduced as one of "*our* folks" from Memphis. I soon learned that they had been there all night.

Shortly after the three men entered, one of them said that he had something to drink in another room, and proposed that we retire by ourselves and "take a smile." So we men folks all repaired to the other room, where we indulged pretty freely. It was not long until the conversation of my new acquaintances flowed as freely as their liquor had done, and I learned from it that they were guerrillas, who had stopped to spend the night on their way to Middleburg, to attend a jollification to come off that day. By this time breakfast was announced, and we repaired to the table. I have rarely eaten a meal that relished better, though it was only a plain one.

When breakfast was over, my guerrilla acquaintances invited and even urged me to accompany them; but I declined, stating as a reason that I had business of great importance, the nature of which I was not at liberty to divulge, and that several of our *most reliable* friends were waiting in anticipation of my arrival at the house of Dr. Coleman, in Bolivar. My mule was got ready, and, having bid them farewell, I resumed my ride back to camp.

Two days after, I accompanied an expedition to Middleburg to capture the guerrillas, but without success. My report at head-quarters caused an increase in vigilance on the part of scouts and pickets. On the 31st of August, the enemy, 6,000 strong, was found to be advancing in the vicinity of Middleburg. General Leggett, with less than one thousand men, mostly from the 20th and 78th Ohio regiments of infantry, met them there, and a desperate fight ensued, in which our loss was trifling and that of the enemy severe. So badly punished was the enemy that he withdrew his forces.

CHAPTER VII.

Attempts to visit the enemy's camp—Learns the strength and position of the enemy—Return intercepted—Perilous situation—Loses his mule—Frightened by men of his own regiment—The plan to capture the enemy—The negro's report—The forces discovered—Disposes of a rebel picket—Reports his discovery.

AFTER the fight in the vicinity of Middleburg, a part of the enemy went into camp between the battle-ground and Van Buren. Soon after, General Leggett requested me to visit the enemy's camp and learn his force, and whether he had any artillery. He gave me a pass to go out, in the presence of the field-officer of the day, who said that no passes were being given out at division head-quarters, and objected to my going out. General Leggett told the officer that I was a privileged character, and that he would take the responsibility of passing me out, but that he would give passes to no others.

Dressed like a citizen, and mounted on a mule, I went out and made my way to the rebel picket line, where I tried to pass in, but was informed by the pickets that they had orders forbidding them to pass citizens in or out. I passed along the line to other posts, but found that they all had the same orders. I made myself quite familiar with the pickets, and those not on duty did not hesitate to enter into conversation with me, by means of which I learned that the force consisted of three regiments of cavalry, and that there was no artillery.

Having gathered up what information I could, I went to visit the battle-field, and while there I came across a young man who was on his way from Saulsbury to Somerville, and had met with the same difficulty I had encountered about getting through the lines, and, in order to continue his journey, he had made a detour round the lines. My own observations and his gave me a correct knowledge of the rebel lines on three sides, and also the position of the rebel camp.

After completing my visit to the battle-ground, I returned toward Bolivar. On my way out to the rebel lines, I had seen and conversed with an old man, a Mr. Knight, who lives about three miles from Bolivar. As I approached his house, on my return, and when within one hundred yards of it, I saw in his front yard two persons dressed like rebel soldiers, who had squirrel rifles. The moment they saw me, they brought their pieces to a ready, as if preparing to fire. I remembered distinctly that General Leggett had said that he would pass nobody else out; besides, I was a little suspicious of the old man Knight's loyalty; so I very naturally concluded that he, knowing that I had gone out, had went and got two soldiers to watch for me as I returned.

I immediately wheeled my mule about and went back behind a rise of ground, and then turned to my left into a corn-field. I dashed ahead about three hundred yards, when I discovered a company of rebel cavalry coming in a line toward me. I turned to my left again, and was dashing ahead toward Bolivar, when I unexpectedly encountered a deep water-gulch that was impassable to my mule. In my flight through the corn, I had already lost my hat. There I was, surrounded, with the enemy to my right, left, and rear, and a frightful ditch in front of me; it was no time for hesitation. I jumped off from my mule and left it, and clambered down into the ditch and then out on the other side, and ran for Bolivar as hard as I could go, bare-headed.

I made my way into camp, and procured a detachment of men and returned, hoping to find my mule, but did not succeed. I learned, however, that the two men that had caused my fright were Daniel Harris and Columbus Johnson, *of my own regiment*. They had been permitted to visit the battle-ground without arms, but, contrary to their instructions, had taken their arms with them.

On my return, I reported the force and position of the enemy, and also a plan for its capture. So well pleased was General Leggett with my plan, that he sent me with it to General Crocker, who was then commanding the post, during a temporary absence of General Ross. The position of the enemy was as follows:

Five miles from Bolivar, on the road leading south to Van Buren, the road forks; the right-hand road leads to Middleburg, a distance of two miles. On the left-hand road, at a distance of two miles from the fork, is a cross-road, called "Wash. Newbern's road," leading into the right-hand road at Middleburg. The three roads inclose a section of country in shape like a regular triangle. We will call the Wash. Newbern road the base, and the right and left-hand roads the sides of the triangle; Wash. Newbern's house stands on the south side of the road constituting the base, and about three hundred yards from the left-hand road. On a line parallel with the base, and three hundred yards south of it, was the rebel camp. Two of the regiments were on the west side of the left-hand road, and one on the east side; the regiment occupying the left of the enemy's line was directly south of Newbern's house. In front of Newbern's house, north of the road, is a pasture-field extending north to the road leading from the fork to Middleburg; the fence along the road in front of Newbern's was thrown down. The pasture-field is narrow at each end, but in the center it is much wider, making the space in the center diamond-shaped. At the corner of the cross-road, near the rebel camp, was the reserve pickets, and about one hundred yards north of the reserve was the advance post. On the west side of the pasture-field was a large corn-field, and on the east side a piece of woods.

My plan to capture the enemy was to take four regiments of infantry, and place two regiments on each side of the diamond space in the field, in the morning, before daylight, and have them lay down in the corn-field and woods, so as to be out of sight. Then, at daylight, with what was known as the "mule cavalry," (infantry mounted on mules,) numbering one hundred men, make a dash on the reserve pickets and drive them in; then turn down the Wash.

Newbern road, and, when in front of Newbern's house, break into confusion and disorder, and, with whoops and shouts of defiance, start leisurely down through the pasture. The enemy would naturally mount their horses and give chase, and, when once within the lines of the infantry, they would suddenly rise up, raise a shout, and close in each flank, and have them bagged.

General Crocker thought my plan would work, but, being only temporarily in command, did not like to assume the responsibility of executing it, and so it was abandoned.

The "mule cavalry" above alluded to was organized to facilitate scouting, and watch more closely the movements of the enemy, and to check the depredations of guerillas that infested the country. It was composed of men from the infantry, selected for their daring and gallantry. On account of the thorough knowledge that I had obtained of the country, I was generally sent out with them, to guide them in their scouts.

Not a great while after the foregoing adventure, as the "mule cavalry" was going out on the road leading south from Bolivar, I accompanied them on my own responsibility. After we had got outside of the lines a short distance, I left the mule cavalry and took across the fields to the left, to Mr. Bill's plantation. I had got into a cotton-field on his plantation, and was riding leisurely along, when one of the niggers, who was picking cotton a short distance to my right, called out:

"Hallo, dar, Mr. Bunker! you come dis way."

I obeyed, and rode out to see what the nigger wanted.

"Mr. Bunker, hab we got forces down dar in de bottom?"

"No, we have n't got any forces there."

"Wal, dar's forces down in dar; for de horn souns down in dar reg'lar ebery mornin', ebery noon, an' ebery night, an' dar mus' be forces down dar."

"It must be rebel forces, then; probably rebel cavalry."

"Oh, Lord! Mr. Bunker, do n't talk dat ar way, for dey will be up here for sure some night, an' dey will kill all de niggers Massa Bill hab got!"

"Well, I must go and see who is down there. Can you tell me of any path that leads down there?"

"Thar's heaps o' hog-paths dat leads down in dat ar way as yer go through de gate in de fur en' de field," said the nigger, pointing to the fence.

I rode on through the field in the direction pointed out, and following one of the hog-paths, I descended a hill, and was just rising to the top of another, when I discovered, on a ridge in advance of me, fourteen mounted rebels. They evidently had not seen me. I immediately backed my mule down the hill so far as to be out of sight, and then turned to the left and went down into a hollow, and then up a narrow ridge, or hog's back, leading in the direction of Bolivar. When I had rode along about four hundred yards through the scattering timber, I saw a fellow dressed like a rebel soldier, about fifty yards ahead, approaching me, with a double-barreled shotgun, which he carried, lying across the back of his neck, resting on both shoulders, with both his arms up over the gun. As he came along he was whistling a very lively tune, apparently perfectly unconcerned at my approach.

The moment I saw him, and before he discovered my movements, I drew my revolver, and held it down by my side out of sight, and when within about six feet of him, I presented my revolver and ordered him to halt. He did so, looking perfectly astonished. "Lay that gun right down on the ground," I continued. He did so, by raising it right up over his head with both hands and laying it down in front of him; then, straightening himself up in the position of a soldier, said:

"Well, sir; what will you have?"

"Step right back, away from that gun!" He did so. "That will do," said I, when about six feet away, at the same time riding up to the gun.

"What were you doing here?"

"I've just been relieved from the look-out post, out thar."

"Look-out post! What's that?"

"Don't you belong to that ar mule cavalry?"

"No, I don't belong to it, but I sometimes go with it. What command do you belong to?"

"Armstrong's 2d Battalion of Cavalry."

"How many are there of you here?"

"There are one hundred and sixty of us."

"What are you doing here?"

"We are sent out here to watch the mule cavalry."

"Where is your look-out post?"

"Well, sir, are you acquainted about here?"

"I am acquainted with all the roads, but not with your look-out post."

"Well, sir, our look-out post is in old 'Squire Knight's wheat-field. There is a big black stump there, with a plank across the top of it; we stand on that. From there we can see your mule cavalry at Joe Knight's, and we can see you at John Ursury's blacksmith-shop, and tell whether you take the Middleburg or Van Buren road; and the next place that we can see you is at Wash. Newbern's lane, and we can tell whether you go to Van Buren or to Wash. Newbern's. If ever you get down past Beaver's lane, going to Van Buren, it will be the last of you and your mule cavalry."

I then dismounted and picked up the shot-gun. What to do with the soldier was hard for me to decide. If I undertook to take him to Bolivar, it was quite probable that I would lose my prisoner, and perhaps my life. To let him go would endanger my life and that of others; particularly my own, in case he should ever recognize me within their lines. I reflected a moment, and then disposed of him in the only way that I thought my own safety and the good of the service would admit; then shouldered the gun and started for Bolivar. I did not feel safe in carrying the gun, lest it should betray me in case I should be captured by a squad of the rebel cavalry; so, at the first stump I came to, I dismounted and broke it, and then went on. If I had had a gun of long range, I should have tried a pull at the man on the look-out post, but as it was, I did not think it advisable to molest him.

On reaching camp, I concluded that it was my duty to report to some body; but not having been officially sent out, I reported to Colonel Force. He listened to my report, and when I had finished, told me to report to General Ross. I did so, and he told me to have myself in readiness the next morning to guide a force of cavalry around to the rear of the rebel force, and that he would send a regiment of infantry in front, and try to capture the whole of them. Morning came, and I was ready to go, but received no orders. I have since learned that the plan fell through because the Colonel wanted his regiment to go, and the General wanted his old regiment to go, and finally did not send any.

CHAPTER VIII.

Sent to find the enemy's pickets—Suspicious circumstance—Sick child—Captures three citizens standing picket—Releases them—Falls asleep—Perilous situation—Fortunate turn of affairs—Attack on the pickets—A very pious man—He proves a rebel spy.

ABOUT a week after my attempts to get into the rebel camp near Wash. Newbern's, General Ross sent me down to the corners, at Newbern's lane, to ascertain whether the enemy had any pickets there. I was ordered to take three men with me, and to be very cautious in my movements, and, if I found any pickets near the place designated, not to fire into them, but to come immediately back and report. The place I was to visit was seven miles from Bolivar; we started out after 9 o'clock in the evening; I was mounted on a mule, but the three men that accompanied me were on foot. It was a starlight night—not so dark but that we could discern objects at a considerable distance, and yet dark enough to facilitate our movements.

Five miles from Bolivar, we came to a house occupied by Mr. John Ursury, and, as we approached it, we observed in it a light. We had moved along very slowly, and it had then got to be past 11 o'clock. Thinking it was rather strange that a light should be burning there at that hour of the night, I resolved to ascertain the cause of it.

Taking one man with me, and sending the other two to the rear of the house, to capture any persons that might undertake to escape, I rode up to the front door, with my revolver drawn, and, without dismounting, lifted the latch and shoved the door wide open. The persons present were Mrs. Ursury and children, one of them a small child, and a brother of John Ursury, about fifteen years old.

"What are you doing here with a light at this time of night?" I inquired.

"We have got a sick child," replied Mrs. Ursury, "and we are doctoring it."

"It's best to see whether the child is sick or not," said the man that accompanied me. He then went in and found it awake in the cradle, and, stranger as he was, soon had the child in a frolic, laughing and playing.

"It's a curious sickness that that child has got," said the man, coming out.

I then called the brother out, and, pointing my revolver at him, said: "There is something going on here besides doctoring a sick child, you young d—l, you! and if you do n't tell me in a minute what it is, I'll blow the heart right out of you!"

"Mr. Bunker," said he, "is there any forces coming along here?"

"Yes, there is a large force coming."

"Well, my brother is standing watch up by the railroad. Had n't I better go up and tell him to come down?"

"No; you go into the house and stay there. I'll go after him myself."

I then called my men and went into the road, where I ordered them to remain until I should call. I then rode forward to see what was going on. When I came in sight of the railroad crossing, I saw five men; three of the men were mounted and two were not; they did not seem to have any arms. I called to my men to come on, and then dashed up to them with revolver drawn, and demanded of them to surrender. As I was dashing up, the two that were not mounted fled, and the other three stood their ground.

"Don't shoot us, Mr. Bunker! Don't, for God's sake!" called out Mr. Ursury, who at once recognized me.

"March down into the road, then, if you don't want to be shot! Fine business, this! Good loyal men standing picket for rebel soldiers! March down there! I'll see about this."

I then marched them over to where I had left my men, who, failing to hear me call, had remained where I left them. One of the prisoners was an old, gray-headed preacher, by the name of Parson Hamer; I have forgotten the name of the other. The two that I have named I had seen several times before.

"What were you doing there at this time of night?" I inquired.

"We were watching for some niggers to come along that ran away from my brother-in-law," said Ursury.

"Who were those two men with you that ran away?"

"I do n't know," replied Ursury.

I asked the other two, and they denied knowing who they were.

"Well, I can tell who they were," I continued. "There are rebel forces over in Mr. Dickens' woods, and those men belong to them, and you men were standing picket for them." This they stoutly denied, and said that if there were any rebel forces there they did not know it.

Addressing Parson Hamer, I said; "You are an old, gray-headed man—a preacher of the Gospel; you ought to be ashamed of yourself. An old man like you, with one foot in the grave and the other just ready to slip in, out at this time of night *watching for niggers!* That's a fine excuse! It do n't look reasonable. You are a d—d old rebel, with the oath in your pocket, and you deserve to be shot!"

I did not know what to do with them; I had two miles further to go, and it was necessary for me to take all my men with me, and to be encumbered with prisoners, in case we should run into a force, would be hazardous. I finally took down their names and released them, and then went on.

Finding no pickets at Newbern lane, we returned. On arriving at the railroad crossing where I had captured the prisoners, I sent my men to camp by way of the railroad, which was a much shorter route than the wagon-road, and kept on myself the way I had come out.

Having slept but very little for several nights, by

reason of being out on scouts, after parting company with my men I became very sleepy, and experienced considerable difficulty in keeping awake, and at last fell asleep.

All at once my mule came to a sudden halt, throwing up its head as if something was wrong. The movement woke me up, and there, stretched across the road, was a line of soldiers bringing their pieces to a ready. I could plainly hear the click-ick-ick as they cocked them, for they were not more than fifteen yards from me. I can not describe the horror and alarm that I felt at my situation; it was of no use to run, so I resolved to put on a bold front and sell my life as dear as possible. Surrender! no, never! thought I, if I die the next instant.

"Who comes there?" said I, drawing my revolver.

"Advance and give the countersign!" said the officer in command of the soldiers.

"Who are you?" said I.

"No matter!" said he; "advance and give the countersign."

"I sha'n't advance a step until I know who you are!"

"Well, you advance one," said he, "and I'll advance one."

"Very well; come on!"

As we met, each with revolver cocked, the officer exclaimed, "Why, Bunker! Is that you? I am frightened to think of it! Why did n't you stop? In an instant more my whole company would have fired into you!"

"I was asleep, Captain! It *was* a narrow escape, was n't it?"

"Indeed, it was!"

It was no other than Captain Ayres and company A, of the 20th Ohio, sent out as a support for me to fall back on if I was discovered by the enemy and pursued. They had been sent out after I left, and I had no knowledge that they were coming. The result of it was, I came *very near falling back without any support!*

My suspicions of a rebel force being in Dickens' woods was confirmed in the morning by an attack on our pickets, by a force of five hundred men, by which two men of the 23d Indiana were wounded. After firing into the pickets, the enemy made a detour to the north-west of Bolivar, and there encountered a large Federal foraging party, that fired into them and killed seven, which made them skedaddle.

The next day I was sent out with a party of nine men to procure forage. Having found a fine lot of honey, some fresh butter, and a quantity of chickens, we loaded them into an open buggy, confiscated a mule to draw it, and then bent our way back to camp. We had proceeded but a little way, when I discovered a man a short distance ahead. As soon as he saw us, he sat down in the shade of a tree in a bend of the road, pulled out a Testament, and commenced to read. Coming up to him, I said, "Daddy, how do you do?"

"By the grace of God, I am well, and I hope you enjoy the same blessing," was his answer.

"You are mighty good, a'n't you? You are a soldier, I suppose."

"No, gentlemen, I am not a soldier. By the providence of God, I am a preacher of the Gospel pure."

"Look here, daddy; don't you know that this country is invaded? Over there lies the Federal army, and yonder the Confederate army. What business have you to be prowling about between the lines of the two contending armies?"

"I have got a Federal pass," said he, handing me one signed by General Ross, "and I have taken the oath. I have no connection with the Confederate army."

"Well, daddy, you do n't look like a man with a clear conscience; we must search you." We proceeded to search him, which resulted in finding, in a leg of his pantaloons, between the outside and lining, a map eighteen inches by twenty-two, representing exactly our fortifications, intrenchments, camp, and picket line at Bolivar. It was skillfully executed, and was as accurate as it could well be made. Our discovery of the map took away the old man's sanctimonious dignity. "This is one of your sermons, I suppose!" I remarked, as I drew out the map. "A fine subject for a minister of the Gospel!" He dropped his head and made no reply.

"Now, daddy, you look tired; you get into the buggy and ride." So the old man got in. "Now, boys, take the rope from the mule's neck and put it on the old man's neck." So they changed places with the rope. By this time the man looked terribly frightened, and as white as a ghost. "One of you that is good at climbing mount that tree." There was a limb from the tree where the old man had been sitting, that extended out over the road where we had halted the buggy. To this the rope was made fast. Every thing being ready, I said, "Daddy, you are in a hurry to get to Canaan, and we are in a hurry to get to camp, so good day, sir." Our mule then gave a desperate plunge, leaving him to travel his journey alone to that place where, by the grace of God, he'll have no use for maps of Federal fortifications.

I carried the map to General Ross, and related to him the circumstances of its capture.

"Did you bring the man in?" he inquired.

"No, sir; we have brought in several disloyal characters, and they have all managed to get released; for that reason we thought it not worth while."

"You let him go, did you?"

"Yes, we let him go—*by the jerk!*"

General Ross sent the map to General Grant, then at Jackson, Tenn., accompanied with the particulars of its capture.

CHAPTER IX

Sent to Somerville—Finds himself a prisoner—Taken to Cold Water—Meets with old acquaintances—Is paroled—Runs with the 2d Arkansas Cavalry—Goes to Lumpkins' Mills—Interview with General Price—Stays all night with his brother, the rebel General—Return to Bolivar—Reports to General Ross—"Steals the Colonel's horse," and returns to the enemy—Runs away from the enemy.

ABOUT the middle of September, the enemy having disappeared from our immediate front, General Ross sent me to Somerville, with instructions to reconnoiter the country all about, and find out, if possible, where the enemy had gone to, and such other information as I could obtain.

I started out quite early in the morning, mounted on a mule, dressed like a citizen in easy circumstances. Whenever I met a planter, I would stop and converse with him about the "news from our army," and the prospects of the war, and the "d—d thieving Yankees that were robbing us of our cotton and niggers." In the course of such conversation, I learned there were no rebel forces in that immediate vicinity. About noon, I reached Somerville. There I found every thing quiet as a Sabbath morning. Passing through the town, I took the road to Moscow. Coming to a large, fine brick house that stands near the railroad depot, I drew up and alighted from my mule, and went in, in pursuit of some dinner.

"Stranger," said I, addressing an elderly gentleman that I found on entering, "can I get some dinner here?"

"I reckon so," he said, handing me a chair; "dinner will be ready in a few minutes. Sit down."

I complied.

"Where do you belong?" he inquired.

"My home is in Memphis, Tennessee, but"—

Just then I was interrupted by the entrance of two men, who came in from an adjoining room, one of whom asked me where I belonged.

"I was just saying to this gentleman," I replied, "that my home is in Memphis, Tennessee, but I came from Bolivar here."

"Do you belong to the Federal army?"

"No, sir; I am a citizen of this State, and my home, as I said before, is in Memphis."

"How came you to be in Bolivar?"

"I went out there to see General Neely and Doctor Coleman, and the Adamses, and several others that I am acquainted with, and when I got in there the Yankees would not let me out when I wanted them to, and I had to remain there several days."

"Did you get a pass from the Yank's to get out with?"

"Yes, sir; but it only passed me out, and was retained by the pickets."

"Have you got any fire-arms or papers with you?"

"No, sir; I had a nice navy revolver that I carried to Bolivar, but I was obliged to leave it with an acquaintance when I left, to keep the Yankees from taking it away from me."

"Well, sir, you may consider yourself my prisoner, and after dinner we'll go down to Cold Water and see what they can do for you there."

"Gentlemen," said I, "I am no Yankee soldier. I am a citizen, and I can't see what object you can have in taking me there."

"It don't matter whether you do or not. I think that they will have some use for you."

Dinner was then announced as ready, and we all sat up. "*I think that they will have some use for you!*" reverberated through my brain, and set me into a train of thought any thing but agreeable. *I'm to be a conscript then!* thought I. I tried to suppress my feelings, and feigned to be cheerful, as if nothing had occurred to disturb my equanimity. In fact, my only hope was in appearing cheerful.

When dinner was over, the two men had their horses brought out, and we all three mounted and started for Cold Water, forty miles distant. On the way I kept up a cheerful conversation, and on several occasions I had my butternut friends convulsed with laughter. I found out that the man who had made me a prisoner was Captain Daniels, a noted guerrilla, and the other person was a Quartermaster.

At 2 o'clock, A. M., we reached the outpost near Cold Water, where we halted until daylight, and then went in. As we were going in, we met a soldier, who, when he saw me, called out, "Hallo, Ruggles, is that you? Where in the h—l have you been? I hav'n't seen you since we made shingles together on White River!"

"I'm a prisoner," said I.

"A prisoner? the h—l you are!"

"Yes, Captain Daniels, here, captured me at Somerville, yesterday."

"Ha, ha! captured *you*? Why, Captain, I have known that man for years, and made shingles for him on White River, in Arkansas, and he is as loyal to the Confederate cause as you are! There are five or six other boys here that know him as well as I do!"

Captain Daniels then took me to the head-quarters of the regiment, and there I found, in the Colonel, another man that I was well acquainted with. His name was Slemmens; he used to be prosecuting attorney at Napoleon, Arkansas. When I entered his quarters—

"Lord bless me!" he said, "if here a'n't Ruggles! How are you?"

"Pretty well, I thank you. I am glad to meet you. I did n't know that you was in the service. The last time we met was at Napoleon, I believe."

"Yes; but pray what fetched you here?"

"Captain Daniels captured me and fetched me here."

"*Captured* you?"

"Yes; I told him I was a citizen of the South, but he did not believe me."

"I have known Ruggles these six years, Captain; he's all right. But, then, never mind—I see! we'll make him count one in exchange. I'll parole him. Where did you capture him?"

Daniels told him the particulars of my capture, and that I had been in Bolivar several weeks.

"Well," said the Colonel, "I'll parole him."

"Do you know the name of any Colonel in Bolivar, and the regiment that he commands?"

"Yes, I know one; his name is Force, and he commands the 20th Ohio Infantry."

"Well, that will do as well as any."

He then paroled me as belonging to the 20th Ohio Infantry, commanded by Colonel Force.

Captain Daniels and the Quartermaster then left me with Colonel Slemmens, and returned toward Somerville. My old acquaintances all got together at the Colonel's quarters, and we had a right lively visit. They were all urgent to have me join the regiment, and I finally consented to run with them awhile, and promised to join if I liked the regiment. I had found out, by this time, that the regiment was the 2d Arkansas Cavalry, and was there on outpost duty. It had been raised in a part of Arkansas where I was well acquainted. There was no other regiment there at that time. The principal part of the rebel forces in Northern Mississippi were then camped at Lumpkins' Mills, seven miles south of Holly Springs.

Among the acquaintances that I made during my stay in the regiment, was the Lieutenant-Colonel and the regimental sutler. The former was a Methodist clergymen, by the name of Rosebrook. He was very urgent in his endeavors to have me join the regiment.

Two days after my arrival, the regiment received orders from General Villipigue to move to Gun Town, on the Ohio and Mobile Railroad, seventy miles distant. I went with it. There it received orders from General Van Dorn to go to Ripley. We remained at Ripley a few days, during which time we made two or three cotton-burning trips. We then received orders to go back to Cold Water.

From Cold Water I accompanied Colonel Slemmens on a visit to Lumpkins' Mills. While there we called on General Price, and I was introduced as a brother of General *Ruggles.* In the conversation that was had with Colonel Slemmens and myself, General Price learned that I did not belong to any organized regiment, but that I had temporarily attached myself to the 2d Arkansas Cavalry. He told me that I would have to be assigned to some regiment as a conscript. I objected to that. He said that it would have to be done, and unless it was done I could not draw any pay or subsistence from the Confederate Government.

"General," said I, "the Southern Confederacy is of *more consequence* to me than *pay.* I did not come into the army for *pay.* I have got six hundred dollars in my pocket, and I intend to fight on that until it is gone. I have got a rich sister in Memphis, and when that is gone, I will go to her and get more. Besides, I can do more good as I am, because when there is a fight coming off any where, I can go into it, but if I am fast, I can only go where the regiment goes to which I belong."

"Well," said the General, "perhaps you can do the most good as you are; you may remain so."

In the afternoon of the day before we were to return, General Price sent me word that my brother, General *Ruggles,* had arrived. I immediately went to head-quarters to see him. He expressed great delight at meeting me, and called me "Bub," as he used to do when at home, though I was forty years old. The Adjutant-General assigned us a tent by ourselves, and I remained with my brother all night. He had not been to Ohio for a great many years, and he was very much interested in learning the changes that had taken place in the neighborhood where he was raised. All I learned of him about the army was, that his command was near Baton Rouge, La., and that he had come there on business pertaining to his command. He did not ask me where I lived, nor allude to the subject of the rebellion. He knew that I had spent a great portion of my life in the South, and, naturally enough, supposed that I was identified with her interests.

In the morning I returned with Colonel Slemmens to Cold Water. I had learned, by this time, a great deal of information, and had been absent a much greater length of time than I had calculated on when I left Bolivar, and I began to feel anxious to get back and report. I had become quite a favorite with Colonel Slemmens, and I could generally get from him any favor that I asked for.

"Colonel," said I to him, the next morning after we returned, "all the rest of the boys have got horses of their own, and I have got nothing but that little mule of mine to ride, and I want something else. Can't you make a cotton-burning trip up into the vicinity of Bolivar? While I was there I found one regiment of Yankees camped out a little distance from the other regiments, and the Colonel of it has got a splendid horse; if you will go, I can get in there and capture it."

"Pshaw! You could not get into the lines if you were there!"

"Yes I can; I know right where to get in, and if I don't get *that* horse I'll get some other. I'm bound to have a horse."

"Well, I can't go now, but I'll see about it."

I waited two days, and then tried him again.

"Colonel," said I, "what do you think about that cotton trip to Bolivar now? I'm getting *very* anxious for that horse."

"If I thought you would succeed, I'd go."

"I *know* I'll succeed."

"How close can we get without getting into the Yankee pickets?"

"We can get as far as Jonathan Herse's place, and there you can halt until I go in and return."

"Well, then, I'll take five companies and we'll go up there to-day, and we'll have every thing ready to start at 10 o'clock A. M."

At the appointed time we started, and moved along rapidly until we reached Herse's plantation. It was in the night when we reached there. The Colonel retained three companies, and sent two, under command of a Captain, with me, with instructions to stop at such a place as I should designate, and wait three hours for me to return, unless I returned sooner, and if I did not come back at the end of that time, to return without me.

We went on until we came within about four hundred yards of the pickets, where I had the Captain halt his men, and, leaving my mule, I went on. I found the advanced picket right where I expected to. He was on the alert, and challenged me as I came up. There I cautioned the officer in command of the pickets to be on the alert, for two companies of rebel cavalry were within rifle-shot of him. The pickets were all called up, and I was sent, under guard, to General Ross. I had him called up, and reported to him what I had learned, and told him that, in order to carry out my plans, I wanted an order on the Quartermaster for a number one horse. I also told him that I would leave my mule on Mr. Herse's plantation, and requested him to send a forage party out the next day and bring the mule in. He gave me the order, and I went immediately to C. C. Williams, Assistant Quartermaster, and woke him up, and told him I was in a great hurry and wanted the horse then.

However strangely he may have thought of my movements then, I am sure that when he reads these pages he will know why I disturbed him at that unusual hour of the night. He furnished me with a beautiful nag. With an old gun-sling and canteen strap I rigged up a sort of bridle, mounted the horse, and returned to my rebel escort.

On my return, I was in ecstasies of delight over "my captured" nag. I told the Captain that I had stolen it from a Colonel, and that I found it not twenty yards from his quarters, and that I tried to steal his saddle, bridle, and holsters, but his d—d nigger was sleeping with his head on the saddle and I could not get them without waking him up.

The men were all highly interested with the narration of my exploit, and not only conceded that I "was a h—l of a fellow," but "that I had got a d—d good horse." We then returned to Herse's plantation, and I awoke the Colonel to show him my prize. He was as much delighted as the rest had been.

It was by this time daylight, and we started for Cold Water; I left the mule, as I had agreed to do, on Mr. Herse's plantation. On our way back we burned considerable cotton. I remained a few days longer at Cold Water, and then accompanied a detachment to Saulsbury to burn cotton; from there I ran away and returned to Bolivar. My mule had been brought in as I requested, and so I exchanged my horse for it. I had been gone in all twenty days

CHAPTER X.

Sent to Grand Junction to capture guerrillas—Suspicious incident—Strategy to get out the guerrillas—Orders disobeyed—The rebel flag—The very kind secesh lady—The mistake—Out of the frying-pan into the fire—Guerrillas watching for them—The attack—The prisoner—The result of the trip.

A PART of the duties assigned me, in the many trips I made to Bolivar, was to hunt up guerrilla organizations, learn their intended movements, and make arrangements for their capture. During my scouts, I had learned that there was an organized band of guerrillas at Grand Junction. On reporting the fact to General Ross, he requested me to go down and capture them, and gave me for that purpose a force of one hundred infantry, under command of a Captain, and forty cavalry, under command of a Lieutenant, with instructions to the officers that they should obey my orders in whatever plans I should choose to adopt. I was also furnished with a train of ten four-horse teams and wagons, and was instructed to let the infantry ride out, and, on my return, to load the wagons with forage.

It was about sundown when the detachment moved out from Bolivar. I rode about one hundred yards in advance, then came the cavalry, and in the rear the train bearing the infantry. My dress on this occasion was that of a citizen.

When the last lingering rays of daylight had disappeared, the night became extremely dark—so dark that it was impossible to distinguish friend from foe by the powers of vision. While crossing a piece of bottom land, with a forest of trees on each side of the road that seemed to make the darkness still more impenetrable, I met three persons. I saluted them with a "Good-evening," and inquired of them where they were going, and was told that they were going after some horses that had strayed away, and that they wanted to go on to Mr. Dickens' and stay all night, and resume the search for the horses in the morning. By this time the Lieutenant of the cavalry came up, and, on further inquiry, found that they had passes. He took their passes to examine, but could not find a match with which to make a light. He then concluded, from the feeling of the paper, that they were our passes, and allowed them to go on. When they passed the train, the infantry soldiers were sitting down in the bottom of the wagon-beds, and the most of them were asleep, and the men, in passing, probably did not discover any force but the cavalry.

When within three miles of Grand Junction, we halted and waited until nearly daylight, and then moved on to within a mile of the place. There I had the teams turned about, facing toward Bolivar, and gave the teamsters instructions to remain by their teams, and, if we were driven back, to push forward to Bolivar, if possible. I then moved the cavalry and infantry forward as noiseless as possible into the lane, within half a mile of town, and instructed the officers to remain there just half an hour, and, if I did not return, to make a dash into the town, for they might know by my absence that I was captured.

My plan was to leave my men there, and ride into town myself and find the guerrillas, and, if they were not concentrated, to find their leader and have him get out his men, to capture a small squad of Lincoln cavalry that I would report as feeding their horses near town, and while he would be getting out his men, I would reconnoiter to see if they were still there, tell the Federal officers where to place their men, and then go back and act as guide to the guerrillas.

Having given all the instructions that I thought were necessary, I rode on into town. As I drew up in front of the Percy House, the doors of the house were being opened, and "mine host" came out.

"Good morning, sir," said I, as he made his appearance.

"Good morning, sir," said he, eyeing me closely.

"Have we got any cavalry here?"

"No, there is none nigher than Davis Creek, three miles from here."

"Have we got any guerrillas here?"

"Yes, some. Why, what do you want?"

"Thar's a squad of Lincoln cavalry right up thar," said I, pointing toward my own men.

"Where are you from?" he inquired, as if uncertain whether I was right or not.

"Oh, *I* am all right. I am just from Memphis, and, as I was coming in this morning, I saw a squad of Lincoln cavalry feeding their horses, and I would like to get out a squad of *our* men and go and capture them."

"Well, I do n't know how many guerrillas there is here; but there is Captain Robison, that keeps the corner grocery, and lives across the street as you go round the corner; he is Captain of the band, and he can tell you all about it."

"Thank you;" and I started off to find him.

When I got round the corner, I saw a nigger coming from a house that I took to be the Captain's; so I waited till he came out to me. I learned from him that it was the Captain's house, and that he was at home. Just then I was startled by the tramp of horses. Knowing that it was not time for my men to come in, I very naturally supposed that it was rebel cavalry. I went back to the corner to see what it was, and there came my own men, the cavalry on a gallop and the infantry on a double-quick. Instead of waiting *thirty* minutes, they had only waited *eight!* I was vexed to have my plans, through disobedience of orders, spoiled; and more so, because I had learned from experience that all attempts to convict a guerrilla after he was captured would be futile unless he was caught with arms in his hands fighting against us. With the oath of allegiance in their pockets, and the use of their oily tongues, they invariably managed to get released.

We then arrested Captain Robison, and such other persons as, from their actions, we had reason to believe belonged to the band.

Captain Robison kept, in addition to the grocery, a billiard saloon, which had been a favorite resort in the summer for the Federal officers, while the place was being garrisoned by the briade under command of General Leggett. One day, while engaged in playing a game of billiards, Lieut. P. M. Hitchcock, regimental Quartermaster of the 20th Ohio, having occasion to look under the table for something, discovered, fastened up underneath the table, a large rebel flag, which he captured and carried to camp. The flag had been secreted there when the Federal troops first took possession of the place, and the officers had played on that table every day for weeks without having discovered it.

Having secured our prisoners, we proceeded to make the citizens of the place furnish breakfast for the detachment. This they were reluctant to do, but finally submitted. When all had been supplied, we re-returned to the teams. The teamsters had not fared so well, and, as soon as I returned, they requested me to make arrangements for their breakfast. I told them to drive on and I would do so. I then rode on, to find a house that looked as if its occupants had a supply sufficient to furnish the breakfast, and forage for the horses and mules.

About four miles from Grand Junction, I came to a large brick house on the right-hand side, a short distance from the road. I opened the gate, entered the yard, and rode up toward the house, and, as I drew up to the door, an elderly lady came out, whom I addressed, and inquired if I could get breakfast there for sixteen men, and feed for a hundred and fifty horses.

Supposing me to be a secesh Colonel, she replied, " Well, yes, so far as breakfast for the men is concerned; but really, Colonel, about the corn, I do n't know as I have got enough here to feed so many; but if you are a mind to be to the trouble to send over to my nigger quarters, about three-quarters of a mile from here, you can get all the corn you want."

"Thank you, madam. I will ride down and halt the train, and send the men up for their breakfast."

As I rode away, I heard her order the niggers to get the breakfast. I halted the train, and set the niggers (who were returning with us from Grand Junction) to cutting up corn from a field on the opposite side of the road for the teams. The infantry soldiers immediately began to scatter about the plantation, in search of horses and mules, of which we had gotten several at Grand Junction.

The thought now occurred to me that I had been supposed by the lady to be a secesh Colonel, and that as soon as she saw the blue trousers, the getting of breakfast would be stopped; so I went back to the house to see about it. As soon as I came up, she met me at the door and commenced to complain.

"I thought that it was *our cavalry* coming; I was mistaken. Instead, I find that it is nothing but a *parcel of confounded Lincoln jayhawkers!*"

"We are all liable to mistakes, madam."

"Now, could you," she continued, "demand of a *poor lone widow*, like I am, breakfast for sixteen men and feed for a hundred and fifty horses?"

"The subject has changed appearances considerably since I was here before. I'll see about breakfast myself."

I dismounted and fastened my mule, and then went to a wood-pile and procured a big club, and then repaired to the cook-house. The niggers had evidently commenced to get things ready for the breakfast, but had stopped.

"What are you about, you black, woolly scoundrels! Why a'n't you cooking breakfast?" said I, addressing the niggers.

"Missus dun tole us not to get de breckfust!"

"Well, you go right to work and get the breakfast, or I'll thrash h—l out of your black hides! Start right away!" At that I made for them with my club.

"Hole on! hole on, massa! we'll dun an' get de breckfust!"

They all sprang to work in good earnest. One of the niggers told me that the woman had locked up the meat. I started for the smoke-house door, with my club, to break it in, but the woman, who had been watching me, followed with the keys, and, when she saw that I was going in any way, *begged* of me to let her unlock the door. On inquiry of the niggers, I found that she had butter locked up in a cupboard. I told her to get out some butter, and she declared she had n't got a bit in the house. I walked toward the cupboard, with my club raised, without saying any thing further, when she came running to the cupboard, with the keys in her hand, saying, "Do n't break it! do n't break it! I'll get it out! I'll get it out for you! Do give a body time!"

By dint of perseverance, using a good many threats and some motions, I succeeded in having the breakfast made ready; which, having been accomplished, the teamsters were called in to enjoy it. While the teamsters were eating, a squad of soldiers came through the yard, with about thirty geese that they had confiscated. The lady saw them, and came to me to plead for them.

"Now, *do n't* let the men take those geese; *do n't!* they are *great favorites* of mine, and I *hate* to part with them!"

I had noticed, a few minutes before, a large, close pen in one corner of the yard, filled with nice, fat turkeys, which one of the darkeys had told me were being fatted to send to the rebel officers. The boys had not yet discovered them.

"Boys, put down those geese; do n't be packing geese from here to Bolivar! Throw them down!"

"Why, Bunker!" they exclaimed, "you said we might get any thing that we wanted!"

"*Throw them down!*"

Down they went.

"Now, if you want any thing of the feathered tribe, pitch into those turkeys in that pen yonder," said I, pointing to it.

Away the boys went, a-flying.

"*Good Lord! Now do n't! do n't* get those *turkeys!* I'd rather you had took *every goose* on the place!"

"You *are* in a bad fix now, a'n't you?" said I. "Right out of the frying pan into the fire!"

Just then a little nigger girl came running in, and said:

"Missis, de Yankees dun got Lucy!"

"Where?" inquired the lady.

"Right out dat ar way," said the girl, pointing in the direction.

"*Well now, I declare! Do n't* take that riding nag away from me, a poor lone widow, as I am; *do n't!* Have a *little* mercy on me; *do!*"

"Yes!" said I, "you are a *mighty poor widow!* worth two hundred thousand dollars, and paying an overseer a thousand dollars a year; you are *mighty poor!* Soldier, fetch that mare back, and let the *poor widow* keep the d—d p-t-g-tt-d thing! It a'n't worth riding to Bolivar!"

As soon as breakfast was over, we again moved on. When within two miles of Van Buren, near where the Whitesville road takes off to the left, a little incident occurred to attract our attention. As I was riding along, in advance of the detachment, I saw a nigger coming up the road toward me, with his hat in his hand, and running as fast as he could, and appearing to be wonderfully excited about something.

"What's up?" said I, as I met him.

"Thar's a heap ob de secesh cavalry down by Massa's house, and dey are gwine to git you all!"

Here, then, was something to do. I was well acquainted with the features of the country all about there, and I knew where they would most likely be posted, and which way they would retreat if we were too much for them. I was also well satisfied that the enemy consisted of Hall's guerrillas, from Saulsbury, and that the men that we had met on our way down belonged to them, and, instead of going to Mr. Dickens' to stay all night, had gone down to Saulsbury and got out the band to capture our train, not knowing that we had any infantry force along.

I sent the Captain, with fifty men, to the right, to get to their flank in a piece of woods, where I was sure they would attempt to escape if we overpowered them. The Captain had a corn-field to cross, in reaching the woods, that would cover his men from view. I was to watch from the top of the fence, and see the Captain deploy his men in the woods, before ordering an attack in front.

I watched until I knew that the Captain had had plenty of time to have reached the woods; but, for some reason, he had not made his appearance. I waited as long as I thought it would do, and then, leaving ten men to guard the prisoners, I ordered the cavalry to charge, supported by the balance of the infantry.

As we dashed over the hill toward the house, a man was seen on the top of a large gate-post, watching for us to approach. He evidently had underestimated our force, and had not looked for a charge. In the yard by him was a splendid mule and a new saddle. He gave a look at them and then at us, and then broke for the corn-field on foot, leaving his mule and saddle for us. The saddle was a new one, and, I learned by the people in the house, belonged to Captain Richardson, who happened to be there, and was helping Hall's guerrillas to capture us. The saddle cost him thirty-seven dollars, and he had just received it the night before. As soon as the guerrillas discovered that we were charging on them, they fled to the woods where I had ordered the Captain to deploy his men, and they all escaped but one. The Captain had halted his men in the cornfield, and did not take them into the woods; had he done so, we might have captured the whole band, numbering, in all, thirty men.

The prisoner that we captured declared that he was no guerrilla, but a citizen; he told us that he lived in Memphis. At Van Buren, Mrs. Moore told me that she knew him, and that he was one of their nearest neighbors, and one of the finest men living in the county. At Mr. Marshall's we found a collection of neighbors, engaged in burying a child near the road-side. Mrs. Marshall, whom I saw there, told me that she knew him, and that he lived in Tupelo, Mississippi, and that he and his wife were out there on a visit, and that his wife was present somewhere in the gathering.

Just then the wife saw her husband, a prisoner, and she began to make a dreadful fuss, crying and wringing her hands, and begged of the Lieutenant to let him go; "for," said she, "I know that he will *never* take the oath, and they will *hang him, sure*, and I shall *never, never see him again in this world!*"

The Lieutenant passed on with his prisoner, and I remained behind until after the detachment had all passed, when I started on. Before overtaking them, I met the prisoner, coming back, with a written statement, signed by the Lieutenant, stating that he had been released. Before reaching Bolivar, the wagons were loaded with forage. Aside from the forage, mules, and contrabands that we gathered, the expedition was a failure.

The men we arrested at Grand Junction all managed to get released. I felt mortified at the result, because I felt sure that, if my plans had been carried out, we might have made a brilliant little affair of it. General Ross reprimanded the officers severely for not having obeyed my instructions.

The reader can see by the foregoing what might have been done on that expedition; yet it was a failure, because the parties concerned neglected to obey orders. It is a parallel case, on a small scale, to numerous others of greater magnitude, in the prosecution of the war.

Captain Richardson, who made his escape in the corn-field, has since been made a Colonel of a rebel regiment, raised near Lafayette, Tenn.

CHAPTER XI.

Sent to Lagrange—Observes two cavalrymen—Arrival at Lagrange—Waits for the cavalry—Accompanies them out—Takes his departure—Is pursued—Evades the pursuit—Finds himself cornered—Crosses the Cypress Swamp—Robbed by outlaws—Disloyal citizen—The fate of the robbers.

NOT long after my return from running with the 2d Arkansas Cavalry, General Ross requested me to make a general reconnoisance of the country along the railroad as far as Lagrange, and to examine carefully the trestle-work and bridges of the railroad, and to watch for any movement that might be intended as an attack on the post or a raid upon the railroad.

I went out, disguised as a citizen, mounted on a mule. Ten miles from Bolivar I stopped at Mr. M———'s, where I spent an hour or more in conversation with the members of the family. Mr. M——— was absent in the hospital, he having been wounded in the battle of Shiloh, and had not yet sufficiently recovered to enable him to get home.

While there I received an introduction to Miss Armstrong, a sister of the rebel General Armstrong. I found her a very frank, open-hearted woman, and very hopeful of the Southern cause. She did not evade the fact of the gloom and darkness that seemed to envelop the cause, but spoke cheerful and hopeful of the result. She inquired if I had any late news from "*our*" forces, and I, in turn, gained as much general information of Southern matters as I could.

When passing myself as a citizen of the South, I have always found the people affable in their manners, sociable, and extremely liberal in their hospitality. Whenever an occasion was offered them of rendering any assistance which they supposed was furthering the cause they had espoused, their kindness and generosity knew no restraint.

Two miles further on is the residence of Captain Rose, to whom I paid a visit. Captain Rose had served in the United States army eleven years, and is one of your genuine Union men, and has always been loyal to the Government. I have visited him frequently since, and was always made welcome. I did not disguise the fact of belonging to the Federal army to him, and have several times received from him valuable information. It was of rare occurrence that I found among the citizens of that locality such genuine sentiments of loyalty and devotion to the Federal Government as I found in Captain Rose.

I moved on leisurely, examining the railroad as I went, but saw nothing worthy of attention after I left Captain Rose until two miles west of Van Buren, where the road from Whitesville comes in. As I came near that place, I saw two rebel cavalrymen, who had been coming up the Grand Junction road, turn off toward Whitesville.

"Halloo, boys!" said I, hailing them, "stop a minute; I want to see you."

"We haven't time to stop," answered one; "our company has gone on to Whitesville, and we want to overtake it."

They dashed ahead without stopping. Their reply, however, answered my purpose. "A company of cavalry had gone to Whitesville," and it remained for me to find out what it had gone *for*. The two men were without luggage, from which I concluded they would return the next day; and, knowing that the rebel forces were principally at Lumpkins' Mills, it seemed probable that when the company returned it would pass through Lagrange, so I resolved to go on to Lagrange that night. It was then nearly dark.

I arrived at Lagrange about 11 o'clock at night, and halted at the depot. It was very dark, and every body had retired for the night, and, not liking to blunder about the place for lodgings, lest I might encounter some rebel cavalry, I lay down upon the depot platform, with my bridle over my arm, ready to spring up at the slightest alarm, and went to sleep.

In the morning I repaired to a house of entertainment, kept by a Mr. Lee, and procured some breakfast for myself and feed for my mule. There I waited for the return of the cavalry. About 1 o'clock, P. M., they came in and halted to feed.

I did not think that it was prudent to mingle with the cavalry while they remained in town, so I had my mule got ready, and remained at the public house until the cavalry commenced to move out, when I mounted and moved out on the same road in their rear, and, at a short distance from town, I came up with them. I rode along in company with them, as if I were a citizen returning to my home from town.

I asked the boys how they liked soldiering, and whether they had ever been in any fights, and what regiment they belonged to, and various other questions, such as I supposed a citizen would naturally ask; and, finally, I inquired where they had been, and was told that they had been to Whitesville, on a scout, to see whether the Yankees had been committing any depredations on the property of the citizens. In that manner I kept up my conversation until we were within three miles of the Cold Water Creek, without having excited any suspicion but what I was all right.

I had gone as far as I cared about, and began to think up some plan by which I could make my exit from their company without exciting suspicion. To accomplish my object, I gradually fell back to the rear, and the first rise of ground that the cavalry went over, that was large enough to hide me from view until I could get a good start on my way back, I turned about and left them.

I moved along on a good fast trot, occasionally looking back to see if I was pursued. I had made about four miles, when, on looking back, I saw a squad of fifteen or sixteen cavalry in full chase after me. My sudden departure had excited their suspicions. I put the spurs to my mule and dashed ahead

at the top of its speed. My pursuers gained on me.
I urged my mule still harder, and still they continued to gain. My situation seemed a hopeless
one. I could not outstrip them in the chase, and
they were rapidly gaining on me. If captured, my
flight under the circumstances would be conclusive
evidence against me. Still, on I pressed, the distance between myself and pursuers growing rapidly
less. My mule, too, was becoming exhausted, and
my pursuers were within five hundred yards of me.
I had come full three miles since I saw them giving
chase. Passing a bend in the road, with a growth
of small trees and brush along the fence that hid me
from view, I came to a gap in the fence, through
which I passed into a field. The field was covered
with stubble and tall weeds. I dashed ahead at
right angles with the road for about two hundred
yards, when I entered a basin or depression in the
surface of the ground, that in a wet time would have
been a pond, but at that time it was dry. The
ground was considerably lower than the surface of
the field between the basin and the road. There I
dismounted and sat down, and, in an instant more, I
heard the tramp of horses as my pursuers passed on.

I had despaired of making my escape, but as my
pursuers passed on, hope began to revive. It was
then about sundown. I waited there until dark, and
then mounted my mule and started on. I knew that
my pursuers would soon return, and I must manage
so as not to be seen. When I arrived at the place
where the road turns off to the right, that goes to
Davis' Mills, I turned to the left into the edge of a

piece of woods, where I could see without being seen, and halted.

In a few minutes I heard my pursuers approaching, who, when they came to the corners, took the road to Davis' Mills. I remained under cover of the woods until I thought all stragglers of the party, if there should be any, had passed, and then went on, watching carefully as I went.

As I was riding along, the thought occurred to me that, perhaps, my pursuers might have mistrusted that I had turned out into the field to evade them, and had placed a picket on the bridge across Wolf River, near Lagrange, to capture me if I attempted to cross. I rode on to within two hundred yards of the bridge, and there I left my mule and went forward to reconnoiter. When within a few paces of the bridge I stopped and listened, but did not hear any thing. I moved a few feet further, and then I thought I heard a footstep. I crept up still closer, and peered forward in the black distance, and there I could see, on the bridge, the form of a man. I watched and he moved. There was no mistake about it! My fears were realized! The picket was there!

The glimmerings of hope that had lightened me up as my pursuers passed me now vanished. I was completely cornered. The only bridge besides that one was on the Davis Mills road, and my pursuers were on that road. Between the two bridges was an extensive cypress swamp, and below the bridge that I was at was another swamp still worse. The only possible way that I could see to get away from my pursuers was to cross the swamp between the two bridges. To think of the undertaking was horrible!

I crept cautiously back to my mule, mounted, and rode through a dense growth of brush to my right, until I reached the edge of the swamp, where I halted. To undertake to cross in daylight would be hazardous, and in the dark utterly impossible; so I concluded to wait until morning before making the attempt. I laid down upon the ground, with my bridle over my arm, with the venomous insects and serpents as my companions, and the intervening brush over my head and the broad canopy of heaven, curtained with black clouds, my only covering. Such surroundings are not very conducive to sleep, but exhausted nature soon yielded, and I slept, and slept soundly—so soundly that when I awoke in the morning the sun was two hours high.

The mule, to satisfy its hunger, had eaten the boughs on the bushes, around where I lay, as far as it could reach, and yet it had neither pulled away from me nor disturbed my slumbers, but had been as careful of me and manifested as much attachment for me as a faithful dog would for his master.

The mule had been presented to me by General Ross, and had been a common sharer with me in the exposures and dangers that I had experienced, and had borne me safely thus far, and was, perhaps, to be the only friendly companion to witness the end that would befall me. When I thought of my situation, and witnessed the careful attachment expressed for me by that dumb animal, I could not control my feelings, but embraced the neck of that mule with joyous affection and wept.

I had not tasted a mouthful of food since I had eaten my breakfast, at the public house, the morning before, and I was not in a very fit state of body or mind to accomplish such an undertaking as was then before me. The tug of war had come, however, and the Rubicon had to be crossed.

Leading my mule by the bridle, I started in, sometimes at midsides in mire and water, and then on top of a bog or root, and then—splash into the water again! On I went, clambering, wallowing, splashing, and plunging! As all things earthly have an end, so had that swamp; and, in spite of venomous moccasins, tangled brush, cypress trees, mire and water, I arrived on the bank of the river. There I mounted my mule, and forded the river to the opposite bank.

Myself and mule were frightful looking objects, from the mire we had wallowed through, and, before going any further, it became necessary for me to clean off the mule to prevent suspicion. Several hours were spent in cleaning and drying before I felt safe to venture out.

As soon as I thought prudent, I mounted my mule and rode on across the country. I passed to the east of Lagrange, in sight of town, keeping a sharp look-out for cavalry. When I reached the Memphis and Corinth stage road, I took my course toward Bolivar.

When about two miles from Grand Junction, I saw approaching me from the east, and a long way ahead, three persons on horseback. I resolved to face the music this time, let come what would. My recent experience at running had satisfied me. As they came nearer, I saw that they were dressed like citizens, which very much relieved my anxiety.

One of them was a very large man, of roughly-defined outline, with light hair and a red face; the second was a medium-sized man, of fair appearance, and the third was a little man, with small, round face, black hair, and sharp, black eyes. Their clothing was made of homespun cloth. As they met me, two came up on one side and one on the other, and halted; so I halted.

"Good afternoon, stranger!" said the big man, as we halted.

"Good afternoon, gentlemen!" I replied.

"That's a fine mule you are riding," continued the big man.

"Yes, it is a tolerable good one."

"Well, mister, we want that mule, and we are going to have it. Get off from that mule," said the big man. Each of them, at the same time, drew out a derringer and pointed it at me.

"You are the strongest party," said I, "and I suppose that you must have it."

I dismounted, and, at the same time, they dismounted, and the big man took possession of the mule. It was like parting with a last friend to give up my favorite, but "it had to be did."

"Have you got any money?" said the little man, coming up and thrusting his hands into my pockets. He took out every thing that I had in them, and then, casting his eyes toward my feet, said: "You have got a good pair of boots there; we want them."

"Strangers," said I, "that's going a little too far. You have got my mule and got my money, and now to take my boots and leave me to walk twenty miles to my home barefooted is *too much*. You *can't have* them, *unless you take them off from my dead body; by G—d, you can't!*"

"That *is* a little too hard," said the big man; "you may keep your boots."

They then mounted and rode away, leading my mule with them, in the direction from which they came, and I followed behind them, on foot. It is not often that I pray, but then I prayed. My prayer was, "*that the* 11*th Illinois Cavalry would come dashing down on the road from Bolivar, and capture the lawless villains that had robbed me of my mule and my money.*"

Hungry and fatigued, with twenty miles to travel on foot, and that, too, upon the top of my misfortunes of the night before, made me any thing but good-natured, and I muttered vengeance to the robbers that had taken my favorite, if ever an opportunity occurred.

When I reached the house of old Mr. Pruett, hunger impelled me to stop. I found the people absent, except a daughter and a young lady from a neighboring family, that had called in. I found them obliging and sociable, and in a few minutes their fair hands, secesh as they were, had spread for me a bountiful repast, much to the delight of my ravenous appetite. I told the ladies that I had been robbed of my mule and money, and described to them the villains that had done it. The lady that had called in said that they answered the description of three outlaws that had robbed her uncle, a few days before, of $3,600 in gold, that he had just received for his cotton, and then they beat him on the head with their derringers, until they supposed he was dead, for having sold his cotton to the Yankees. She also said that they were supposed to live near Ripley, Miss.

Having satisfied my hunger, I resumed my walk toward Bolivar. When I came to the railroad crossing, I followed the railroad. I was too tired to make rapid progress, and made frequent stops to rest myself. When I arrived at Middleburg it was between 9 and 10 o'clock at night. As I was about passing a well near the depot platform, I saw a person drawing a bucket of water. Being thirsty, I stopped and asked for a drink. I recognized the man as the merchant that kept the brick store near by; he, however, did not know me. He handed me a drink, and when I returned him the cup, he inquired if I had any news. I told him there was no news.

"Have you got a Southern paper?"

"No, sir."

"I would give *ten dollars* for a Southern paper. I feel anxious to hear from Baton Rouge."

"I have no paper and no news from Baton Rouge."

"Where are you from?"

"Holly Springs."

"You from Holly Springs, and ha'n't got any news!"

"Look 'e here, mister, you are a stranger to me; I do n't know who you are."

"Oh! I am all right!"

"Well, I do n't know you. I am sent up here on special business," said I, in a confidential way.

"*Oh! that's it, is it?* I did n't know that!" Then, patting me on the shoulder, he said, "Go on! that's right! I hope you will have good luck and get through."

Before daylight next morning I was once more in camp at Bolivar.

The next January, as the army was on its way back from its campaign in Mississippi, while riding on ahead of the division to which I belonged, I came across my favorite mule. It was in company K, of the 7th Kansas Cavalry. I went to Captain Bostwick, who was in command of the company, and told him that he had my mule, and how I came by it and how I lost it, and also described the men that took it away from me. The Captain returned me the mule, and told me that, while making a raid near Tupelo, Mississippi, during the fall, he had captured three men of the description I had given, and with them eighteen mules, including mine, and that the men had been sent to Alton, Illinois, as guerrillas; so I never had an opportunity of retaliating on them for their outrage to me. I am fully convinced that they were professional robbers, and belonged to neither army.

CHAPTER XII.

Starts to find General Bragg's forces—"Wools" the secesh farmer—Receives a bottle of rum—Guerrillas washing stockings—Finds Bragg's advance—Recognized as a Yankee spy—Ordered off his mule to be shot—The clamor of the crowd—Recognized as a Confederate spy—Rebel Surgeon vouches for him—Is released—Gray-headed rebel brought to justice—The Sutler of the 2d Arkansas Cavalry a prisoner—What became of the guerrillas that were washing stockings.

THE next trip that I made was under the following instructions from General Ross:

"I understand," said he, "by report from citizens, that General Bragg is coming this way with his forces, and I want to know whether he *really is* coming or not, and on what road and with how much force he is coming. I want you to go to Somerville, and if you find nothing there, go to Lagrange, and thence to Grand Junction, Saulsbury, Middleton, and Pocahontas, and then back. If you find a force at any place in your route, you will come immediately back and report. You will make the trip with as little delay as possible.

I received my instructions in the evening, and early the next morning, in the disguise of a well-dressed citizen, mounted on a mule, I was on my way. During the cool of the morning I traveled along at a smart trot, and by sunrise I had made about eight miles. When about twelve miles out, I was about passing a plantation house, when an old planter, who was feeding some hogs near the road, motioned me to stop.

"Good morning, stranger," said he, as I reined up.

"Good morning, sir."

"Where have you been?"

"Oh, ho, ho, ho; I have been to Bolivar," said I, laughing. "I have been there a week, and I know all about the Yankee forces in there, and now, if I can only find General Bragg, then I am all right!"

"Oh, indeed! I am delighted to hear it. Won't you alight and come in?"

"Well, yes, I do n't care if I do; for I have been riding since before daylight."

I dismounted and went in, and, as soon as I was seated, the old man inquired who I was.

"I have been acting the Yankee, and I belong to General Bragg's command."

"You do?"

"Yes, sir!"

"Well, do you ever drink any?"

Oh, yes, I drink when I can get it; but a man is very fortunate to get it these times."

"I have got some nice rum here; will you try some of it?" (offering me a glass and bottle.)

"Yes, sir! I 'll take a drink of *rum*."

"How did you manage to get into Bolivar?"

"Oh, I told them that I was a *Union* man, and wanted to go in and take the *oath!*"

"Well, there is right smart of them gets in that way, but there a'n't many of them that thinks it binding."

"You have taken the oath, I suppose."

"Yes, we *all* do that, in order to get along smoothly. But, come, breakfast is ready; sit up and eat some breakfast."

"Thank you; my ride this morning makes me quite hungry."

The breakfast was just what I wanted, and his invitation saved me the trouble of asking for it. When I had finished, said I,

"Mister, look 'e here; have you got any more of that 'divine, adorable stuff?'"

"Yes, I have got more of it in the cellar."

"Well, can't you bestow a little more of your hospitality on a fellow, in the shape of about a pint, to put in my pocket and take along?"

"Yes, certainly you can," spoke the planter's wife. "if I can find any thing to put it in." She then went in search of a bottle, and soon returned with a pint bottle filled with it, which she stowed away in my coat pocket with her own hands.

With a profusion of thanks and good wishes to them, I bade them adieu, and resumed my journey. Somewhere near three miles east of Somerville is a beautiful spring, that makes its exit from the ground beneath a group of shady elm trees. There I saw three men, engaged in *washing their stockings!* It is not usual for *men* to wash their own stockings in the ordinary peaceful avocations of life, and the fact of their being so engaged, and also dressed like citizens, was conclusive evidence to me that they were guerrillas. Riding down to the spring and dismounting, I said, pulling out my bottle, "Look 'e here, boys; here is a present that I received this morning; won't you try some of it?"

One of the men took the bottle and drank, and the other two declined, saying that they never drank. I then took a "little smile" myself, mounted my horse, and rode on.

Finding no troops at Somerville, on my arrival there, I continued on, taking the road that leads south to Lagrange, which place I reached late in the afternoon. There I found four regiments of infantry and two regiments of cavalry. They had just arrived, and had not yet thrown out any pickets. The advance cavalry had but just entered the town, and the other troops were coming in the distance.

I rode along into town among the soldiers, as familiarly as if I belonged in the place, and stopped near the drug store. Standing within a few feet of the drug store, was a large, corpulent, red-faced old man, with hair almost white, leaning upon a walking-staff; near by was a Colonel, dismounted, and leaning with his left hand upon his saddle; all about were cavalry soldiers, dismounted. As I reined up, the old man pointed to me, and said, "Colonel, there is a d—d Yankee spy; he ought to be shot. I know him, Colonel, and know that he is a Yankee spy."

"If he is a Yankee spy he shall be shot."

"I have seen him before. I *know* that he is a Yankee spy."

"A Yankee spy!" "A Yankee spy!" "Shoot

IF HE IS A YANKEE SPY I'LL HAVE HIM SHOT.

him!" "Hang the d—d son of a b—h!" cried out the soldiers, rushing up to get a sight of me.

"Where do you belong?" inquired the Colonel.

"My home is in Osceola, Mississippi County, Arkansas; but I am from Memphis now."

"What are you doing here?"

"I have been out to Somerville, and beyond toward Bolivar, to see some friends."

"Yes, *Bolivar!*" cried the old man; "the d—d rascal has just come from Bolivar, and *there* is where he belongs. I tell you, Colonel, I *know* him; I *know* that he is a Yankee spy."

"Well, if you know him to be a Yankee spy, I'll shoot him. (Addressing me, and drawing his revolver and cocking it:) "Get off from your mule."

I dismounted, and one of the soldiers led my mule to one side, and the crowd opened behind me. The excitement was intense, and the crowd dense, and, in its excitement, it swayed to and fro like an angry mob, and cries went up from every direction, "Hang him!" "Shoot him!" "Shoot the d—d rascal!" I can not picture the horror that filled me. In all that vast multitude, there was not a friendly eye to witness my doom. To escape was utterly impossible! Die I must by the hands of traitors, and my fate be wrapped in oblivion to my comrades and relatives! The color left my face and a cold tremor crept over me, and such indescribable sensations filled me as makes me shudder at this when I think of it.

Just then Doctor Biggs, surgeon of the 4th Tennessee Infantry, stepped out of the drug store to learn the cause of the excitement. As he came out, he saw me and recognized me as the Confederate spy that had been captured by the Federal pickets near his house, and who had eaten breakfast with him.

"Colonel, you are gwine to shoot the wrong man thar," said the doctor. "I know that ar man, and I know who he is and whar he belongs. He is *no* Yankee spy."

"I know that he *is* a Yankee spy," said the old man.

"*I know better*," said the doctor; "and if you kill him, you kill the *wrong* man. You ar not a gwine to find out his business; and if you kill him, he'll not tell you. I *know that he is all right*. I have seen him in a *tighter place* than he is in now." Then stepping to the soldier that held my mule, he snatched the bridle out of his hand, and, turning to me, he said: "Here, take your mule; they are not a gwine to shoot you." Then turning to the Colonel, and stamping his foot on the ground, he said: "*You are not a gwine to shoot that man, for I* KNOW *that he is all right!*"

"Well, doctor, if you know that he is all right, and are willing to vouch for him, I'll let him go."

"I *will* vouch for him, for I know who he is." Then turning to me, he said: "Get on your mule and go about your business; they are not a gwine to hurt you."

I mounted my mule and the soldiers opened the way for me, and I went *a sailing* out of town; and I don't think I was very long in getting back to Bolivar.

I tell you, reader, in that Doctor Biggs I fully realized that "a friend in *need* was a *friend indeed*." His appearance at that critical moment was as unexpected as would have been a visit from an angel in heaven. When I reported to General Ross, I narrated to him my adventure.

"Bunker," said he, "do n't you know that when you go out as a spy, you go, as it were, with a rope round your neck, ready for any body to draw it tight?"

"Yes, I think I had a *slight hint* of that fact on this trip."

I resolved that if ever an opportunity offered, the old, gray-headed rebel at Lagrange should be brought to account for his treatment; so I went to the Provost-marshal and gave him a narrative of the adventure, and a description of the rebel, so that in case he should ever visit the place he might be captured.

About two months after the foregoing adventure occurred, Lagrange was occupied by Federal troops, and the same officer that was Provost-marshal in Bolivar now commanded the post at Lagrange. As I was passing along the streets, one day, I saw, not ten feet from the place where I first saw him, the old, gray-headed rebel, with his staff in his hand. His appearance was permanently stereotyped in my mind, and I could not be mistaken in the man who had so nearly deprived me of my life.

Drawing my revolver, I walked up to him, saying, "You d——d old, gray-headed rebel! do you remember the '*Yankee spy?*' Do you '*know him*' now? Have you '*seen him before?*'"

"What do you mean?" said he; "I do n't understand you!"

"You do 'nt know what I mean! You do n't remember telling the rebel Colonel, standing in the tracks where you now stand, '*I know him; I have seen him before; I know that he is a Yankee spy!*' Do n't tell me, you old, gray-headed villain, that you *do n't know what I mean!* You start with me to the commander of the post, or I 'll blow your brains out here!"

The old fellow led the way and I followed, with my revolver cocked.

"Colonel," said I, as we entered his office, "here is the old, gray-headed devil that said to the rebel Colonel, 'Kill the Yankee spy;' and I have brought him in for you to dispose of."

"Bunker," said the Colonel, "a'n't you mistaken?"

"No, I a'n't! I know him, and I found him standing in the very place where he tried to have me shot!" Then turning to the old man, I said: "Did n't you tell the rebel Colonel that I was a Yankee spy, and try to have him shoot me? *Tell me the truth, or I 'll kill you right here!*"

"Ye—yes, I—believe I—d–do—recollect it now."

"*You old whelp! you deserve to be shot!*" said the Colonel. "Here I have been guarding your house, and guarding your mules, and boarding with you; and you representing yourself to have *always been a Union man, and the oath in your pocket that you took last summer!*" Then turning to me, he said: "Bunker, I 'll dispose of him as he ought to be."

"Thank you, Colonel, I wish you would."

The next morning the guards were removed from the old man's premises, and he was put aboard the cars, in irons, destined to go North.

A day or two afterward I happened to be passing by where a number of rebel prisoners were confined, and there I saw the sutler of the 2d Arkansas Cavalry (the regiment that I run with so long). The sutler knew me, and motioned to me to come in; so I got permission of the officer in charge to go in and see him. He still supposed that I was secesh.

"Ruggles," said he, "I am here under arrest as a guerrilla. Now, you know that I am *no guerrilla*, but a regularly authorized sutler in the 2d Arkansas Cavalry. I wish you would see the commander of the post and explain that fact to him, so that I may be treated as a prisoner of war, and not as an outlaw."

"Well, I will tell him what I know about it. Perhaps he will recognize you as a prisoner of war."

"Thank you! Do what you can for me. But, between you and I, (speaking confidentially,) I quit sutlering and joined a band of guerrillas, because I thought that I could make more money at it. It was all bad management that we got captured."

Just then another prisoner came up, and, taking me by the hand, said, "Don't you know me?"

"No, I don't remember you, as I know of."

"Do you remember of seeing three men at the spring, three miles east of Somerville, last summer, when you was riding by, and of offering them some rum to drink?"

"Oh, yes! I do recollect it now."

"Well, I am the man that drank with you, and the other two are here."

"Are they?"

"Yes. Now, you know that we are only citizens, and that we do n't belong to any guerrilla band."

"Of course I do! You are no guerrillas!"

"If you please, I want to have you go and see the commanding officer, and tell him that we are not guerrillas, but *peaceable, quiet citizens.*"

"Certainly, boys! I'll help you out of this, if I can?"

I went to the commander of the post and told him what "*I knew about them,*" and did all I could to "*get them out of that,*" and a few days after they were all sent North in irons.

CHAPTER XIII.

Reconnoiters Hickory Flats with a squad of seven men—Shoots at the mark—Orders to march with two days' rations—Cause of the alarm—Reconnoiter beyond Whitesville—Major Mudd's trap—"Bunker" entices the rebs into it—Rides into the trap behind a rebel Captain—Sent out beyond Pocahontas—Passes as a rebel artillerist—Secesh citizen stands guard for him—The very kind secesh lady—The anxious wife—Discovers guerrillas burning a human being.

NEAR the close of September, General Hurlbut arrived at Bolivar, with his division, from Memphis, and assumed command of the post. General Ross recommended me to him as a reliable and successful spy. I knew the General, but had never worked for him. I will here acknowledge that I am indebted to General Hurlbut for some of the best lessons that I have ever received in regard to my duties as a spy.

The first time that I went out for General Hurlbut, he told me that he wanted I should go out to the Hickory Flats, and scout all over the flats and see if I could find any rebel cavalry. I asked the privilege of taking seven men with me, which was granted, and I was told to select such men as I preferred. At that time detachments of the enemy, mostly cavalry, were scattered about the country, watching for opportunities to annoy us, by attacking our forage parties, and making raids upon the railroad that we depended upon to transport our supplies. It had been extremely difficult to find such detachments, because they usually stayed but a short time in a place, and generally encamped in some back, out-of-the-way place, concealed by swamps, woods, and cane-brakes, reached by unfrequented roads or paths. The object of my trip was to examine thoroughly the Hickory Flats and its vicinity for any such detachments.

I selected my men, and proceeded to the place and examined it, so far as I could, on the day that I went out. I remained there over night, and in the morning resumed my work, and by noon had thoroughly reconnoitered the locality, without having discovered any detachments of the enemy. We then eat dinner, and prepared to return.

As we were about to leave, Sergeant Downs, one of my squad, proposed that, inasmuch as we were fifteen miles away from camp, I allow the men to shoot a few rounds at a mark, for practice. Not thinking that there *might* be any serious consequences resulting from it, I consented. We all engaged in shooting, following one after the other in quick succession, until we had fired, in all, forty-seven shots. I was not aware that any other scouting party had been sent out. Having finished our shooting, we returned to camp. It was late when we arrived, and, being very tired, I deferred reporting to General Hurlbut until the next morning.

About 2 o'clock in the morning the troops were

wakened up, and given orders to put two days' cooked rations in their haversacks, and be ready to march at a moment's notice. It seemed a strange move for me, for I thought that I was as well posted as any body of the whereabouts of the enemy. I could not comprehend what the move meant.

My curiosity became so excited about it, that I started for head-quarters to report much earlier than I otherwise would have done. As I passed the different camps, every thing was bustle and hurry, with preparations for a march. The cavalry horses were saddled and the artillery horses harnessed, in preparation for a move. Something was up, sure, and I wondered what it could be.

"What's up? What do you think is the matter?" said I, calling to an artilleryman, as I passed.

"The cavalry that went out yesterday reported a large force of rebel cavalry on the Hickory Flats, and I expect that we are going out there," was the reply.

It was all clear enough then! I had done the mischief! I felt badly worked up about it. I knew that I had no business to fire a gun; but I was so far away that I did not suppose any of our forces would hear it. It was my first scout for General Hurlbut, and I expected that it would destroy his confidence in me. I expected a severe rebuke, at least, and I dreaded to report. I determined, however, to face the music, let come what would; so I went in.

"Good morning, General," said I, saluting him as I went in. "I have got back."

"Good morning, Bunker. What's the news?"

"Nothing; I have n't got any news this morning."

"Where did you go?"

"I went right where you told me to go—out to Hickory Flats, and back, by way of Middleburg, to camp."

"Have you been out to the Hickory Flats?"

"Yes, sir."

"Did you see any rebel cavalry there?"

"No, sir, I did not."

"Well, Bunker, your report and that of the cavalry do n't agree at all."

"I can't help it, General; I have been right where you told me to go, and I did not see any rebel cavalry."

"*Bunker!*" said the General, with emphasis, "*do you come here and tell me that you have been down on the Hickory Flats, and that there is no rebel cavalry there?*"

"Yes, sir, I do. I know what the trouble is. I expect that I'll catch "Hail Columbia" now! I caused the mischief."

"How so?"

"After I finished my reconnoissance yesterday, before starting back, I allowed the men to fire at the mark, and they kept up a pretty brisk fire until they had fired forty-seven shots. I suspect that the cavalry has been out there and heard it. I knew that we were fifteen miles away from camp, and I did not think that we might cause an alarm by it."

"That's a *fact*, is it?"

"Yes, sir."

"Very well; that will do. Be careful the next time."

An hour later all was quiet in camp; the horses were unharnessed, and every thing moved off as usual.

A little incident took place during a reconnoissance to a small town on the right bank of the Hatchee River, west of Whitesville, some time in September, 1862, that I will here narrate.

A brigade of infantry, a regiment of cavalry, a battery of artillery, and the detachment known as the "mule cavalry" constituted the force. The cavalry was the 2d Illinois, under the command of Major Mudd. When within four miles of the town, the infantry and artillery halted, and the 2d Illinois and mule cavalry went on to the river.

On several occasions, scounting parties of cavalry had dashed into the town, and they had always found some rebel cavalry, who, on the approach of the Federal cavalry, would skedaddle, taking a path that led to a ford across the river, and hide themselves among the canes that grew upon the bottoms along the river. To prevent their escape, on this occasion, Major Mudd sent two companies and the "mule cavalry" by the road into town, and took the balance of his command down the river to the ford that I have mentioned, and disposed his men among the canes in such a way as not to be seen from the side of the river next to the town, and, at the same time, be able to capture all that crossed at the ford.

I accompanied the Major, and, after he had got

his men satisfactorily arranged, I undressed and waded to the opposite side to see how things looked there. Having dressed myself, I proceeded to examine the locality. I found that, at a few paces from the river, there was a path that turned down the stream and crossed at a ford below where the Major had set his trap. It was then too late to change the disposal of the men, so I resolved to act as "stool-pigeon" to the Major's trap. I stationed myself where I would be in plain view of any person that might take the wrong path, and whenever a man would incline to turn down the river, I would motion to him to come toward me, as if I mistrusted there was something wrong down below, and as he came up, I would say to him, as if by way of caution, "There is Lincoln cavalry down there; you had better cross here."

Some rode across the ford without any enticing, and others inclined to take the wrong path; such I would entice to take the right path. In this I was successful at every attempt. My dress being like that of a citizen, they did not mistrust my character. I had succeeded in enticing five men into the trap, when a rebel Captain made his appearance, with a pair of beautiful mouse-colored mules, as sleek as moles, and manifested a disposition to take the wrong path. He was riding one of the mules himself, and a colored boy was riding the other. I motioned to the Captain to come toward me. As he came up—

"There is Lincoln cavalry down that way," said I; "you had better cross here. What's the matter up in town?"

WHOA, MULE! CAPTURED, BY G—D!

"The town is full of Lincolnites!"

"They'll be down here directly, then, I reckon. I had better get out of this. Won't you let me get on behind you and ride across?"

"Yes, come this way." He rode alongside of a bank of earth, and I straddled the mule, behind him. We crossed the stream, and had ascended the bank on the opposite side, when, discovering the Lincolnites, with their carbines leveled at us, he exclaimed, "Whoa, mule! Captured, by G—d! Both of us! I swear, that's too bad! Here I am, within five miles of my command, and captured!"

"That's a fact, Captain, but we can't help it now. I expect we had better ride on up; it's no place to trade jack-knives here!" So we went on.

"Whew!" said the Major, "that's the way I like to see you come; when you come, come double!"

We rode up to the Major, who ordered us to dismount, and, taking possession of the mules, he said, pointing to the group he had already captured: "There, you had better go right down there, out of sight; that's the best place for you. How do you like my trap, Captain?"

"I think it's a very good one; it caught me mighty nice!"

He felt sold over his capture, and doubly so when he learned that *I* had *enticed* him into the trap. The Major having succeeded in entrapping eighteen "very fine" rebs, we returned with the brigade to Bolivar.

On the 3d day of October, General Price attacked General Rosecrans at Corinth, Miss., and, after a severe engagement, was defeated and compelled to retreat. General Hurlbut immediately marched the troops under his command to General Rosecrans' assistance. On his way, he met the rebel army on its retreat, while it was crossing the Hatchie River, and completely routed it.

A few days after the return of General Hurlbut's command to Bolivar, he sent me out to find where the scattered fragments of General Price's army were concentrating. I was allowed to take a man with me, and was requested to make the trip as quickly as possible. As I was about leaving the General's quarters, he called to me, "Here, come back!" I went back, and he continued: "I want you to understand that you are to work for me now. I don't want you to tattle on the picket line. I have been told that you have sometimes reported to your Colonel; you might as well report to a *corporal* as to a Colonel, unless he sends you out. I want you to report to me."

"General, explain to me, if you please, what that means. I have never reported to a Colonel but once."

"Well, *that's once* too much. That's the reason the detachment of Armstrong's cavalry was not captured, that you reported to General Ross, the other day."

I begged the General's pardon, and promised to do better. I have been very careful since not to report to any body but the officer that sent me out.

I selected Sergeant E. W. Quackenbush, of the 20th Ohio, to accompany me. He had been with me on previous scouts. We were on foot, disguised like rebel soldiers belonging to artillery.

Owing to the lateness of the hour of our departure, when night came on we had made but about seven miles. Stopping at the gate in front of a farm-house, just before dark, and, addressing the man of the house, who was standing on the porch, I said: "Halloo, mister, can we get a little supper here, and stay all night?"

"Well, no, sir; the Yankees have done taken all that I had; you can't get any supper here."

"Partner," said I to the Sergeant, "let us go on. Blast that man's picture! he'll hear from me some day to pay for treating his *own soldiers* in that way!"

"Hold on, soldiers!" said the man; "where do you belong?"

"I am Orderly Sergeant of Price's 1st Battery of Artillery," I replied, "and this man with me belongs to the same battery. We were captured by the Yankees, and have succeeded in getting away from them; we have been without any thing to eat for twenty-four hours."

"Yes, yes!" said the man's wife, who had heard what had been said; "you *can* have something to eat, and you can have the best bed in the house! Come in, boys, come in."

We went in and sat down. "You were in the fight on the Hatchie, the other day, were you?" said the man.

"Yes, till we got captured."

"Well, how did the fight come off?"

"I can't tell you very much about it. When we had fired only three rounds, some Lincoln cavalry charged right up to us, and captured us and our battery, and immediately sent us to the rear; consequently, I do n't know much about it."

"I declare!" said he; "I *would like to hear* from the fight!"

"Have you lived in these parts long?"

"Yes, I was raised in this county."

"You have taken the *oath* to the Lincoln Government, I suppose?"

"Yes, we *all* do that. I was obliged to do it, but I do n't consider it binding at all. I have been in the Confederate army fifteen months! You did n't know that, did you, boys?"

"No; you had better keep that thing to yourself, for if the Yankees find it out they 'll hang you."

"Pshaw! I am not afraid of their finding it out. But, come boys, I see that supper is ready; sit up and eat some supper."

The lady of the house had prepared us a meal worthy of veterans in a nobler cause than we feigned to represent. The table was bountifully supplied. In times of peace a better table would rarely have been set. It had been a long time since our eyes had rested upon such a meal. I think, however, that we did the subject justice.

Having finished our supper and shoved back, the Sergeant began to show signs of drowsiness, and in a few minutes was asleep in his chair. "That's a *brave, gallant soldier,*" said I. "Very few men have the *daring* and the *courage* that he possesses; but I see that the *poor fellow is tired out with his hardships, and has gone to sleep.*"

Poor soldier!" exclaimed the lady. "*How the poor soldiers do have to suffer!*"

"Yes, and there are very few persons, outside of the army, that realize the hardships and sufferings that the soldiers have to endure."

"*God bless their brave hearts!*" she exclaimed; "*how I do pity them!*"

The "poor soldier" was wakened up and shown to bed. Before retiring, I took off my belt and revolver, and, handing it to the man, I said: "Now, mister, I would like to ask another favor of you. Can't you take this revolver and keep watch for us to-night, while we sleep, so that we can *both* get one good night's sleep? Can't you afford to do that much for us? We have got away from the Yankees, and we don't want to be captured again."

"Yes, I'll stand guard for you. How did you keep the Yankees from taking your revolver?"

"I had it rolled up in my coat, and I carried my coat under my arm; they did not suspect that I had one."

"Well, that was lucky, wasn't it?"

"Yes, it was lucky for me, but my partner lost his."

I then retired to bed. Before I had gone to sleep, the man visited my room, and said: "If the Yankees come, you must unhook the window-blind, shove it open, and jump out, and run down into a gully behind the stable and hide, and when the Yankees are all done gone, I'll come down and tell you." For some time before closing my eyes in sleep, I could hear the man pacing back and forth across the floor, like a sentry pacing his beat. The night passed away and we enjoyed a most refreshing sleep, under the *"guarding influence"* of our secesh friend. We arose early in the morning to renew our journey, and found our guard still on duty. We were about to leave, when the man said, "You'll stop with us to breakfast, won't you?" "No, I thank you; we should be glad to, but we *must* go, for I am afraid that the Yankees will be after us by-and-by, and we do not want to get captured again. We are under very great obligations to you for our excellent supper and the refreshing sleep that we have had. You have been a soldier, and you know, by experience, *how very grateful* a soldier feels for such kindness." We then shook hands with him and his wife, bade them a good-by, and went on.

When we had traveled about six miles, we came to a large, fine, white house, with every thing about it that indicated wealth and refinement. Our walk had created an appetite for breakfast, and we concluded to give the people of the house a call. I noticed, as we entered, that breakfast was about ready. Addressing myself to the lady of the house, said I, "Can we get some breakfast here this morning? We are in rather a tight place. We were captured by the Yankees in the fight on the Hatchee, and we have run away from them; they have robbed us of all our money, and we have got nothing to pay you with."

"Why, certainly you can have some breakfast. How you *poor soldiers do have to suffer!* Sit down and rest yourselves."

We sat down, and but a few minutes elapsed before breakfast was ready, when we were invited to sit up with the family. The Sergeant was seated next to the lady, and I next to him. I had finished my breakfast, and was about shoving back, when the lady of the house said: "*Do n't be in a hurry, my dear soldiers; eat all you want;* we have got plenty. You do n't know when you will get any thing to eat again."

I thanked her, and shoved back. When the Sergeant had finished, she said: "*Now, dear soldiers*, fill your pockets with those nice wheat biscuits. The Lord only knows when you will get any thing more. *How I do pity you!*"

The Sergeant declined, but she insisted. "You *must* take some. As likely as not you won't get any thing again for several days; *do* take some. Here, take these," (and she began to stuff them into his pockets, which she continued until she had filled them full.) "*There;* how nicely they will relish."

"Partner," said I, "we had better be getting back to the woods again, for the Yankees might come along and find us."

"Yes," said the lady, "*do be very careful*. Do n't let them take you if you can help it, for you do n't know how much you might have to suffer. *How glad I am to help you!*"

Thanking her for her good wishes and kindness, we proceeded on our way.

That lady was a *noble, generous-hearted* woman, and her eyes sparkled with crystals of sympathy while she was bestowing upon us those little acts of kindness. So full had she filled the Sergeant's pockets with cakes, that they rendered him uncomfortable while walking, and he was obliged to throw part of them away.

The next house that we stopped at was occupied by an elderly lady, who, when we entered, was engaged in churning. She invited us to be seated, and then said: "Have you been in the fight?"

"Yes, we were in the fight and were captured, and have made our escape."

"Dear me! how anxious I do feel about my husband!"

"Was he in the fight?"

"Yes, he took his gun and went down to help whip the Yankees; I am so afraid that he is killed that I do n't know what to do! What a dreadful thing it would be if he should get killed!"

We listened to the lady's expressions of anxiety about her husband until the churning was finished, when she gave us some buttermilk to drink, which, with some of our nice wheat cakes, made us an excellent lunch.

From there we went on, without seeing any thing of interest until we came to the vicinity of Middleton. As we approached that place, we saw a dense smoke arise, and smelt a peculiar odor, which was so strong and peculiar as to attract our attention, and lead us to suspect that all was not right. We moved along cautiously, keeping a sharp look-out for soldiers or guerrillas. As we rose to the top of the hill to the west of the town, we could see a large fire, and about thirty men standing around it, with long poles in their hands. The odor that arose was almost intolerable. This was about 3 o'clock in the afternoon. We crept up as near as we could without exposing ourselves to full view, and then—*oh, horrible to tell!*—we could see the men move about excitedly, and push with their poles something into the fire. Then sparks would fill the air, and we could hear screams like those of human beings. Amid the screams would arise horrid oaths, and cries of "*Bring on another!*"

I did not see a human form in the fire; but that *odor, those screams,* intermingled with such *horrid blasphemy,* was *unmistakable evidence* that some poor mortal was suffering the *hellish torture* of a band of guerrillas! Perhaps some brave soldier, unable to keep up with his command on its return from the late battle; or some citizen, whose loyalty made him dare to breathe his sentiments; or, some poor mortal so unfortunate as to possess a sable complexion, was there, immolated upon the altar of fiendish revenge. As much used to sights of suffering as I have been, the recollection of that scene, as I call it to mind, makes me shudder to think of it.

We did not dare to remain there long, lest it might be our turn next to gratify their hellish barbarism. We went back down the hill, and took off in another direction. We soon found the country full of guerrillas and squads of soldiers, that had become routed during the fight. They were gathering together in small squads wherever they could, some with arms and some without. The victory to the Federal troops had been a complete route of Price's army.

I did not go as far as I had intended to go, because the state of the country was such that I deemed it imprudent to venture further; so we returned to camp the next day. I did not find out where the scattered troops were concentrating.

CHAPTER XIV.

Starts on a trip for General Lauman—His instructions—A Confederate widow—Discovers a squad of rebel soldiers—Captures part of their arms—Learns the whereabouts of guerrillas—Attempt to capture them—Guerrillas escape—Captures a prisoner—Cause of guerrillas' escape—The "General" and squad get arrested—The charges and specifications.

WHEN General Hurlbut took command of the District of Jackson, with his headquarters at Jackson, Tenn., Brigadier-General Lauman took command of the post at Bolivar.

On the 13th day of October, 1862, I reported to General Lauman for orders to go out on a scout. I received instructions to take with me a squad of ten men, and reconnoiter thoroughly a strip of country that lay south of Bolivar, between the road to Grand Junction, which would be on my right, and the road to Pocahontas, which would be on my left. I was ordered to kill all the guerrillas that I could find, bring in all that I had strong suspicions were guerrillas, and capture all the straggling rebel soldiers and arms that I could find. The General also told me that he would send out cavalry on my right, on the Grand Junction road, and, on my left, on the Pocahontas road. He did not limit me in time, or the distance to go, nor instruct me to take rations. I have usually, when out as a scout or spy, got my subsistence wherever I went.

The men that I selected to accompany me were Sergeants W. G. Downs and Thomas Watson, and eight privates, all of them from the 20th Ohio Infantry. It was nearly noon of the day I received my instructions before we were ready to march. The day was extremely warm, and we made but slow progress. We did not follow any road, but took our way across the fields and woods, and examined all the valleys that lay along our route for any signs that might exist of cavalry or guerrillas.

At 5 o'clock in the afternoon, we called at a house about eight miles from Bolivar, which we found to be owned and occupied by a widow lady by the name of Cheshire, who, by the way, is what might be called a Confederate widow. Her husband had belonged to the Confederate army, but had deserted. He came home and took the oath of allegiance, but, unfortunately for him, was captured by the Confederate authorities, and the oath found in his pocket. He was carried back to the rebel army and hung. In my scouts in the Southern Confederacy, I found that *widows* were of frequent occurrence, and the proportion of them to the population remaining at home was *astonishingly large*. I am inclined to think that many of the ladies chose to call themselves widows, rather than admit to Union soldiers (if they knew them to be such) that their husbands were in the rebel army. I call them all, whether real or professed, that have become such on account of the war, *Confederate widows*.

At Mrs. Cheshire's we procured our supper, which was provided and served up by her with a cheerfulness and willingness not characteristic of an enmity to the Federal Government. I offered to pay her, but she positively refused to receive any compensation.

After we had finished our supper, we moved a mile and a half, to Mr. Campbell's, where we halted for the night. Mr. Campbell was absent from home, but his wife extended to us every assistance that she could to make us comfortable. She gave us a room in the house to occupy during the night, and in the morning a bountiful breakfast was prepared for us, of which sweet potatoes and chickens formed no inconsiderable part. I offered to pay her, but she refused to accept any remuneration, and expressed astonishment at the gentlemanly behavior of the whole party. She said that it was the first time that Federal soldiers had ever visited her house, and she had heard that they were nothing but a set of thieves and robbers, and, for that reason, she had been happily disappointed in our behavior.

Thanking her for her compliments and hospitality, we bade her a good morning, and resumed our march. We had proceeded only about two miles, when we discovered a small squad of rebel soldiers, in a large cotton-field, at some distance in advance of us and to our right. As soon as they saw us, they broke for the woods; the distance that they had in advance made it useless for us to pursue.

Near the road, and between where we saw them and ourselves, stood a dwelling-house. Having observed that but one of the rebs had arms, the thought occurred to me that the others might have left theirs at the house, and that our approach had been discovered too late to allow of a return for them; so I determined to institute a search. On entering, I inquired of an elderly man present if there were any arms about the house. He said there was not. I told him that I had reason to believe that there was. He insisted that there was not. A search was made, and three guns were found, which we carried with us.

At night we halted fourteen miles from Bolivar. On former trips, I had learned that a squad of guerrillas were stopping somewhere in that vicinity; during the day we had obtained a partial list of their names, and had learned that they were harbored by a Mr. W. S. Perry, who was also supposed to be one. This information we gathered from the people that we saw in our route.

At 3 o'clock the next morning we were again under way, on a road leading direct to Mr. Perry's. When we had gone about a mile, we came to a farmhouse, where I halted my men, and aroused the inmates by rapping upon the door, which was answered by, "Who is there?"

"A friend," I replied.

"What do you want?"

"I want you to get up and come to the door." Hearing some one come to the door, I inquired where Mr. W. S. Perry lived, and was asked,

"Who are you?"

I sha'n't tell you," was my reply.

"Then I sha'n't tell where Mr. Perry lives," was the response.

Fearing to make any disturbance that might spoil my plans, I proceeded on my way, without obtaining the desired information. At the next house I inquired again for Mr. Perry, but the occupant refused to inform me. These refusals increased my suspicions that he was not all right. Not knowing certainly but that I was already at his house, I distributed my men among the negro-quarters in the yard, to capture any persons that might attempt to escape. It was time for daylight to make its appearance, but a dense fog had arisen, which made it difficult to see.

Having arranged my men to my satisfaction, I returned to the door of the house, which I found open, and was met by an aged woman, who told me that her name was Tabitha Perry, and that she was grandmother of W. S. Perry, and that W. S. Perry lived in the next house.

While I was engaged in conversation with the old lady, two men were seen to run out of one of the outbuildings that stood in the yard; the density of the fog prevented shooting them, or observing whither they went; so, they made their escape. On examining the building they were seen to emerge from, it was found to have the appearance of being nearly filled with cotton-seed, but in the center of the building there was a large vacant space, and in it was a bed that was yet warm from the animal heat of the persons that had occupied it.

We then searched carefully all the buildings in
11

the yard, but without success. From there we went to the residence of W. S. Perry, only a short distance from the residence of the old lady. We found Mr. Perry at home, and arrested him. In searching his house, we found considerable quantities of goods, that looked as if they might have been remnants from some dry goods store; or, what is more probable, the booty of some band of outlaws.

We captured at W. S. Perry's one horse and two mules, and at the old lady's house one horse and one mule. The bed that we found in the cotton-seed at the old lady's we gave to the niggers on the place, except two quilts that we used to put upon the mules' backs, to ride on.

Very much against Mr. Perry's wishes, I compelled him to furnish myself and men with breakfast, which was no more, perhaps, than he would have done willingly to as many guerrillas, if we had not been seen in the neighborhood.

When breakfast was over, we commenced our return to camp, taking with us our prisoner and captured property. The men were much in need of saddles and bridles, with which to ride the captured mules and horses, and requested the privilege of taking them if they could be found; to which I consented, providing they could be found on the premises of the man who refused to give me information about Perry. The man's name, I had learned, was Dougherty.

When we arrived at Dougherty's place, we halted, and the men commenced to search for saddles and bridles, and, in a few minutes, reported to me that they had found twelve United States army saddles and as many bridles. I told them to take five of them. Dougherty remonstrated, but the men told him that he had no business with that kind of property in his possession, and took them along.

On our way back to Bolivar, I learned the reason why we did not find any more guerrillas at Perry's. A colored boy, belonging to Mr. William Moore, of Van Buren, had been sent to mill, and, while on his way, he happened to see us. On his return, he told his master that he had seen some Yankee soldiers in the woods, and that they were going south. Dr. Tansey Russel, a man of disloyal proclivities, happened to be present, and heard what the colored boy said. The doctor had some Enfield and Whitney rifles in his possession, that he had managed to get of unprincipled Federal soldiers, which he had collected for the benefit of the guerrillas. As soon as he heard of the Yankee soldiers being in the woods, he concluded, readily enough, what their business was; so he took his guns, eight in all, and carried them over to Perry's, and gave them to the guerrillas, and warned them that there were Yankee scouts in the vicinity. There was eleven of them, besides W. S. Perry. On hearing about the scouts, they all left and went to Saulsbury, except W. S. Perry, John Shaw, and Gid. Galloway. The two latter were the persons that escaped from the out-building in the old lady's yard.

When we arrived within six miles of Bolivar, I sent the five men that were not mounted across the country, by the shortest route, to camp, and the rest of us went on by way of the road. At Mr. Lawhorn's, near Dunlap's Springs, we halted a short time, and three of us went into the house. Mr. Lawhorn was absent from home. One of the men asked Mrs. Lawhorn for some milk, which she refused, saying that she had none. From the colored people about the house the man learned that she had milk in abundance, and where it was, of which he helped himself, and then passed some to the rest of the squad. None was wasted and nothing else was disturbed.

Having rested ourselves, we went on to Bolivar. I immediately turned over my prisoner to the Provost-marshal, Lieutenant W. S. Dewey. I also gave him a list of the names of those that I had been informed were guerrillas. It was after noon when we arrived, and we had eaten nothing since breakfast, and, being very hungry, I took my men into camp to get my dinner, before reporting to General Lauman. On my arrival in camp, I told Colonel Force what property I had brought in, and asked him what I had better do with it, and was told to turn it over to the post Quartermaster. I told him that I would, as soon as I had eaten some dinner.

I had eaten my dinner, and was on my way to see about turning over the captured property, when I was met by some guards, with an order from Lieutenant W. S. Dewey, Provost-marshal, to arrest me. I accompanied them to the Provost-marshal's office, where I found Lieutenant Dewey, in a dreadful rage.

"What do you want of me?" I asked.

"I want to hang you, and all the rest of the G—d d—d robbers that were with you!" was his reply.

"What is that for?"

"For going through the country and deceiving the people, and representing yourself as a citizen of Tennessee."

"I have never been through the country, except as I have been sent on scouts by my commanding officer."

"I'll *scout* you, d—n you! I'll scalp you! What's the names of the men that belong to your band?"

"I hav'n't got any band."

"What's the names of the men that were out with you?"

I then gave him a list of the men that accompanied me, and was then ordered to be put in the guard-house. The court-room of the court-house was used as a guard-house. The Provost-marshal's office was in one of the lower rooms of the court house.

The Provost-marshal had all the men that had been with me arrested, and when he had got us all together in the guard-house, we were marched, under guard, into his office. Addressing us, he said:

"There has been a great deal of stealing and robbing going on in the country about here, lately, and I believe that you are the men that have done it, and I mean to make an example of you, and I shall use my *utmost endeavors to have every man of you shot.*"

"What have we done," I inquired, "that you should have such an awful antipathy against us?"

"You will see when I make out my charges and specifications. Guards, take them back to the guard-house."

When back in the guard-house, and left to reflection, the words, "*I shall use my utmost endeavors to have you shot,*" seemed to force themselves upon my mind with vivid impression. What could it mean, that an officer in the United States army should express himself so emphatically, as committed against us, when justice every-where holds a man to be *innocent* until he is *proved* to be guilty.

While I had been in camp getting my dinner, the Provost-marshal had released Mr. Perry, and had administered to him the oath of allegiance, and returned to him the property that we had taken. On being released, Mr. Perry found Doctor Russel, Parson Hamers, and Mr. Lawhorn—who happened to be in town at the time—and, in company with them, went to the Provost-marshal, (who tolerated their complaints,) and fabricated such statements as they chose to make against us, and upon those statements the Provost-marshal based his charges and caused our arrest.

It was humiliating in the extreme, for us, after having served our country with devoted patriotism, and imperiled our lives for its preservation, to be thus made the victims of revenge by those whom we knew were at enmity with the Government.

Two days after our imprisonment, we received a copy of the charges against us, of which the following is an exact copy:

"CHARGES AGAINST CORPORAL RUGGLES, AND TEN OTHERS, OF THE 20TH OHIO INFANTRY.

"CHARGE.—*Indiscriminate plundering and pillaging of citizens in the country.*

"SPECIFICATION FIRST.—That Corporal L. Ruggles, Corporal D. W. Huxley, Sergeants W. G. Downs and Thomas J. Watson, and privates John Lawrence, Jacob W. Snook, H. Chryst, S. Rosebaum, Granville Cassedy, John Sessler, and B. F. Wannamaker, did, on or about the 14th day of October, 1862, enter the house of one W. S. Perry and break the locks of two trunks, and take from them W. S. Perry's clothes; also, the clothing of his children, some finger-rings, some jaconet cloth for children's clothes, and rummaged through every part and portion of the house; also taking two mules, one horse and one saddle, and one double-barreled shotgun, both tubes being broken.

"SPECIFICATION SECOND.—That Corporal L. Ruggles, and ten others, named in specification first, did, on or about the 14th day of October, 1862, enter the house of one Mrs. Tabitha Perry, took from her possession two bed-quilts, one sheet, a pair of pillows, and a bolster; also, one mule.

"SPECIFICATION THIRD.—That Corporal L. Ruggles, and ten others, named in specification first, did enter the house of Mr. Lawhorn, break the door of the ladies' wardrobe, searched through the whole house, brandishing their pistols. Mrs. Milliken endeavoring to save her property, they threatened to shoot her, and used insulting and threatening language to the same; also, taking the milk in the house, prepared for sick and wounded Federal soldiers at Dunlap's Springs, of which they were notified.

"SPECIFICATION FOURTH.—That Corporal L. Ruggles, and ten others, named in specification first, did, on or about the 14th day of October, 1862, at the farm-house of W. S. Daugherty, enter his outhouse, and take therefrom three saddles and three bridles, threatening to take said Daugherty's life in case of his interfering.

"SPECIFICATION FIFTH.—That Corporal L. Ruggles, and ten others, named in specification first, approached the house of B. N. Hendricks, at which place Mrs. Goforth was staying, and demanded their dinner, frightening Mrs. Goforth to such an extent as to cause a miscarriage, after being *enceinte* seven months, her life placed in a very dangerous condition.

"SPECIFICATION SIXTH.—That Corporal L. Ruggles did forcibly take a pair of gloves from W. S. Perry and wear them to town. That Sergeant T. J. Watson did take from W. S. Perry's trunk one razor-strop and shaving-box. That Private B. F. Wannamaker did take from same one pair of men's shoes.

"All the above charges being calculated to destroy the good character of our army and soldiery, being contrary to the laws of war and army regulations, demoralizing in their tendency, I submit them.   W. S. DEWEY,

"*Provost-marshal 4th Div., Bolivar, Tenn.*

"The witnesses are as follows: Doctor Tanzy Russel, Parson Hamers, W. S. Perry, Mr. Lawhorn, W. S. Daugherty.

"SPECIFICATION SEVENTH.—That Corporal L. Ruggles did, after being entertained gentlemanly for the night by Parson Hamers, take said Hamers' *watch, which hung on the mantel-board.*"

This last specification occurred in the original in the same order in which it is here placed.

CHAPTER XV.

Unfortunate state of affairs—Informality of charge and specifications—Assistance of friends—Fails to get a trial—Gloomy prospects—Evidence accumulates—Guard-house incident—The "General" concludes to help himself—Narrow escape from guerrillas—The capture—Reaches his regiment—Himself and squad released.

THE reader will remember that I once arrested Parson Hamers, while standing picket for the enemy, and released him. Doctor Russel, I had learned from reliable sources, had been engaged in contraband trade between Federal soldiers and guerrillas. Mr. Lawhorn had tried to induce one of the men under arrest with me to desert, and, to prevent suspicion of desertion, offered to carry him in his own carriage to a rebel paroling officer, and get him paroled and bring him back. Perry had been captured on suspicion of being a guerrilla. Such were the men that were allowed to make statements against me.

It is easy to conceive how such men would connive together for the injury of Federal soldiers, if they could only get the military authorities to tolerate their complaints and give them a hearing. Under such a state of affairs, it would be an easy matter for any disloyal citizen to cause the imprisonment of any soldier, however spotless his record.

When men are mean enough to attempt the destruction of the fairest and the best Government that ever existed, and to insult that national emblem which has called forth the honor and respect of the world, it is no wonder that they should resort to falsehood, or any other dirty means, to work their revenge upon those that love and fight for their country.

It was extremely unfortunate for us that we were thus imprisoned during the command of a temporary post-commander, to whom I was an entire stranger, and that, too, at a time when a new and extensive campaign was about to commence.

The charge and specifications, as preferred against us, were *very informal*, and it is doubtful whether any court-martial would have attempted a trial based on such informalities. But, nevertheless, there were grounds for our arrest and confinement.

About two weeks after our arrest, a general court-martial convened, and our friends used every exertion in their power to have our trial come on, but did not succeed. Soon afterward the principal part of the forces stationed at Bolivar moved to Lagrange, Tenn., to which place we soon followed them. A second and a third court-martial was convened at Lagrange, and still we failed to get a trial.

On the 28th day of November, the Army of the Tennessee commenced to move from Lagrange, on its campaign into the State of Mississippi, and with it was crushed all hope of our immediate trial. With the movement of the army, the court-martial had been dismissed, and our witnesses, friends, and counsel scattered beyond a probability of rendering us any assistance for a long time; and, to make the matter still more unpleasant, we were confined in a dirty, filthy building, extremely loathsome and unhealthy, and too small for the number of men confined.

During our confinement, up to the time the army moved, evidence continued to accumulate in our favor. The list of guerrillas that I had given to the Provost-marshal, he had destroyed the same day that it was handed to him. During our confinement, W. S. Perry, and all the persons named in the list that I gave to him, were captured by a detachment of the 7th Kansas Cavalry and sent North as guerrillas, showing conclusively that I had not been mistaken in supposing them such. In taking their property, under the circumstances that I found it, I did no more than any detachment of troops would have done under the same instructions.

The property found at W. S. Perry's was evidently plunder that had been seized by himself and band. Very much of the specifications against us were grossly false. What property we did take, I was making arrangements to turn over to the Quartermaster when I was arrested, showing conclusively that I did not take it for my personal benefit.

The lady that we were charged with having frightened not one of us had ever seen; neither had we ever been nearer than three-quarters of a mile of Mr. Hendrick's house. Mrs. C—— visited us twice while we were confined at Bolivar, and spoke very complimentary of our behavior while at her house, and assured us that we need not feel at all uneasy about the charge of frightening Mrs. Goforth, because that it could easily be proven that "*her husband was in the rebel army, and had not been home for more than a year!*" Doctor Russel was the man that trumped up the charges about Mrs. Goforth. A soldier by the name of William Goodhart, of the 20th Ohio Regiment, visited Dr. Russel, one day, and, in the course of conversation, remarked, "Doctor, you have got some of the Yankee soldiers in rather a tight place, hav'n't you?"

"Yes, I have had some of them shut up awhile."

"Well, it will be apt to go pretty hard with them, won't it?".

"No, I think not. I do n't expect to prove any thing against them. They will probably get clear in the end; but it will keep *Ruggles* from running all over the country and representing himself as a citizen of the State of Tennessee.

Parson Hamers, in specification seventh, accuses me of stealing his watch, but neglects to fix the date of theft. He afterward fixed the date as the 30th of September. My company commander was able to show that I was in camp on the 29th and 30th of September and on the 1st of October. In a conversation with Parson Hamers, had in the presence of Sergeant E. W. Quackenbush, of the 20th Ohio Regiment, a few days before I was arrested, he spoke of having had his watch stolen, and said that he was so sick at the time that he *did not know who took it.*

During our confinement we were under the custody of four different Provost-marshals. As a general thing, we met with kind treatment from those that were guarding us, and oftentimes, through the kindness of officers and men, we received favors not usually given to soldiers under arrest. There were a few exceptions to our kind treatment, and I will narrate an incident illustrative of it:

The whole number of prisoners confined in the guard-house at the time I allude to, including my own squad, was forty-three, and we all occupied the same room. Among the prisoners confined with us was a very young soldier—a mere boy—by the name of George S——, of the 18th Ohio. He had been in confinement much longer than myself and squad, and was noted for being decidedly a "hard case." His recklessness sometimes caused restrictions to be placed upon all confined, thereby causing the innocent to suffer for the guilty.

One night, George took a rail from off the banisters that surrounded the stairway and placed it from the portico in front of the court-house into a tree that stood close by, and, by that means, got out of the guard-house, unobserved by the guard, and spent the evening in town. On his return, he neglected to take the rail away. In the morning the officer of the guard discovered it, and concluded correctly what it had been placed there for. He commenced an inquiry of the prisoners to find out who put it there. None of the boys would acknowledge having done it. Several told him that they supposed George had done it. George denied it, and nobody had seen him do it.

The officer would not take suppositions as to who did it, but told us that he should hold us all responsible for a correct report of who did it, and would give us till roll-call at night to find out; and at that time, if we did not report, we should all live on nothing but bread and water until we did.

We told him that we had already said all that we knew about it, and that we did not feel like submitting to punishment as a body for the acts of an individual. Roll-call came, but nobody was able to report. We were then told by the officer that we should have nothing but bread and water until we reported who did it.

During the night, the boys took several pocket-handkerchiefs and made a black flag, about three feet square, and fastened it to a long strip of molding, which they tore off from the wood-work of the room, and hoisted it upon the top of the court-house cupola. In the morning it attracted every body's attention, by its disgusting appearance, as it floated from the most conspicuous place in town. It created universal indignation throughout the town.

The officer of the guard came up and ordered us to take it down. We replied that as long as we had to subsist upon bread and water, it was the flag that we rallied under. He then ordered the guards to make us remove it. As they were attempting to come up the stairs, George, who had armed himself with an armful of bricks from the fire-place in the room, opened fire upon them from the head of the stairs, which made them beat a hasty retreat, and the officer could not induce them to renew the attempt. In about half an hour, a detail came, armed, not with guns and bayonets, but with mess-pans and kettles, filled with *soft bread, beefsteak, and coffee.* It is needless to add, the "additional reinforcements" compelled us to "surrender" and take down the flag. As long as we remained in charge of that officer, we continued to receive an abundance of good, wholesome rations.

During our confinement in the guard-house at Bolivar, quite a number of rebel soldiers, that had been captured by the Federal cavalry, were temporarily confined with us. Several of them were men that belonged to the 2d Arkansas Cavalry, and I had become acquainted with them during the time that I was with that regiment.

On the 3d day of December, 1862, five days after the army had advanced from Lagrange, I came to the conclusion that I had been confined long enough, and that my only way of getting myself and men released, without delay, would be to visit in person my commanding officers, and lay the case before them. One inducement that I had was, I had learned that there were no papers in the hands of the Provost-marshal with charges against us. They had either become lost, or, what is more probable, were returned to the officer that preferred them, on account of informalities. In the absence of such papers, I felt convinced that I could get an order for the release of myself and men. It was an unmilitary way of doing business, but, nevertheless, I resolved to leave the guard-house, *without authority, to obtain authority for my release and that of my men.*

We had been in confinement *fifty days*, and before I could reach the army it would be more than a hundred miles from Lagrange. It was a great undertaking to leave the guard-house without authority, and, without rations, to run a gauntlet of that distance, through Federal pickets and railroad guards, stationed at frequent intervals along the whole route, every one of whom would halt me to examine my pass, or would turn me back if without one.

Sergeant T. J. Watson volunteered to go with me. *How* we got out of the guard-house it is not necessary for me to mention. From Lagrange we took a south-east course, across the country toward Davis' Mills; we struck the railroad where the wagon road crosses it. There we found some pickets, belonging to a detachment of five companies stationed at Davis' Mills, under command of a Major, and charged with guarding a portion of the railroad. At the time we approached them, they were all, except the sentry, engaged in cooking a part of a fat porker that they had confiscated during the night. We halted and entered into conversation with the boys, as though we had no intention of going on. Having finished their cooking, they asked us to eat with them, which we were no way backward about doing. We finished our breakfast, and were about starting on, when the sentry, who had been more attentive to duty than we had hoped, asked us if we had passes. I told him we had not, and that we were on our way to the front, and had not been asked for passes before, and did not know as it was necessary to have them. With that explanation, the sergeant of the guard let us pass, but told us that it would not do to let the Captain in command see us.

Not liking to run our chances with him, we crossed the railroad and left it to our right, and crossed Davis Creek on a log, and, a short distance from the creek, turned to our right, so as to reach the bridge across Wolf River, near Davis' Mills. As we were passing through the cleared field, I discovered to my left, on a rise of ground, a squad of guerrillas, mounted on horses. We were within easy shot of them. We were then within half a mile of the detachment camped at Davis' Mills; they probably did not wish to alarm the Federal pickets. They had evidently discovered us first, and were watching for an opportunity to "gobble us up."

"Tom," said I to the Sergeant, "what kind of soldiers do you call them?"

"What kind are they, Bunker?"

"They are a band of guerrillas, and they will have us in less than a minute, if we do n't get away from here."

Just then the guerrillas started for us.

"Come on, Bunker; for God's sake, let us run!" said Tom. "They are coming now!"

Turning square to the right, away we went, as hard as we could run, toward Davis Creek. A hundred and fifty yards brought us to a dense growth of brush and briars, so thick as to seem impenetrable. There was no getting around it, for our pursuers were close upon us. With all the strength we could muster, we sprang into that briar patch and scrambled through. It was no time to mind scratches, and so we dashed on to the creek. Our pursuers could not get their horses through the briars, and before they could get round them, we were across the creek. We made our way to Davis' cotton-gin, where we found a picket post. A few paces from the post, the guerrillas were in sight. I showed them to the pickets, and told them I would go and report the guerrillas to the Major in command.

Having found the Major, I said: "Major, there are about thirty guerrillas just across Davis Creek, not half a mile from here, and if you will get out your men, you can surround them and capture them."

"Who are you?" he inquired.

"I am a scout for the Government."

"Where are you from?"

"Why, I am right from the guerrillas," said I, getting out of patience; "they have just chased me through a briar patch. Look at my hands and face, if you want any evidence of it. You can *see* the guerrillas from the cotton-gin."

"Who is that man with you?"

"Which is of the most importance, Major: for me to sit down and tell you my history, or for you to get out your men and capture those guerrillas?"

By this time the pickets had become alarmed, and sent in for support. The long roll began to beat, and every thing was excitement. Then was my time to get away.

"Come on, Tom," said I to the Sergeant; "we must pass the pickets at Wolf River bridge during the confusion incident to this alarm, or we will not get away from here without trouble."

As I had expected, the confusion enabled us to get by the pickets at the bridge. We continued on until about 7 o'clock in the evening, when we were halted by a railroad guard. The guard allowed us to come up, and we stayed at the post all night. Before we went to sleep, a messenger came along on a hand-car, with orders to double the guards during the night, for an attack on the railroad was intended, and that thirty guerrillas had already been captured at Davis' Mills, and that more were supposed to be in the vicinity.

At daylight I tried my persuasive influence upon the guards, and succeeded in getting leave to pass. From that on we had very little difficulty in passing the guards. When we had gone about half a mile, we met six rebel soldiers, of the 8th Kentucky Regiment, on their way to give themselves up. They had become tired of the rebellion, and were anxious to return to their homes. From them I learned that a raid upon Holly Springs was in contemplation by the forces of Generals Van Dorn and Tighlman. The rebel deserters were so candid in their statements that I deemed them reliable; and when we reached Waterford, where General Ross' division was encamped, I called at his head-quarters, to report what I had learned. General Ross was absent, so I reported to the Adjutant-General. We then resumed our journey, and in five days from the time we left Lagrange, we reached our regiment, then at Oxford, Miss.

I immediately reported to Colonel Force, who inquired if I had been released from the guard-house.

I said, "No, sir; we ran away."

"Well, Bunker, I am sorry to say it: I can't harbor you in my regiment."

"I suppose, then, Colonel, that the best thing that we can do is to get away from here; a'n't it?"

"Well, I do n't know but it is."

I then left him, and went to General Leggett, commanding the brigade, and told him the situation of affairs. He told me that we need not go back to the guard-house, and that we might stay with the regiment. I told him that I did not wish to stay, unless the men of my squad were released. He assured me that they should be, and immediately went in person to Major-General McPherson and explained the situation of affairs to him. He issued an order releasing the whole of us. When the order reached the men in the guard-house, they had been in confinement fifty-eight days. They reached the regiment when it was encamped about three miles south of the Yacona River.

During our confinement, very much interest and sympathy was manifested for us by both officers and men, and many of them rendered us valuable assistance. To General M. D. Leggett and Colonel M. F. Force, and to Captains F. M. Shaklee, E. C. Downs, and B. A. F. Greer, of the 20th Ohio, we are under very great obligations; and to the officers and men of the 78th Ohio and the 17th Illinois Regiments, who guarded us during the greater part of our confinement, I will here take the opportunity to express, in behalf of myself and squad, sincere and heart-felt thanks for their kindness and assistance.

CHAPTER XVI.

Starts for Grenada—Instructions—Is captured—Returns to Water Valley—Starts again—Arrives at Grenada—Condition of Price's army—He returns—Again sent to Grenada—Proposes some fun—Plan of strategy—Plan unnecessary—Returns with rebel cavalry—Bivouac at Big Springs—The attack—More fun than bargained for—The result.

Soon after I joined my regiment, the army advanced to the Yacona River, and the brigade to which I belonged was made the advanced post of infantry, and was stationed three miles south of the river. I had been with the brigade but a few days, when General Leggett requested me to make a trip to Grenada, a distance of thirty-two miles.

As General Grant's army had advanced, General Price's army had been forced back, and the movements of the Federal forces had been so skillfully managed as to cause Price, after evacuating his strong position at the Tallahatchie River, to make a hasty and rapid retreat to Grenada, which place he then occupied.

General Leggett wanted me to find out the strength and condition of Price's army; of what his force consisted, and, if possible, what were his intended movements.

I started out on foot, disguised like a rebel soldier, with a pass to Colonel Lee (since Brigadier-General), of the 7th Kansas Cavalry, stationed five miles in advance of the infantry, at a railroad station called Water Valley. I carried with me a request to Colonel Lee that he would pass me through his lines, if it would not interfere with his arrangements. The Colonel detained me over night, and then passed me through.

I went on through Cofferville, and to within a mile of Grenada, without being molested. Not liking to venture in on the direct road from Water Valley, I turned to my left when within a mile of the place, calculating to enter the town on some other road. I had proceeded but a short distance, when I met three soldiers, dressed exactly like rebel soldiers, who captured me and made me turn back.

When we came back to the Water Valley road, I was surprised to find that I was being taken toward Water Valley instead of Grenada. I then found that I had been captured by soldiers belonging to *the 7th Kansas Cavalry.* I tried to make them believe that I was a Federal soldier, and was scouting for the Government, but it was of no avail; they were not to be *persuaded* out of their prisoner.

We had traveled but a few hundred yards after taking the Water Valley road, when we met a negro, who was riding a splendid mule, with a nice saddle, bridle, and spurs, and was carrying on the mule, in front of him, a sack of corn-meal.

"Halt, you black devil!" said one of the soldiers. "Get off from that mule and let white folks ride!"

The negro dismounted and turned over his establishment to me, and then, shouldering his meal, he resumed his way. I mounted the mule with a somewhat lighter heart than I had had at the prospect of walking all the way back.

When we arrived at Water Valley, I was taken to Colonel Lee, who, on inquiring of the soldiers where they caught me, elicited the fact that they had *ran away from camp and gone to Grenada without leave*.

"Go to your quarters, men," said the Colonel; "I'll take care of your *prisoner now*, and take care of *you in the morning*."

The next morning I started again for Grenada, mounted on the mule taken from the negro the night before, with a letter to Captain Townsend, who had been sent to the vicinity of Coffeeville, during the night, with a detachment of cavalry, requesting him, if admissible, to pass me on. On reporting to the Captain, he informed me that he had men deployed all through the country about Coffeeville, watching for rebel scouts and stragglers, and that it would be hazardous for me to undertake to get through, and advised me to remain with him until his men came in before attempting to go on.

It was so late in the afternoon when the cavalry came in that I concluded to remain with the Captain all night. In the morning I resumed my journey, and at 1 o'clock, P. M., without having experienced any difficulty in passing the rebel pickets, I entered Grenada.

The first thing that attracted my attention, was

the suffering and destitute condition of the infantry and artillery soldiers. Very many of them were lame and foot-sore. Hundreds of them were barefooted, and very many of them were bare-headed, and all of them more or less ragged and destitute of blankets. Sickness prevailed to a great extent. The soldiers were loud in pronouncing curses upon General Sherman, whom they represented as having brought on much of their suffering by attempting to execute a flank movement upon them while in their intrenchments at the Tallahatchie River, which caused them to make a precipitate retreat to Grenada.

A Sergeant, in describing to me the retreat, said: "So closely were we pressed, that while camping at Water Valley for the night, after a hard day's march, we undertook to get some breakfast before resuming our march in the morning, and had hardly commenced when the Yankees commenced shelling us, and we had to leave. We then marched to the vicinity of Grenada, and there worked several hours at cutting down timber and forming abattis, to protect us from the Yankee cavalry, before resting long enough to get any thing to eat."

From such hardships and exposures, and the prevailing destitution of clothing at the worst season of the year, the men had become sick and disheartened. Artillery horses were in as bad a condition as the men, having been worked and short-fed until nearly starved. Large numbers of sick, lame, and foot-sore men were being sent on the cars to Jackson, Miss. The heavy artillery and commissary stores were also being sent there. Every thing indicated to me that General Price did not expect to hold the place.

As near as I could learn, General Price had had at the Tallahatchie 18,000 men; but the force then in Grenada did not exceed 12,000. What cavalry troops there were in the place seemed to be much better clad and in better spirits than the infantry or artillery.

I remained in Grenada two nights, and then started back. I took the road that leads to Pontotoc. I came out, and had proceeded but a short distance, when I was overtaken by three regiments of rebel cavalry. As they came up, I fell in with them and accompanied them. In conversation with one of the Captains, he told me that "they were on their way to assist General Van Dorn to make a raid upon Holly Springs and the railroad, to cut off the Yankee supplies." He expressed himself as very confident of success, and remarked that "if we can't whip the Yankees by force of arms, we can by starvation."

About twelve miles from Grenada, we came to a large plantation, owned by a wealthy planter by the name of Leggett. Mr. Leggett had evidently expected the cavalry along, and had caused to be prepared a large wagon-box of corn cakes, of about a pound and a half weight each, and a large quantity of fresh beef, cooked and cut up into pieces of about a pound each. As we passed, two large negroes handed each man a cake and a piece of meat. I received a share the same as the cavalry.

I continued on in company with the cavalry until

about the middle of the afternoon, when I concluded I had gone far enough on that road. I then dashed on ahead of the cavalry to a piece of woodland, where I dismounted and sat down, as if to rest myself, and remained there until the cavalry had all passed on out of sight. I then mounted, and started across the country toward Water Valley. A few minutes travel brought me into a road that led direct to the place.

When I arrived at the picket lines, the guards arrested me and took me to the Colonel of the 3d Michigan Cavalry, who sent me to Colonel Lee. I reported to him the three regiments of cavalry that I had accompanied out, and he immediately started in pursuit of them. I learned afterward that the chase was kept up to the Rocky Ford, on the Tallahatchie River. On reporting to General Leggett, he expressed himself well pleased with the result of my trip, and requested me to make another to the same place, which I accordingly undertook to do.

Early the next morning I was again on my way to Grenada, mounted on a mule, and disguised as before. At Water Valley I found the 3d Michigan Cavalry still encamped, and called upon the Colonel, whose name I have forgotten. I told him that I was going into Grenada, and that if he wanted a little fun, I would decoy out a regiment of rebel cavalry to a place within twelve miles of him, on the Pontotoc road, known as the Big Spring. The spring, from its distance from Grenada and the abundance of water that it afforded, and the excellent ground about it for camping purposes, made a fine natural place for troops passing out from Grenada to halt for the night.

I told the Colonel that I would go into Grenada and see what cavalry was in there, and select the regiment that I wanted; and then I would go to General Price and tell him that I knew of three companies of Lincoln cavalry, camped near the Pontotoc road, a long distance from support, watching to pick up "our" couriers and small parties that happened to pass that way, and if he would let that regiment go, I would guide it so that it could surround the Lincolnites and capture the last one of them. I also told the Colonel that he could take his regiment over to the place the next night, and then, early next morning, crawl close up to the rebels, and suddenly rise up and pour in five volleys into them, in quick succession, from their five-shooting carbines (the regiment was armed with five-shooters), which would so surprise and terrify them that they would break and run without stopping for guns, horses, or any thing else, and that he would be able to capture the most of their arms and horses, and very many of the men.

The Colonel seemed pleased with my proposals, and promised to have his regiment there in time. I had no doubts whatever about my ability to decoy a regiment out there, but I was not so sure that the Colonel had confidence enough in me to keep his promise. With the understanding, however, that I was to return the next day with a regiment of cavalry, I resumed my journey.

I halted for the night a short distance out from

Grenada, and early the next morning I started in. At the bridge across the Yallabusha River, about half a mile from town, I came to the rebel pickets. They manifested some hesitation about passing me, and asked me various questions about where I lived and what I wanted to go in for, etc. While they were questioning me, a regiment of cavalry made its appearance, coming out. I did not press the pickets to pass me, but remained in conversation with them until the cavalry came out, and then fell in and went along with them.

My prospects now seemed bright. The regiment coming out would answer my purpose, provided it went far enough, and had saved me the trouble of carrying out my strategy. I soon found out that it was a Texas regiment, and, like the three regiments I had accompanied on a former trip, they were on their way to report to General Van Dorn. Having found that out, I felt almost sure that they would halt for the night at the desired place.

The sun was about an hour high when we arrived at the Big Spring, and my anxiety was considerably relieved by the regiment coming to a halt. Preparations were made for the night—horses fed, supper prepared, and a picket thrown out on the road to Water Valley, but on no other.

Long before daylight in the morning, the men were up feeding their horses and preparing breakfast for an early start. At the approach of daylight, the pickets were drawn in. My anxiety for the appearance of the Federal cavalry now became intense. Not a movement could I see that indicated their approach.

Not a suspicion had yet been excited among my grayback companions. How I longed to hear the crack of those revolving carbines!

Breakfast was now ready, and all fell to work at it with a hearty relish. I took some in my hands, and seated myself near a large oak tree, and began to eat, wondering whether the Colonel really would come. The moments seemed unusually long, and, as I occasionally glanced my eyes toward the place where I had hoped the cavalry would make its appearance, all was quiet. I had come to the conclusion that the Colonel had failed to fulfill his promise, when, Bang! bang! crash! crash! went the carbines in a perfect roar of musketry, and the air was filled with whizzing bullets. I instantly sprang behind the oak tree and stood there. So sudden had been the attack, that, although I had been looking for it, a volley was fired before I was aware of the approach of the regiment. The leaden messengers came in much greater profusion and closer proximity to my person than I ever want them again. But such a panic, such confusion, such running, such scrambling was never seen before! It was beyond description. Some fled without horses or arms; some cut the halters of their horses and mounted without arms or saddles—*all* were *terribly* frightened.

Myself and sixty others were captured, and as many horses and twice as many saddles and arms, with their accouterments. Eight men were killed, and several horses and quite a number of men were wounded. The rebs fired but a very few scattering shots, and not a man of the Federals was injured.

It was a brilliant success, but for a few minutes *rather serious fun*. The Colonel played his part with admirable ability. After the stores were gathered up, I was released, and we returned to camp. During my absence, the brigade to which I belonged had advanced to Water Valley, at which place I found it.

CHAPTER XVII.

The forage party—Runaways—Daring scout—Narrow escape--The line of battle--Safe return—Scout reports—Assumes the character of a rebel prisoner—Finds a friend—How he introduced himself—Where he belongs—The burning of Holly Springs—The heroine—What she captured—Shows partiality—Offers assistance—Rebel doctor executed.

WHEN the army fell back behind the Tallahatchie River, General Leggett's brigade remained at Abbeville, as advanced outpost of the army. It was while we were there on outpost duty, that the troops experienced the inconvenience of short rations, caused by General Van Dorn's cavalry raid into Holly Springs. While the scarcity of rations prevailed, the troops were under the necessity of frequently sending out foraging expeditions to obtain assistance for both men and animals.

On one occasion, an expedition was sent out to the east of Abbeville after forage. After it had been gone a short time, I took a notion that I would go; so I mounted my mule and started out. Soon after passing the pickets, I overtook two men, who, I found, had run away from camp, and, by representing to the pickets that they belonged to the detail guarding the train, had succeeded in passing. They were going out on their " own hooks " to forage a fat sheep.

About a mile from the pickets, the road forked; the left-hand road, or main road, led straight ahead to the east, and the right-hand road led to the southeast. The forage party had taken the left-hand road: the runaways took the right-hand road, and I followed them out a piece to see what I could find. About a mile from the forks, both roads pass through a belt of timber-land, several hundred yards in width, and then emerge into an open space of country, inclosed in fields. After passing through the timber, we halted and mounted the fence to look for the forage party on the other road. They had halted at a plantation-house, and were engaged in loading the train. While on the fence, the two runaways espied some fat sheep in the field near by us. They immediately gave chase, and I remained on the fence to watch the forage party. We had been discovered by the forage party while on the fence, and directly a man was seen dashing across the fields toward us, on horseback, to reconnoiter. In the brigade was a chaplain, not very brave, who sometimes undertook to perform the duties of a scout. As the man on horseback approached, it proved to be the chaplain scout. The field, on the side where we were, was covered with tall weeds, as high as a man's head, and for that reason the runaways did not see the chaplain until he was within fifty yards of them. The boys had not yet captured a sheep, but were trying to corner one, when they discovered him.

"There comes our chaplain, as sure as h—ll!" said one. "We must frighten him back, or we'll both be arrested for running away."

"I'll stop him," said the other, aiming his piece.
"Snap!" went the cap, but the gun did not go.
"Are you going to *shoot* him?" said the first.
"Yes, by G—d!" said the other.
"Then I'll shoot," said the first. Bang! went his gun.

That was too much for the chaplain; he wheeled his horse about, and went *flying back*. The chaplain did not see the boys, but saw me on the fence, dressed in rebel uniform, and my mule hitched to the fence. As soon as he got back and reported, the men not engaged in loading the train were formed in line of battle, ready to repel an expected attack.

The runaways succeeded in capturing a fine, nice sheep, and carried it on their shoulders back to the forks in the road, to wait for the train. There I left them, and joined the forage party, which I found drawn up in line of battle.

When the train was loaded and ready to return, flankers were thrown out on each side of the road, and in that way, succeeded in reaching camp without the loss of a man. The runaways got into camp with their forage without being detected.

I felt curious to know what sort of report the chaplain would make; so, on my return to camp, I immediately repaired to head-quarters and awaited his arrival. When he made his appearance, it was with a countenance indicating that something *serious* and *impressive* weighed upon his mind.

"Has the forage party come in, chaplain?" said General Leggett, as he entered.

"Yes, we *made out* to get back."

"Well, what luck did you have?"

"We had a very *narrow escape*, indeed."

"Why so?"

"Well, I'll tell you; we halted about four miles out, to load the train, and, while thus engaged, some rebels were seen about a mile distant, across the field, on the fence, watching our movements. I was sent to reconnoiter and find out about them, and when I had got within a short distance of them, I saw a long line of them dismounted, behind the fence. Several of them snapped their pieces at me, and one went off, and the ball came whizzing by my head. I wheeled my horse and ran back as fast as I could go. I tell you, General, it was a *providential escape for me!* We then formed a line of battle, to repel any attack until the train was ready to start; then we threw out flankers on each side of the road, and in that way we marched in, without being attacked."

The joke was a serious one, but, inasmuch as nobody was hurt, I concluded not to expose the roguery of the runaways, or the bravery of the chaplain.

* * * * * * *

While the army was on its march from the Tallahatchie to Lagrange, I had an amusing little adventure with a secesh lady. It was on the day that General Leggett's brigade left Holly Springs. I was riding along behind my regiment, in company with Levi Hood, of the 20th Ohio, when I observed, to the left of the road, and about half a mile back, a large, fine white house. I told Levi that, from the fine appearance of things about the house, I presumed we could get feed there for our mules; so we rode out to see.

The house was built with a porch extending across its entire front. As we approached, we saw a Federal guard standing on the porch, near the main entrance to the house, and two Federal officers, one of them a Captain and the other a Major. The officers were engaged in conversation with a lady belonging to the house. We halted in front of the steps leading on to the porch, when Levi, addressing the lady, said: "Madam, have you got any corn or fodder here?"

"Yes, I expect there *is some* out there," she replied, pointing to an outhouse; "go out and get it. Take it *all*, if you can; don't leave any. I shall be glad when it is *gone;* then you won't *bother* me."

We rode to the outhouse and procured what fodder we wanted, and, having fed our mules in a yard in front of the house, we repaired to the porch, where the officers and lady were still engaged in conversation. They were talking about the burning of Holly Springs, and as I came near, I heard the lady say:

"If General Van Dorn and General Price can't *thrash* you out of Mississippi, they can *starve* you out, or get you out in some way; *you are going out, anyhow.*"

"Yes," said I, "that's one of General Van Dorn's capers; he is just the man to do such tricks as that."

The officers left as soon as I came up, and the lady turned her conversation to me:

"Do you know General Van Dorn?"

"Yes, I know *all of our* Generals; and I know you, too."

"Where did you ever see me?"

"A'n't you the lady that sent Colonel Slemmens the boquet last summer, when he was on outpost duty, with his regiment, at Cold Water?"

"Why, yes, I believe I was; where was you?"

"I was sent from Lumpkins' Mills, by General Villipique to Colonel Slemmens, with orders."

"Where do you belong?"

"I belong to the 17th Mississippi Zouaves, the pride of the Confederacy."

"Who is the Colonel?"

"Colonel Hanner."

"Yes, yes! that's a fact! I thought that you was fooling me, at first, but I do n't think you are now. How in the world did you come to be up here?"

"I was captured near Grenada."

"You was? That's too bad! Oh, tell me, have you received your new guns yet?"

"Yes; we received them on the 18th day of last August."

"They were so long coming, that I was afraid they never would get through the Federal lines. How do you like them?"

"Very much, indeed. They are Colt's six-shooters, and are a most excellent gun."

"Well, I am glad of it; they ought to be a *good*

gun, for they cost the Confederacy sixty dollars apiece. You are really a prisoner, then, are you?"

"Yes."

"Well, come into the house."

"I would if I could; but that man is my guard, and I do n't think he 'll let me."

"Oh, no!" said Levi, "I can't; I am instructed not to let him go into any houses nor out of my sight."

"Well, you can see him at the end of the porch; let him go there. He won't run away. Come this way, soldier." She led the way and I followed.

"Now," said she, speaking low, "*do tell* me how the Yankees like the burning of Holly Springs."

"Well, as near as I can find out, they hate it like blazes, and it makes some of them real heartsick."

"Good! I am glad of it! I am getting back pay for my trouble now!"

"Did you help take the place?"

"No, I did not help to take it, but I was chief of the signal corps, and signaled the town all night. I had nearly all the ladies of the town out, and had them watching the movements of the Yankees. We sent up rockets, every hour, all night. I tell you, I felt *so much* relieved at the approach of General Van Dorn, and when he captured the Yankees I was *perfectly delighted!* Then I just *went* for things! I had four mules and a yoke of steers and a cart in there, and I just *loaded them down* with stuff! I got a hundred overcoats, and lots of pants and blankets, and nice canvased hams, and other things, until I had the garret of my house *stowed full*."

"Did you do *all that alone?*"

"Oh, no! my husband, Captain McKisic, was there—he is captain of company A, of Bragg's 1st Battalion—and my servants were there, and they all helped. Oh, I really do wish that you could come into the house!"

"There is no use talking about that, for the guard *won't let me.*"

"Well, I'll tell you," said she (casting her eyes at the man who was guarding her house, and speaking still lower); "I was suspicious that some of the Yankee soldiers might ransack my house and find out what stuff I had got, and so I went over to the Colonel of the —th Illinois Regiment and sung him a few songs of love, and he sent me over a guard, to keep the soldiers from going into my house."

"You are all right, then, if you keep things to yourself."

"I can do that, I assure you; I have run with the army almost two years, and I have learned how to do that."

"*Come,* prisoner," said Levi, manifesting impatience; "a'n't you getting about through with your conversation?"

"Wait! wait a minute, if you please, guard," said the lady, and away she went into the house. She soon returned with a lot of apples, and commenced to stuff them into my pockets. "There, you eat them yourself. Give the guard these *three little ones;* don't give him any more; eat those nice ones yourself. But, pray tell me, what is your situation for money?"

"I have got about five dollars."

"Is that all? Really, that a'n't enough! Sha'n't I help you to some? I am sure that you can't get along with that?"

"No, I thank you; I can get along in some way."

"*Do* let me help you; I have got three thousand dollars in the house, and I'd just as leave help you as not. *Do* take some."

"No; I won't take any. I might never return this way to repay it."

"I should think that you might get away. Why don't you get paroled, or run away from that guard?"

"I might, but, on account of a plan that I have got, I don't want to get away yet."

"Why, what is it?"

"Well, I'll tell you. I want to go with Grant's army to Lagrange, and see which way it goes from there, and then I'll come back and report it."

"That's a good idea, certainly; get all the information that you can."

"*Prisoner!*" called Levi, getting more impatient; "the mules are done eating and we must *go!*"

I then bade Mrs. McKisic good-by, and we resumed our march. On my return to the regiment, I related the incident to the Colonel, and he replied: "If the *women* are a mind to take advantage of the *disgraceful surrender* of Holly Springs, I don't know as I have any objection."

During the march of the army north-west, from its campaigns against General Price, and when we were near the Tennessee line, thinking that an opportunity might occur of retaliating upon a certain doctor living in the State of Tennessee, who had been instrumental in causing the arrest and imprisonment of myself and ten others, by false accusations, I called upon General Grant and told him what we had suffered by the doctor, and asked him if I might take the same men and go through the lines some night and kill him.

The General said, "I can not give you leave to take a man's life, except under such circumstances as are warranted by the rules of war; if you wish to capture him, I'll give you the countersign."

The next evening a party of eleven men, without the countersign, went through the lines, unobserved, and repaired to the house of the said doctor. Stopping at a neighboring house, about a mile from the doctor's, was a Miss Armstrong, a sister of the Confederate General Armstrong. I had paid some attention to her the summer before. When we came near where she lived, I said to the men, "I have an old acquaintance living about a mile from here that I want to see. You go on and capture the doctor, and wait there until I come." I found the lady at home, and passed the evening with her very pleasantly. Before I was aware of it, two hours had passed. Recollecting my promise to meet the men at the doctor's, I bade the lady adieu and hastened on, fearing, perhaps, my long absence had caused them to return to camp without me. When I arrived, I found the men impatiently waiting for me. Seeing only my own number of men, I inquired: "Was the doctor at home?"

"Yes."

"Where is he?"

"This way, Bunker." (I followed to the far end of the yard.) "There he is."

The reader can judge of my horror and surprise at the sight before me. There lay the trunk of the man in one place and the head in another, looking as if pulled asunder by fastening the neck to a tree and the feet to a span of mules. The mules were still fastened to the feet of the lifeless form.

As much used to scenes of blooodshed and slaughter as I have been, and as much as I felt myself wronged by the ill-treatment of the doctor, the sight was revolting indeed. While I have no doubt but that the doctor would have rejoiced to have caused the death of myself and ten others, I am clear from ever having desired his death by acts of babarism and cruelty. I regret very much that Federal soldiers have ever felt constrained to resort to such acts of retaliation.

It is a fact, however, in the prosecution of this war, that oftentimes the worst of traitors, after having been captured, have escaped the penalty of the law, and then, in their last state, have acted sevenfold worse than in the first. It is in consequence of such evasions of justice, that individuals have felt compelled to deal out punishment themselves. In the face of the cruelties that our men have suffered at the hands of the rebels, contrary to all the rules of war, it is a wonder to me that they have committed so few acts of retaliation.

When arrested, the doctor declared, with most

emphatic assertions, that he was a loyal man, though the men that confronted him knew, by sad experience, that such assertions were false. Such provocation, coupled with the fear that he would escape punishment, caused this summary execution. I only regret that a more civilized mode was not resorted to. The next day the troops moved on toward Memphis, and no complaint was ever made about it at head-quarters.

CHAPTER XVIII.

Arrival in Memphis—Daring robbery—Detailed by the Provost-marshal General—Assumes the character of a rebel Major—Secesh acquaintances—Captures a rebel mail—A jollification—A rebel trader—Plan to run the pickets—Escape of the outlaws.

ON the 22d day of January, 1863, General Logan's division arrived in Memphis, Tenn., preparatory to moving down the Mississippi, to join in the campaign against Vicksburg. While there, as I was passing through the city, accompanied by William Goodhart, of the 20th Ohio, I saw a splendid carriage approaching, drawn by a fine pair of black horses, with silver-plated harness. In it were Captain Daniels and the Quartermaster that had captured me and taken me to Cold Water to be paroled.

As the carriage came up, we sprang into the street toward it, to capture the inmates. Recognizing me, they sprang out at the opposite side, and ran in different directions and made their escape. Supposing that the carriage and horses belonged to them, we unfastened the horses, mounted them, and started for camp, leaving the carriage standing in the street. We reported, with the horses, to division head-quarters, and thence was ordered to brigade head-quarters. At brigade head-quarters we were ordered to turn them over to the Quartermaster of our own regiment, which we did. The next morning, the following article appeared in the Memphis *Bulletin:*

"DARING ROBBERY.—Yesterday, some time during the day, two soldiers entered the stable of a citizen on Adams street, and took therefrom a valuable span of black horses, and a set of silver-plated harness, and succeeded in getting away with the stolen property.

"Such outrages upon citizens of this city have become frequent of late, and it is high time that the military authorities took the matter in hand and suppressed such disgraceful proceedings."

The same day that the above article appeared, an order was procured by a citizen of the city for the release of the horses and harness. From what I could learn, the horses belonged to him, and not to the persons driving them.

With nothing to do about Memphis but idle my time away in camp, I began to get restless and uneasy, and was about contriving some way to get outside of the lines to work, when I received word that General Logan wanted to see me. I immediately reported to him, and was handed a sealed envelope and ordered to report with it to Colonel Hillyer, Provost-marshal General on General Grant's staff. I carried the communication to the Colonel, as directed, and, when he had read it, he immediately sat down and wrote me an order, of which the following is a copy:

"HEAD-QUARTERS DEPARTMENT OF THE TENNESSEE,
"OFFICE OF THE PROVOST-MARSHAL GENERAL,
"MEMPHIS, TENN., February 6, 1863.

"The bearer, Lorain Ruggles, is in scout service of the Government. He will be passed through all lines, at all hours. He will be furnished with whatever assistance he may require.

"He has authority to make arrests, reporting the same to the nearest military commander or Provost-marshal.

"All officers and soldiers of this command will, in every way, facilitate his operations.

"By command of Major-General U. S. Grant.
"WILLIAM HILLYER,
"*Provost-marshal General.*"

Handing me the order and some money, the Colonel told me to procure a place to board, and then commence operations. He requested me to report every two or three days the result of my labors, and to do my reporting, when practicable, at night.

I selected a boarding-house on Adams street, kept by a Mrs. W——s. There I represented myself as a Major in the rebel army. My former residence in the city, at intervals of time, gave me an acquaintance that enabled me readily to carry out the character of a rebel officer, without exciting any suspicion to the contrary.

Having established myself in my boarding-house, I proceeded to drum up the acquaintance of such persons as I had reason to believe were of suspicious loyalty.

My first acquaintance of that sort was a Captain Wells, who formerly commanded an independent company in Vicksburg, Miss., but who had resigned his commission in the Confederate army and established himself in business in Memphis. He was at that time a "*Union man*," with the oath of allegiance in his pocket, but engaged in buying horses of Federal soldiers, and smuggling them through the Federal lines.

My acquaintance with him soon led to an acquaintance with others, variously engaged—some as guerrillas, some horse-stealers, some smugglers, some as mail-carriers, and others in various disloyal capacities. They all knew me by my assumed rank, and always addressed me as Major Ruggles.

On one occasion, while looking about the city, one of my disloyal acquaintances informed me that there was a large mail in town from Missouri, to go to General Price's army; and, said he, "Major, I thought that, perhaps, you would be going down that way soon, and if you are, why not take it with you? I presume it is a mail of considerable importance, and undoubtedly General Price would compensate you well for it.

"Perhaps I will take it down," I replied. "But I must make some arrangements with my wife before I go, and I will let you know in the morning."

"Very well. Come up in the morning."

I then went and told the Provost-marshal General what I had learned. He told me to keep watch, and when it started out, to capture it.

The next day I went to see about carrying it out myself, and was told that a man had already made arrangements to carry it, and that it was packed up, ready to go. While talking about the mail, another of my new acquaintances came up, and I invited the two to walk over to the Italian saloon with me and take something to drink.

"You go with me," said the new comer, "over to the saloon where I get my drinks."

"Very well," said I, and we all went over.

In front of the saloon was hitched a horse and buggy. In the saloon, besides the proprietor, was a very gentlemanly-looking man, who, soon after we entered, asked the proprietor of the saloon if he had any word that he wanted to send to Hernando. The man said he was going down that way, and if he had any thing to send he would take it.

The proprietor had nothing to send, and the gentleman, without making any further business, went out. The thought now occurred to me that the mail was in the buggy at the door, and the man that went out was the mail-carrier. I excused myself from my companions, as soon as I could, and started out to watch the suspected gentleman. When I went out, he had unhitched and started down the street. I followed along, through one street after another, until the buggy stopped at a provision store. There the gentleman purchased a demijohn of something, and a side of bacon. I saw him place them in the buggy, and then return to make other purchases.

I then went to Captain Taylor, who had charge of the Government horses in the city, whom I found sitting on his horse at his stables. I told him that a rebel mail was going out through the lines, and that I wanted his horse long enough to ride out to the picket line, on the Hernando road, and stop it. He lent me his horse, and I soon found myself at the picket line.

I found a Lieutenant in command of the pickets. I told him that there would be a rebel mail attempt to pass his lines, and that it would be in a one-horse buggy, driven by a very gentlemanly-looking man, and that the buggy that contained the mail would contain a demijohn and a side of bacon. I told him to be thorough, and search the man's person and his buggy and the cushions, and every thing else about the buggy and to do it in such a way as not to lead the man to suspect that any information had been given him. I then took another road and returned to the city.

I had not been gone more than an hour, when the man described drove up to the pickets, halted, and handed out his pass for examination. The Lieutenant, having examined it, told him that he presumed he was all right, but attempts had been made to carry contraband articles through the lines, and his instructions were such that he was under the necessity of making a thorough search before passing him. The man assured the Lieutenant that he had no objections to being searched, and that nothing could be found about himself or buggy not mentioned in the pass.

The man's person was searched and then the buggy, and finally the cushions of the buggy were examined, and in them, neatly quilted in, was found the mail. It is needless to add that the gentlemanly personage was furnished accommodations in the Irving Block, and the mail was turned over to the Provost-marshal General. I never learned what became of the man afterward.

A few days after the arrest of the rebel mail-carrier, I invited several of my new acquaintances down to my boarding-house, to have a little jollification. They all accepted the invitation, and, at the appointed time, made their appearance.

14

When I went to Mrs. W——'s to board, I took with me a yellow boy that had been in my Captain's employ nearly a year. I had trained him so that he understood me perfectly, and, being naturally of a smart, ready turn of mind, and quick to comprehend my meaning, was of great assistance, when I was visited by rebel friends, in helping me to carry out my assumed character.

On this occasion, he represented to perfection the character of a negro waiter. I called him "Spence." Whenever his name was called, he would promptly enter the room, with his hat under his arm, and approach me with as much manifestation of profound respect as if I had been a king, receive my orders with marked attention and execute them with wonderful agility, and then immediately retire from the room.

I had procured a supply of whisky, and Spence was frequently called in to exercise his masterly skill at preparing slings, punches, etc., for which my guests had a peculiar relish.

From my rank, my companions seemed to regard me as possessing peculiar advantages over them, and all seemed desirous to secure my advice and my personal assistance in their individual projects. By that means, I was enabled to find out very much that was going on, that I otherwise would not have done.

Among my guests of that evening was a man that had been in the Confederate army, and had been severely wounded in the shoulder in the battle at Fort Donelson. On account of his wound he had been discharged. As a sort of compensation, to enable him to make a living, for which his disability had seriously disabled him, General Price had given him a paper authorizing him to trade and sell goods in the Confederate army.

After showing me his paper, signed by General Price, "Now," said he, "Major, you can render me some assistance, if you feel disposed, that will be of great help to me in my circumstances."

"Indeed! I should be very happy to do so; but you must remember that I am under bonds to the Federal authorities, and I have to be very careful what I do; if I am caught in any scrape, they will surely hang me."

"I am well aware of that, Major, but I think you can do it, without subjecting yourself to any great danger."

"Well, what is it that you want I should do?"

"I'll tell you. I have been engaged, for some time, in purchasing, in small quantities at a time, various articles of goods, to take through the Federal lines to sell, and I have now got about four hundred dollars' worth. The military authorities are beginning to suspicion me, and I have got to move the goods to some place for safe-keeping. Your boarding-rooms are not very public, and you could keep the goods here without exciting suspicion."

"I expect that I might. I have done more hazardous jobs than that since I have been in the Confederate service. I think I can manage it. You may get the goods ready, and then let me know it, and I will send my servant after them."

"Thank you, Major! You are just the man to do it. I will get them ready in the morning."

My friend Captain W——s also had a little scheme in view, which he related to me, as follows:

"I have got six fine horses, that I have purchased of Federal cavalrymen, and I want to manage some way to get them through the Yankee lines. Now, Major, what plan do you propose to get them through?"

"Well, really, Captain, I hardly know what course would be advisable. The 'Yankees' are getting to be mighty strict in their picket duties. A sudden dash upon the pickets, some dark night, by as many plucky riders as you have horses, might take them through."

"That's my mind exactly, Major! and I was thinking if I could get some military man of experience, like yourself, to lead us, the plan might be executed to a charm! What do you say? will you lead us?"

"Well, Captain, the undertaking is a bold one, but I think I am good for it; at any rate, I will try."

"Good! good! Major, here's your health!" and they all drank heartily.

Late at night, the festival broke up, with an agreement to meet at frequent intervals, as opportunity offered.

The next day the contraband goods were brought over to my rooms and secreted.

I will here relate a little incident concerning my servant Spence, to show how well I succeeded in making my secesh acquaintances believe that I was a Southerner and a slave-owner. I was in the habit of finding fault with him, and would reprimand him severely for the slightest neglect, and sometimes imaginary ones, were sufficient to call forth from me the severest rebuke.

A few mornings after the night of our festival, several of my secesh friends called on me to ride out in the city. I ordered Spence to bring out my horse. When he made his appearance at the front of the house, I went out to see that every thing was in proper order, and at once flew into a terrible passion with him, on the pretense that the horse was not properly cleaned. Spence, as if mistrusting something was up, was about to leave.

"Here, you black rascal!" said I; "why did n't you clean that horse's legs? Ha'n't I taught you better than that? Come here, you black lazy calf, till I thrash you! What! lived with me all your life, and *do n't know how to clean a horse!* Ha'n't I thrashed you time and again for that? Come here, I say! I'll fix you!"

Spence, as if apprehending a booting, manifested a wonderful fear of me, and no inclination to approach nearer, and, as I approached him, he involuntarily drew back. I attempted to catch him, and he ran away from me into the back yard, and I after him. "Stop! stop! you black d—l you! Stop! or I'll shoot you!" I shouted.

Mrs. W——s and my companions ran to the back door to see what I was doing. As they came out, I fired my revolver. Spence stopped, and, facing me, implored, "Oh, Lord! Massa Ruggles, do n't shoot dis nigger! do n't shoot again, for de Lord's sake!

do n't shoot! I'll done clean de hoss all off clean de nex' time! I will, I will, for shure, Massa Ruggles!"

"Don't shoot him, Major!" implored Mrs. W———s.

"Don't shoot him, Major! for God's sake, don't shoot him!" implored my friends.

"Well, I won't shoot him this time, but the next time he won't get off so easy. Do you understand that, you black rascal?"

"Yes, Massa Ruggles! I 'spects dat I was careless. I'll done clean him good now!" and away he went to clean the horse.

Many a laugh have Spence and I had, when by ourselves, over my pretense to shoot him.

A few nights after the above occurrence, another jollification was held at my rooms. Before separating, it was agreed that eight of us, including myself and Spence, should take the contraband horses and goods, and, on a night agreed upon, if every thing was favorable, make a dash through the lines.

The time agreed upon came, and with it my rebel acquaintances, prepared for the dash. I was not ready, and apologized by saying that the weather had been so bad for a day or two that I did n't think they would be along that night. I told them that I had left my saddle at a harness shop to be repaired, but if they would wait until I could go and get it, I would accompany them. To this they agreed. Taking Spence with me, I started for the saddle.

I procured one, to prevent suspicion, and, carrying it with me, I went to the officer of the provost-guards. I told him what was going on, and then showed him my order from Colonel Hillyer, and told him that I wanted six men. My plan was to place them where they could throw themselves suddenly across a street that we would have to pass, as we came up, and halt us, and to fire into every man that did not halt. Spence and myself would, of course, halt and be captured. The Captain would not give me any men unless I would take a whole company. I remonstrated. I knew that six men would not be suspected of any thing more than an ordinary patrol guard, if seen on their way to the place designated, and it would be impossible to get so many men into position without their being seen. The Captain would not yield, and I started with a full company, under command of a Lieutenant. After we had started, the Captain halted us, and charged the Lieutenant not to divide the company into squads, but to keep his men compact in a body. That completely spoiled my plans, but I had no other alternative.

Before we got within three hundred yards of the outlaws, they discovered the force coming and mistrusted their object. They raised a yell of defiance, and, swinging their hats with whoops and hurrahs, dashed out of sight before the company could be got into line. They succeeded in dashing through the lines, and I have never heard of them since.

The contraband goods, however, remained in my possession, and I turned them over to the Provost-marshal.

I was heartily vexed with the failure, and disgusted with the detective service, and resolved that I would never have any thing more to do with it. How well I kept my resolution the sequel will show.

CHAPTER XIX.

Reports to Major-General McPherson—Instructions—Disguise—Starts for Vicksburg—Changes his route—Reports to General Denver—Acquaintance with a cotton-buyer—Plan to make money—Visit to guerrilla Sol. Street—The arrangement consummated—Visit to General Price—Arrival at Jackson—Robbed of his field-glasses—Introduction to President Davis—Visit to Vicksburg—Visit to Edwards' Station—Meets his bear-hunting comrades—Visits Black River bridge—Robbed of his horse—The return—Reports to General McPherson—Reports to General Grant.

HAVING fully determined to do no more detective service, I went to Colonel Hillyer, of General Grant's staff, and told him that I was desirous of making a trip to Jackson, Mississippi, and also to Vicksburg, and that General Ross had frequently promised me an opportunity of doing so. The Colonel said that he was not only willing but desirous that I should do so, and that, as General Grant had gone down to Milliken's Bend, I had better report to General McPherson, and tell him what I wanted. I did so, and was informed by the General that, as I was a stranger to him, if Colonel Hillyer wanted me to go, he must give me a written order to that effect. On reporting back to the Colonel, he gave me a written order, and on that authority General Mc-

Pherson at once gave me his instructions, and furnished me with funds to supply myself with an outfit. I also received from Colonel Hillyer a large roll of Confederate money, with which to bear my expenses.

My instructions were to go down on the Hernando road from Memphis to Grenada, and see how many troops were there, and whether the enemy was fortifying at that place, and whether appearances indicated a determination to remain there long. I was then to go on to Jackson, Miss., and see how many troops were there, and ascertain, if I could, from a reliable source, whether the rebs were still operating the Confederate States armory at Columbus, Miss., or had removed it, as had been reported, to the State of Alabama. Then I was to go to Clinton, Miss., and see how many troops were there; and then to Edwards' Station, and see how many were there; and then to Black River bridge, and see its defenses, and gather all the information that I could concerning them, and find out, if possible, how many forces were at Haines' Bluff; and then return to Memphis, and if General McPherson was not there, to follow down the Mississippi River until I found him.

When he had finished his instructions, I said to him, "General, I am confident that I can get to Jackson, Mississippi, easy enough; but what excuse can I make, or business can I pretend to have, that will call me to Black River bridge? Why not instruct me to go on to Vicksburg, and then there can be no suspicion on my visit to the bridge."

He replied, "Ruggles, the Government has sent six men into Vicksburg already, and none of them have returned; it is of no use to send out men unless they return. Act your pleasure about it, but go no further than you can go and get back."

I felt uneasy about trying to go to Black River bridge without going to Vicksburg, and I did not like to assume the responsibility without saying something about it, for fear I might fail to get back. I decided to go in only on condition that circumstances favored a certainty of return.

The disguise that I chose was that of a well-to-do Southern planter, accompanied by a servant—myself on horseback and my servant mounted upon a mule. Spence went with me as servant. We were both of us richly dressed. I carried on my shoulders a pair of field-glasses, and had in my possession a splendid gold watch, which was furnished me as a part of my outfit, and afterward given to me by General Grant. My hair, at that time, was very long, hanging down upon my shoulders. I wore a very broad-brimmed black hat.

Every thing being ready, I started out on the road leading to Hernando on the morning of the 24th day of February, 1863. When we were fairly outside of the Federal lines, Spence began to reflect on what the consequences would be if I were found out to be a spy. After riding several miles without saying a word, and appearing to be more than usually serious, he said: "Mr. Bunker, a'n't you gwine right down in among de rebils?"

"Yes; why?"

"If de secesh dun git us, won't dey hang us both?"

"You keep that to yourself; if you don't they will certainly hang us both. Remember what I say: all you have to do is to obey me promptly at all times. You must be my nigger—raised with me, and just a day and a half older than I am. Do you understand me?"

"I spects dat I do."

"No matter," I continued, "how much I scold or boot you, you must carry out the character of a tiptop genteel nigger waiter; and you must make every body think that you have got the *best master* in the world. Can you do it?"

"I spects dat I can."

Spence was too deeply impressed with the reality of the situation to say much; but, however much he feared the consequences of a discovery, he acted well the part assigned him, and that, too, knowing the certain fate awaiting him if my real character should be found out.

At the time that I started, the weather had been rainy for some time, and the ground had become completely saturated with water, the roads muddy, and the streams very high. I had gone but about twenty miles, when I found that the bridges across the streams had all been destroyed either by the enemy or swept off by the water, and that they were too high for me to ford them.

I then turned to go back to Memphis, but I found that a squad of guerrillas had got between me and the city. Not wishing to encounter them, I made my way across to Lafayette, a town on the Memphis and Charleston Railroad. At that place I found Brigadier-General Lee (formerly Colonel of the 7th Kansas Cavalry). I called on him, and requested him to inform General McPherson that on account of the high water, I was unable to get through on the Hernando road. From Lafayette I went to Lagrange, at which place I found General Denver. I requested of him a pass to go through his lines. He inquired who I was. I told him, and, to convince him, showed him the order Colonel Hillyer gave me to scout, in Memphis; but, for some reason, best known to himself, he took the order away from me. It was raining at the time I asked for the pass, and I requested to have it dated for the next day. The Adjutant remarked that if I had it dated a day ahead it would afford me a *fine opportunity to see how many forces they had before I went out*. A pass was granted me, however, to go out, but not to return, and I remained at Lagrange until the next day. I think that General Denver doubted my being a Federal scout. Not expecting to pass any Federal lines, except when I left Memphis, I had no pass proper for the occasion, and showed the order that I had for want of something better.

I put up at a house of entertainment kept by a Mr. Lee, where I met with a cotton-buyer by the name of Hall, who was boarding at the same place. In the course of our conversation, something was said about a noted guerrilla by the name of Sol. Street. I remarked, "I do n't see how it comes that Sol. Street has managed to make himself so noted; he is a man that very little was said about before the war."

"Do you know Sol. Street?" said the cotton-buyer.

"Yes, I have known him for ten or twelve years. I knew him when he lived in Memphis, and then afterward when he lived on Island 40, and then again when he moved up to the foot of Island 37."

"Now, see here," said Hall; "you want to make money and I want to make money, and now is the time to do it. If you are acquainted with Sol. Street, you can arrange the matter so as to make a handsome thing of it for both of us."

"How so?"

"Well, I will tell you Sol. Street has got about eighty guerrillas stationed back in the country a few miles, and in their rear is a large amount of cotton. I have seen it, and it is worth eighty cents a pound. Sol. Street likes money as well as either you or I. Now, if you will see him, and get him to give you a writing that he will withdraw his men for ten days, and let Government teams in there, without molesting them, to haul the cotton away, I will give Sol. one-half of the proceeds of the cotton, at eighty cents a pound, and I will give you five thousand dollars of my share, and you shall see the cotton weighed and carry Sol.'s money to him."

"That would really be a nice little spec, would n't it?"

"Yes; and now is the time to strike."

"Well, I am going down into the Confederacy to be gone several days, perhaps two weeks, and I will try and see Sol. Street and find out what he will do about it, and I will let you know on my return."

"Well, do. I am sure that you can't make five thousand dollars easier."

In the morning, I resumed my journey, and had proceeded as far as Waterford, when I accidentally come across Sol. Street. He immediately recognized me as an old acquaintance. After conversing awhile, I said to him, "Sol., you like to make money and so do I, and it don't matter much how we make it, either. I know of a chance for both of us to make something."

"Well, what is it?"

"There is a large lot of cotton in the country, to the rear of your men, and there is a Yankee cotton-buyer, that has seen the cotton, who says that it is worth eighty cents a pound, and that if you will agree to withdraw your men for ten days, and allow him, unmolested, to haul the cotton out with Federal teams, he will sell the cotton and pay over to me one-half of the proceeds of the cotton for you, and will give me five thousand dollars. What do you think of that, Sol.?"

"Will you be responsible to me for my share?"

"Yes, I will, and I think it is as fine a chance for you to make a little fortune, and do it easy, as you will ever have. What do you say, will you do it?"

"Yes, I will; I am bound to make money out of this war, and I don't care a d—n how I do it."

"That's the understanding then, is it?"

"Yes, and when you get ready to have the cotton out, let me know it, and I'll withdraw the men."

However well I had completed the arrangements, I had no intention of participating in a traffic of that kind on my own responsibility. I relate it merely that the reader may see one of the internal phases of this monstrous rebellion. Others have made money in that way.

The journey from Waterford to Grenada was a painfully lonesome one. Not a human being, save a few citizens at Oxford, were seen to enliven the solitude that prevailed. Scarcely a living being was to be seen, save perhaps, now and then, a poor, old, blind and crippled mule or horse, in the last stages of starvation. Even the feathered songsters of the forest seemed to realize the utter desolation that prevailed, and lent, by their silence and seclusion, to that inexpressible gloom. Scarcely a fence or plantation-house remained to mark the place where happiness and prosperity had once existed. Huge chimney-stacks pointed out where the consuming elements had been, and stood as monuments of retribution that was being meted out to those whose folly had led them to participate in their own fearful destruction. I involuntarily exclaimed, "Surely, the way of the transgressor is hard!"

On my arrival at the rebel lines, near Grenada, I experienced no difficulty in passing, and, without having met with any obstacles after leaving the Federal lines, I found myself once more a sojourner in Grenada. I found about 14,000 troops stationed there, composed of infantry, cavalry and artillery, and considerably improved in appearance since my last visit to the place.

I repaired at once to General Price's head-quarters, and there I found General Wheeler, whom I have mentioned as having met before in the rebel army, at General Van Dorn's head-quarters. I asked General Price for a pass to visit Jackson, and for the privilege of leaving my horse and mule with his head-quarter horses until my return, which was granted. While there, I found out that General Wheeler had just received a permit to visit Jackson, so I proposed to accompany him, to which he assented, and we both took the cars together.

At the depot I met with an old acquaintance from Arkansas, from whom I learned that three of my old bear-hunting comrades, by the names of Samuel Teel, Henry Thomas, and Lemuel McIntosh, were in the 10th Arkansas Infantry, and that the regiment was at Edwards' Station, four miles from Black River. I knew that Teel had been a regular canebrake ranger, and I concluded that, if I could find him, I could contrive some way to get safely to Black River bridge.

On our way down, General Wheeler told me that President Davis was to be at Jackson, and that his business down there was to see the President. The idea of seeing Jeff. Davis pleased me. I told the General that I was glad to hear that the President was to be there, for I had never been so fortunate as to have met him, and that I should be very happy to make his acquaintance. He promised that if an opportunity occurred, he would give me an introduction.

On our arrival at Jackson, we repaired at once to

the Confederate House, registered our names, and procured rooms. Before I had been shown to my room, a General (I learned afterward) from South Carolina, stepped up to me, and, taking my field-glasses from my shoulders and placing them upon his own, said: "Citizens have no use for such things, and Generals have."

"Take them, General; take them along, sir! I am willing to do any thing for our Government. You are perfectly welcome, sir."

I knew that it would do no good to object, but I should have been better pleased if he had as much as thanked me for them, but, instead, he walked off with as much dignity as if "Monarch of all he surveyed."

Shortly after our arrival, I entered the sitting-room, in company with General Wheeler, where we found President Davis and his attendants, and Lieutenant-General Joe Johnston. Among the attendants were several Generals, whose names I did not learn; one of them, however, had my field-glasses. General Wheeler approached the President and introduced himself, and then introduced me as a brother of General Ruggles. He also introduced me, in the same way, to General Johnston.

I remained at the Confederate House four days, at an expense of thirteen dollars per day for myself and servant. During our stay, Spence came in for his share of notoriety. He was remarkably attentive to my wants and scrupulously exact in all his arrangements of my toilet. His own clothing was richer than that of any body-servant at the hotel,

HE THEN INTRODUCED ME TO PRESIDENT DAVIS AS A BROTHER OF GENERAL RUGGLES.

and he kept it perfectly clean. His superior dress helped him wonderfully in carrying out the character he had assumed. It was really amusing to observe his lofty and dignified bearing among those of his own color.

After having seen what I could to advantage in Jackson, I went to General Johnston and showed him my pass from General Price, and told him that I wanted him, if agreeable to his good will and pleasure, to give me a permit to visit Vicksburg and return. I told him that I had some friends in there, and, as we did not always know what might be the fortunes of war, I was extremely anxious to see them. He made no hesitation about it, but immediately ordered the required pass for a period of ten days, subject to the approval of the Provost-marshal in Vicksburg, whenever I wished to return.

I took the cars the same day, and went into Vicksburg, where I remained two days. I found a force of ten regiments of infantry there, and, as near as I could judge, 2,000 heavy artillery. From what I could learn, there was at Haines' Bluff about 12,000 troops. The batteries along the river were very formidable, and seemed to me sufficient, if well served, to annihilate any water craft that might undertake to pass.

At the expiration of two days, I went to the Provost-marshal and got my pass approved, and returned as far as Edwards' Station, where I had the good fortune to find my old friends, whose names I have mentioned. They were very much delighted to see me. Sam. Teel still carried his old favorite rifle, which he called "Old Bill." Many a bear had I seen succumb to its unerring aim. The next day after my arrival, Sam. Teel procured a pass for himself and three others (mentioning our names) to visit Black River and fish. We went directly to the bridge, and then rambled up and down the stream as much as we pleased. Teel showed me how they had blockaded the river below the bridge by sinking two small steamboats, one a little above the other, to keep our gun-boats from coming up to the bridge. The bridge and its approaches was guarded by a force of 1,000 men. It was nearly night when we returned to camp. At Edwards' Station, I found a force of 40,000 men. I remained there five days, and then returned to Jackson on foot.

At Clinton, a smart little place, ten miles west of Jackson, I saw one regiment of infantry. At Jackson there was but one regiment of infantry; that was the 17th Mississippi Zouaves, called the "Pride of the Confederacy," and armed with Colt's revolving rifles. I was informed in Jackson that the armory at Columbus, Miss., had been removed into the State of Alabama.

Having found out all that had been required of me in my instructions, I thought it was best to return. Accordingly, I again visited General Johnston, and requested a pass to Grenada, which was granted.

On arriving at General Price's head-quarters, I found that during my absence my horse had been stolen. I made no complaint about it, but continued my journey with my mule and servant. Just before night, on the first day out from Grenada, I passed a stable that contained a very good-looking horse. I proceeded on about two miles, and halted until after dark, when, leaving my servant and mule until my return, I went back and took possession of the horse.

We then rode all night, and the next day until nearly night, without halting, for fear that the owner of the horse would get track of us and follow on after. We succeeded, however, in making our way to the Federal lines without difficulty.

On our arrival at Memphis, being unable to procure transportation down the river for my horse and mule, I turned the former over to the post Quartermaster, and left the latter at my old boarding place, on Adams street. It was the same mule that had been given to me by General Ross, and taken from me by the outlaws. I then took a steamboat passage to Lake Providence, La., where I found General McPherson.

Having heard my report, the General expressed a doubt about the two steamboats that I have spoken of being sunk in Black River, below the bridge. In order to test my reliability, he questioned me about what kind of a man General Wheeler was, his stature, weight, complexion, etc., and let on that he was a very large man. I told him that he was mistaken, or else the General Wheeler that he knew and the one that I knew were two different persons. He then told me that he and General Wheeler both attended the Military School at West Point at the same time, and that he knew him well, and that I described him exactly. I afterward had an opportunity of proving to him that I was correct about the sunken steamboats, by taking him in person to the place and showing him the remains of them.

After I had finished my report to General McPherson, he sent me to General Grant, who was then at Milliken's Bend, La. I reported to him all the particulars of my trip, even to the conversation that I had held with Hall, the cotton-buyer, and Sol. Street, the guerrilla. I also asked the General if there would be any harm in such outside transactions. I told him that if I was allowed to do it, I could pay my own expenses in the secret service, and thereby save that much expense to the Government.

Said he, "Ruggles, don't you have any business transactions with outlaws; if you do, I shall certainly disgrace you. Do a straightforward, honest business for the Government, and then, if you should ever need any assistance, come to me about it, and I will see that you have all the help that you need. A good name, well earned, is worth more to you than all you can make by unlawful traffic."

I think the General's advice was excellent. At all events, I have followed it, and saved myself the disgrace that has since fallen upon many, far my superiors in rank. I have never seen the cotton-buyer nor the guerrilla since.

CHAPTER XX.

Return to Mississippi—Instructions—Visit to Troy—Movement of cavalry—Reports to General Denver—Is arrested—Federal Cavalry driven back—Is released—Visits Greenwood—Journey to the Mississippi River—The perilous crossing—Again arrested—Interview with General Prentiss—Takes the oath of allegiance—Meets a friend—Makes his escape—Reports to General Grant.

WHEN General Grant had heard my report of my Mississippi trip, he supplied me with funds, and requested me to return into the Confederacy, to whatever place I thought proper, and remain until I saw a movement worthy of his notice, and then immediately return.

With these instructions, I started for Memphis, leaving my servant Spence to report himself to my Captain.

At the time I undertook to make the trip, a part of the army operating for the capture of Vicksburg was engaged in trying to get through the Yazoo Pass into the Yazoo River. A part was at Lake Providence, a part at Milliken's Bend, and the rest at Young's Point; the three latter places are in Louisiana, and the former in Mississippi.

I made up my mind to visit that part of Mississippi through which any force designing to operate against General Grant's movements might be seen in time to communicate the fact to General Grant.

Supposing that I might have swamps and rivers to cross, which would have to be accomplished in canoes or on rafts, I determined to make the trip on foot.

I left Memphis some time in the latter part of March, in the same dress that I had worn on the previous trip, and directed my course to Grenada, on the Hernando road. I met with nothing of interest on the entire road to Grenada, a distance of one hundred miles.

On my arrival at Grenada, I found the forces that were there on my last visit to the place, under command of General Price, gone, except the convalescents.

General Price, as I learned afterward, had gone to Missouri. At that time, however, I supposed his forces were at Fort Pemberton, near Greenwood, Miss., resisting the advance of the Federal force through the Yazoo Pass.

From Grenada I intended to visit Yazoo City, and left for that purpose the next morning after my arrival, on the road to Troy, which place I reached about 2 o'clock in the afternoon. There I remained until the next morning, and was about resuming my journey, when a force of five regiments of cavalry made its appearance, coming in on the same road that I intended to take out. They passed through Troy, and took the direct road to Coffeeville. I followed them on foot, and on my arrival at Coffeeville, I found them halted for the night. I had been there only a few minutes, when another cavalry force of five regiments came in on the road from Grenada, and halted for the night.

The next morning a council was held by the commanding officers, but I was unable to learn the subject of discussion. The opinion prevailed among the troops that they were part of a force designed to take Memphis.

I was of a different opinion. I did not think that they could bring to bear a sufficient force to take the place, and from what I had heard from some of the officers, I concluded they intended an attempt to capture Fort Randolph, above Memphis, and intercept the supplies being sent below for General Grant's army. I felt convinced that the movement was of such importance as to warrant me in reporting it, and, not knowing how rapid the movement might be, I determined to report to the nearest Federal commander.

Soon after the council of officers was held, the force started—the first five regiments on the road to Holly Springs, and the other five on the road to Hernando. I accompanied the first.

One of the soldiers had an extra horse, which I persuaded him to let me ride. The march was continued to Lumpkins' Mills, where the regiments halted. There I turned my horse over to its owner, and before any pickets were thrown out I was on my way to Lagrange, which place I succeeded in reaching without any interruption.

At the Yacona River a little incident occurred

which amused me considerably. Previous to evacuating that position, the Federal troops destroyed the bridge across the river. The water in the stream at that place was quite shallow, but the mud was exceedingly soft and very deep, and the banks at the immediate edge of the water very steep and high for a horse to step from. The General in command of the force attempted to cross in advance of his command, and his horse, in stepping from the edge of the bank into the water with its forefeet, plunged in so unexpectedly deep that he precipitated the General over his head into the water, all over. By the time he had established himself on *terra firma*, he was, from his sousing in the mud and water, a ludicrous looking personage.

On my arrival at Lagrange, I immediately reported the movements of the enemy to General Denver. For some reason, best known to himself, he did not credit my report, and detained me under arrest until he could ascertain the truth of the matter.

I told the General my instructions, and assured him that I thought the movement of the enemy was one worthy of notice. A regiment of cavalry was then sent out to reconnoiter, and when near Holly Springs they encountered the enemy, and a sharp engagement took place, in which the superior numbers of the enemy enabled them to drive the Federals back, with a loss of eighteen killed and wounded. At the end of three days the regiment returned, and the General was convinced that *a part of my report*, *at least, was true.* He then told me that I had better report the movement to General Grant.

I replied, "I have been of that opinion for *three days.*"

I then determined to penetrate the country between Hernando and Coffeeville to Greenwood, and find out the locality of the other five regiments of cavalry, and see the position and force of the enemy at Greenwood, and, if possible, communicate with General Ross, and then make my way across to the Mississippi River, and then to General Grant's headquarters at Milliken's Bend, La.

In crossing the country, I left Hernando to my right, but learned, by citizens, that the cavalry stopped at that place, and that General Hurlbut had sent a small force of cavalry to reconnoiter, which, like the one General Denver sent out, was driven back with considerable loss.

On arriving at Greenwood, I found that the principal part of the rebel force was twenty miles below; to which place I went. The force there at that time was a division of fourteen regiments of infantry, under General Tighlman, and one other division of infantry, under whose command I did not learn, and some artillery.

At the time of my arrival, the rebs had erected a battery on a flat near the river, which they flattered themselves would do immense execution upon the Yankee fleet. The Yankees, during its erection, cut the levee above, and in the morning the rebs were chagrined to find the flat overflowed with three feet of water.

I was exceedingly anxious to communicate with General Ross, and the cutting of the levee had very much increased the difficulty of doing so. I made a great many inquiries concerning the Yankee fleet and the danger of crossing to the opposite side of the river. The soldiers assured me that every person that had attempted to cross had been fired into by the Federal gun-boats. The overflow of water made it impossible to reach General Ross from the side I was on. My anxiety to do so caused me to make several indiscreet inquiries of the rebel soldiers, which, I was convinced, made them somewhat suspicious of me, and I thought it not advisable to remain there longer than was absolutely necessary.

On reflecting upon what course to pursue, I decided that the safest way would be for me to make my way to the Mississippi River, opposite Helena. With that determination, I left the rebel force in the afternoon of the next day after my arrival, and retraced my way twelve miles toward Greenwood, and there I took to the left on the bluff road that leads to the river, opposite Helena.

So strong had my fears been excited for my safety, by the suspicions caused by my indiscreet inquiries, that I did not feel safe to stop at any plantation-house over night, but stayed by myself in the woods.

Fortunately, the enemy did not suspicion me strong enough to induce them to follow. After seven days' hard walking, I arrived at Crowder's plantation, on the Mississippi River, near the foot of Island No. 60, without any molestation.

I was then three miles from Helena, with the

Father of Waters between, and no means of transportation across. I immediately commenced a search for some means of crossing. After spending several hours in search of a boat, I found a Dutchman, who owned an old leaky dug-out, which was very small and extremely unsafe for even one person to cross in. I concluded, however, that if I could buy it, I would make an attempt. The Dutchman asked me ten dollars for it, and could not be induced to take any thing less. I took it, at last, and paid him ten dollars in Confederate money.

I embarked in it and undertook to cross. The water came in on me rapidly, and by the time I had reached the sand-bar at the foot of Island 60, my frail bark was so full of water that I was in imminent danger of going down.

I landed on the bar, and drew my dug-out up on the sand and emptied out the water. I had still all of two miles further to go, without any intervening place on which to land, and before re-embarking it was necessary to contrive some way to stop the leaks.

Nine years previous to that time I had been engaged in chopping steamboat wood on that very island. Two winters I had chopped wood there; consequently, I was no stranger to the locality.

About a quarter of a mile from where I landed, near an old wood-chopper's shanty, I found an old shirt; with that I stopped some of the worst leaks, which, having accomplished, I re-embarked on my perilous voyage. I kept my bark to the north of the middle bar, and ran into the Sterling chute, and then landed at Helena, near the foot of Main street.

The moment my dug-out touched the shore, two guards stood ready to capture me, and accosted me with:

"Halloo, old fellow! what's the news on the other side of the river?"

"The news is favorable," I replied.

"Well, I reckon we'll have to take you to the Provost-marshal," said one of the guards.

"Boys, I am a soldier, and I want you to take me to the General in command of the post."

"Our instructions are to take all such customers as you are to the Provost-marshal."

"I can't help that I am a Federal soldier, and I want you to take me to the General."

They then called the corporal of the guard. I knew him; he belonged to the 25th Indiana Infantry. I had frequently seen him in Memphis, during my stay there in the winter; but he knew me as my secesh acquaintances had known me—as a rebel Major. I prevailed on him, however, to send me to the General, whom I learned from him was General Prentiss.

As soon as we arrived at the General's quarters, the guards explained how they had captured me, and then returned to their post, leaving me with the General.

When ready to attend to me, he said: "Well, where do you belong?"

"To General Grant's army."

"What are you doing here?"

"I came in from the other side of the river."

"What do you want here?"

"I want to take a steamboat down the river and report myself to General Grant."

"Yes, to General Grant! That would be a nice way to get off! I guess the best place for you to report is to the Provost-marshal!"

"General, I am a Mississippian, and a soldier sworn into the service of the United States; and I belong to the Army of the Tennessee, under General Grant; the 17th Army Corps, General McPherson; the 3d Division, General Logan; the 2d Brigade, General Leggett; the 20th Ohio Regiment, Col. M. F. Force, and to company H, Capt. E. C. Downs; and I am detached as a scout for General Grant."

"Yes, a *Mississippian!* There are a *great many* Missippians coming into our lines nowadays! Have you any papers to show that?"

"No, sir, I have not; but I can tell you all the principal movements of the Federal army on the east side of the Mississippi River, since the capture of Fort Donelson, up to the present time."

"Well, what are they?"

I then told him what they were, and where General Grant's forces then were; and then I added, "I can tell you all about your surrendering at Shiloh, and what Confederate regiments captured you."

"Well, that's quite likely; I suspected you could do as much. Now tell me about the movements of the army in Missouri and Arkansas."

"I can't do that, General."

"No, I don't expect that you can. I will now

give you the following limits: You can go from my quarters to the Commercial House, and from there to the Provost-marshal's office and back; and if you undertake to get away I'll have you shot."

"General, I left papers in General Denver's possession, at Lagrange, Tennessee, that will show who I am and what my business is."

"Well, you can have the limits that I have given you, and if you have got papers to show who you are, the Provost-marshal will write for you and get them."

From the General's quarters I went to the Provost-marshal, and requested him to write to General Denver for the order he took from me, when on my way to Vicksburg and Jackson, Miss. I learned from him that there was an order, from the commander of the post, requiring all citizens within the lines to take the oath of allegiance to the Federal Government by 9 o'clock of the next day, or be sent outside of the lines toward Little Rock.

I went to General Prentiss the next morning, and again assured him that I was a Federal soldier, and asked him if he required me to take the oath of allegiance.

He replied, "Yes; and unless you do, you will have to leave the lines before 9 o'clock this morning." I then went to the Provost-marshal and took the oath.

I had hoped that in doing so I would be released, and allowed the full privilege of a citizen; but, for some reason not known to me, I was not released from the limits assigned to me. I could not make

General Prentiss nor the Provost-marshal believe that I was a soldier. Several of the soldiers in the 25th Indiana Regiment, on provost duty, had known me in Memphis, in my assumed character; but I could not make them believe that I was a Federal soldier. I had very little hopes of getting the order that General Denver had taken from me; but I felt almost sure that among the great number of officers that I knew in General Grant's army, some of them would stop at Helena, either going up or down the river, and, with their assistance, I thought I could get released. It seemed to me as if every steamer would have on board some one of my numerous acquaintances; but one came, and then another, and still another, and in that way day after day passed by, and no familiar face was seen. In that way I spent nine days in anxious suspense.

At the levee, within the limits allowed me, lay the steamer Imperial. She was used for stationary purposes, and on board was kept a saloon and various refreshments. I was allowed to go on board of her whenever I desired.

On the ninth day after my arrest, I happened to be on board of her, when the steamer Continental came down the river, and, stopping, made fast alongside of her. Before the guards made their appearance, I jumped aboard the Continental and ran up into the cabin, in search of some person that I knew.

There I found Colonel Marsh, of the 20th Illinois Regiment. He knew me. I told him how I came to be there, and that I wanted to run away and report myself to General Grant. He was going on shore at the time. He handed me the key to his state-room and told me to make myself at home, and when the boat started he would join me. In the course of an hour we were under way, and without any molestation from the provost guards. Whether the Provost-marshal ever received my order from General Denver, or whether General Prentiss ever found out what became of me, is more than I know.

I reported to General Grant the result of my trip, and why I had been so long in getting to him. He said that I had done right in coming back when I did, but that I should have reported the cavalry movement to General Hurlbut, at Memphis. He then relieved me from duty for thirty days, and allowed me to return to my regiment.

I will here say, that I have no doubt that Generals Denver and Prentiss acted in good faith on their part, and had what seemed to them good and sufficient reasons for detaining me as they did.

All the conversation that I had with General Prentiss was no more than a Confederate spy might have had under the same circumstances.

Papers I very seldom carry about me when inside of the enemies lines; and in the absence of such evidence, it is sometimes very hard to convince one's own friends of his loyalty, and equally as hard for the enemy to make him out a spy.

CHAPTER XXI.

Return to the regiment—The Henry rifle—The march from Milliken's Bend—The tug of war—The army crosses the Mississippi—Capture of Port Gibson—Battle of Raymond—Amusing Capture—The charge on Jackson—Battle of Champion Hills—The rebel courier—Sharp-shooting—The gallant charge—The march to Vicksburg—The place besieged.

It was about the middle of the month of April that I returned to my regiment, which I found encamped at Berry's Landing, five miles above Lake Providence, La. It was while there that I had an opportunity of examining one of Henry's volcanic or repeating rifles, which are capable of discharging seventeen shots without reloading. The one that I saw was in the possession of the Captain of the steamboat Superior.

From my first enlistment I had possessed a strong desire to have a first-class rifle of the most modern improvement. The promise of such a gun was the principal condition on which I enlisted. It was several months after I enlisted before I received in exchange for my "hand-spike" (musket) the Enfield that was promised to me. My company officers, however, did all they could to furnish me with the promised gun. My long experience as a bear-hunter in the Western wilderness had made me expert with the rifle, and my desire to have a piece with which I could excel at sharp-shooting, if ever an opportunity offered, had become intense, and the organizing campaign against Vicksburg seemed to promise the desired opportunity.

I went to General Grant and told him about the gun, and that I wished to purchase it and carry it. He asked me if I thought I could carry so valuable a piece without losing it. "I think I can," was my reply.

"You lose mules, do n't you?"

"Yes, but I *capture mules.* I am several mules ahead of what the Government has furnished me now; but I can't capture Henry rifles."

"Very well; tell General McPherson to get you the rifle."

I saw General McPherson about it, and he gave me permission to purchase and carry it.

It was a most beautiful piece, with steel barrel and chamber. The Captain who owned it was so much attached to it that he hated to part with it, but at last he yielded to my importunities, and sold me the rifle for sixty-five dollars, including what cartridges he had.

My release from duty afforded me a splendid opportunity of practicing with it. I was perfectly delighted with its execution. Its accuracy and long range was a marvel compared with the best feats of marksmanship that I had seen among experienced hunters.

A few days after I purchased the rifle, the grand move of the army against Vicksburg commenced.

Several gun-boats and transports had already run the blockade of the formidable batteries that commanded the river. It was on the 25th day of April, 1863, at 6 o'clock, A. M., that the 2d Brigade of General Logan's Division, to which I belonged, moved from Milliken's Bend. That night the division bivouaced at Richmond, and the following night at Smith's plantation.

A heavy rain set in at the commencement of the march, which filled the ground and water-courses full of water, which made the roads across those rich alluvial bottoms extremely soft, and easily cut up by the artillery and supply wagons. From Smith's plantation to Perkins' plantation, eight miles below New Carthage, was only fifteen miles, but it took us two days to make the march. That march was really a "*tug of war.*" The horses and mules floundered in the mud. At times, it was with the greatest difficulty, after doubling the teams, that the artillery and wagons were extricated from those miry depths. The men, however, kept up an indomitable good-will and courage, which carried us through. It was 9 o'clock, P. M., when we halted for the night, and at 12 o'clock, the same night, we started for Hard-Times Landing, situated a short distance above Grand Gulf, on the opposite side of the river. The march was made by way of Lake St. Joseph, and it was 4 o'clock, P. M., of the 29th, when we reached Hard-Times Landing.

On the 1st of May we crossed the river to Bruinsburg. It was on that day that General Osterhaus' division and two brigades of General Logan's division captured Port Gibson. From that time until the 12th of May, the troops were engaged in following up the enemy and harassing him. Our general course of march was to the north-east, toward Jackson.

On the 12th, General Logan's division being in the advance, when within ten miles of Raymond, the enemy, about 5,000 strong, including two batteries of artillery, under command of General Gregg, was found advantageously posted, with the artillery so arranged as to sweep the road and a bridge that it was necessary to pass.

The division was formed in line preparatory to an attack, with the 2d Brigade, commanded by Brigadier-General Dennis, on the left, occupying both sides of the road; the 1st Brigade, commanded by Brigadier-General John E. Smith, in the center, on the right of the 2d Brigade; and the 3rd Brigade, commanded by Brigadier-General J. D. Stephenson, on the right, and the 8th Michigan Battery, commanded by Captain De Golyer, in the road near the bridge.

As soon as the troops were in position, an advance was commenced, and the battle opened with great energy. The roar of musketry was tremendous. On the left of the 1st Brigade and the right of the 2d Brigade the contest was dreadful. The line had advanced to the ditch in which ran the little stream crossed by the bridge. On the side of the ditch next to the enemy was a dense growth of underbrush; behind that brush, not fifty yards distant, were the enemy. So heavily did the enemy press the left of the 1st Brigade, composed of the 23d Indiana and the 20th Illinois, that they were compelled to give back, but immediately rallied, supported by the 81st Illinois. The giving back of the left of the 1st Brigade enabled the enemy to occupy a portion of the ditch, and exposed the 20th Ohio, occupying the right of the 2d Brigade, to a most galling fire in its flank. At one time the regiment was nearly surrounded, but it gallantly held its ground, in spite of the terrible fire to which it was exposed, and not a man of the regiment fell back.

The 23d Indiana and 20th Illinois now made a dashing charge, and drove the enemy from the ground that they had lost. It was while gallantly leading his men on to victory that the brave Lieutenant-Colonel Richards, of the 20th Illinois, was killed. An attempt was made by the enemy to charge and capture the battery, but they were met by such a terrible fire of grape and canister, that they broke and fled from the field. Our troops immediately commenced a pursuit, and by 5 o'clock, P. M., were in possession of Raymond.

The determined obstinacy with which the 20th Ohio, under the gallant Colonel Force, held its ground, added much to the brilliancy of the victory. Our loss was 69 killed, 341 wounded, and 30 missing. The enemy's was 103 killed, and 720 wounded and prisoners, 2 cannon disabled, besides the loss of a quantity of small arms.

In the morning of the 12th, after the column had commenced its line of march, General Grant sent me out to the right of the column, to ascertain whether a rebel force was coming up from below to intercept our line of march.

After riding out about three miles, I saw, in the distance, a single horseman approaching. As I neared him, it proved to be a Mississippi planter, well advanced in years, armed with a Mississippi Yager, or rifle.

"Whar be you gwine?" he asked, as we met.

"I'm gwine out to jine our forces and fight the Yankees to-day," I replied.

"So am I. I'm jist gwine to turn up sixteen Yankee moccasins with this yer piece o' mine."

"If I can kill six o' them thar Lincoln hirelings, I'll be satisfied."

"Well, I'm gwine to kill *sixteen, now, sure.*"

"Well, take care that they do n't *git you.* Is any of our forces out on this yer road?"

"No. I've jist come eight miles without seeing any. They left for Raymond last night, an' they ar jist a gwine to kill the whole Lincoln army."

"We had better go this way, then," said I, turning back the way I had come.

"I reckon we had," said the Mississippian.

As we rode along, he kept up his boasting of how many Yanks he was gwine to turn up, little dreaming whom he was addressing. Fortunately for me, the road on which the column was moving passed through a piece of woodland, so as to hide all movements of troops. When we came to it, the rear-guard of the 17th Corps had passed along out of sight, and the advance of the corps next in line of march had not come up. As we turned into the right, where our troops had been passing, I caught sight of two Federal soldiers, sitting by the roadside, who had fallen back from their commands. Dropping a little to the rear, I drew my revolver and motioned to the soldiers to help me. I was a little afraid the old fellow would give me battle as soon as he discovered his mistake, and I wanted to make sure of him. The soldiers comprehended my meaning, and instantly leveled their pieces at him, which, discovering, he halted, and inquired, " Is them thar our forces?"

" Never mind whose forces they are," said I, presenting my revolver; " you go right along."

" I thought it was *our* forces," said the old man, quite crest-fallen at his discovery.

" Come in there, old fellow! come in!" shouted the two soldiers.

" Ride along, daddy, or those Yanks will bore you in a minute," said I.

He took my advice, and rode up to the soldiers, where I made him turn his horse over to one of them and his rifle to the other, and then marched him on, at a rapid pace, to overtake the command.

We came in sight of our lines just as the first firing commenced in action at Raymond. As the musket reports became frequent, the old man's courage failed him, and he began to quiver and grow pale; and when the action became general, and the messengers of death came thick around us, his limbs could scarce support him, and he exclaimed, " My God! is that a fight? Won't we all be killed? If I can only get out of this yer scrape, I'll go home and behave myself! My God, I will!"

I turned the old man in with the first squad of prisoners that came back to the rear, and then reported to General Grant, who had a hearty laugh over the capture of the old Mississippian. I presume the old man often thinks of his attempt to *turn up sixteen Yankee moccasins!*

On the 13th we resumed our march for Jackson, by way of Clinton. On the 14th, about five miles from Jackson, the enemy's pickets were encountered, and driven back to within two and a half miles of the city. The enemy was under command of General W. H. T. Walker, and occupied the top of a gradually ascending rise of ground, with a large open space in his front. Many of General Walker's troops were South Carolina and Georgia regiments, and had only arrived there from the east the night before.

Preparations were now made to give the enemy battle. General Sherman's corps had arrived at the same time, on another road, to the right. General Logan's division was placed in reserve. The 7th Division of McPherson's corps, commanded by Brigadier-General Crocker, and part of General Sherman's corps, were formed in close column, by division, to charge upon the enemy. In our having to cross the open field, in full view, the enemy had a decided advantage over us. When every thing was ready, the command was given to charge on a double-quick, and the columns moved forward.

It was a sight that I shall never forget, when those thousands of brave boys, in perfect order, swept across that field! The rustle of garments, and the flapping of scabbards, cartridge-boxes, and canteens, to the tread of double-quick from that large body of soldiers, moving in close column, was like the roar of the tornado when it sweeps across the plain!

Opposed to them was a long line of Rebellion's choicest troops, pouring into them volley after volley of leaden hail. Still, on they went, without a waver! It was a terrible spectacle, and awfully grand! Mingled with the roar of the enemy's musketry was the crash of artillery from both sides.

The charge swept on. Still the enemy held his ground, as if determined to withstand the charge, and a dreadful encounter seemed imminent. A line of fence in front of the enemy was reached, and it vanished like chaff in the wind before those solid columns of Western braves. With the crash of that fence went the enemy's lines, and the pride of South Carolina fled in dismay, followed by the veterans from Georgia, that had been stationed as reserves. Then went up such shouts of victory as only Western lungs can accent. Volley after volley was fired at their retreating ranks, and pursuit kept up until they were driven beyond the city. In five hours from the time the action commenced, the stars and stripes were proudly floating over the capitol of the State of Mississippi.

Our loss was very light compared with that of the enemy—much lighter than it would have been, if the enemy had not overshot us while crossing the open field. For the casualties of the battle, the reader is referred to the official reports of the commanding Generals.

As the troops were going into Jackson, I asked General Grant if I might steal enough to make up for the field-glasses that the South Carolina General had taken from me, when I was there as a spy.

"I can't instruct you to steal," said the General, "but I presume you can find something in Jackson of as much value to you as the field-glasses."

The city had been so completely ransacked by the soldiers before I got in, that I failed to get pay for my glasses.

On the 15th of May we marched west, toward Vicksburg, and on the 16th the enemy was found in large force at Champion Hills, under command of Lieutenant-General Pemberton. He had moved his army out from Vicksburg to attack us. The position selected by the enemy was a strong one, on the summit of an elevation, or ridge of ground, with a line something like a crescent, the right and left of the line further advanced than the center. The face of the hill, in front of the enemy, was an open field, thereby exposing our lines to view as we advanced to the attack. The enemy's lines were in the skirts of a piece of woods that extended to his rear.

Early in the day, the battle commenced, opening on our left, and extending gradually along to our right, until the whole line was engaged, when it raged with intense fury. General Hovey's division, on our left, from the much stronger position occupied by the enemy in its front, suffered terribly; but timely support arrived, and the enemy was driven back. An attempt was then made to crush our center, but made in vain. Support having arrived to the assistance of the center, a dashing charge was made and the enemy routed.

It was a desperate and hard-fought battle, with a heavy loss on both sides, but that of the enemy was much the heaviest. Here, again, I must refer the reader to the official reports for the casualties. It will not be amiss, perhaps, to give the reader some of my personal experience in that battle.

When the action commenced, I was instructed by General Logan to keep to the right of each brigade of his division, as they successively arrived in position and became engaged, and to watch closely for any attempt at flank movement on the part of the enemy. My first position was with the line of skirmishers of the 2d Brigade. About the time our skirmishing commenced, a rebel courier was seen dashing along in a line nearly parallel to the line of skirmishers from the right, and about one hundred yards in advance of the line. When up with and in front of the line, he discovered us and wheeled to the right, and was dashing away at right angles with our line, when six of us brought our pieces to bear on him and fired. He fell from his horse, with one foot fastened in the stirrup. At that instant, the horse gave a leap over a log, and the dangling body struck the log and bounded into the air higher than the horse's back, and then struck the ground with a "thug" sufficient, to all appearances, to have crushed every bone in his body.

A few minutes later, I saw a rebel Major leading his regiment forward to charge upon one of our batteries. When I saw him he was not more than fifty yards distant. In an instant I brought my "repeater" to my face, and while I was looking at the prominent point of his right-cheek bone, a ball took him in the exact spot that I was looking at, and he tumbled from his horse.

I now discovered that, instead of a regiment, a whole brigade was coming, and that our skirmishers had fallen back, and that I was in range between McAlister's Battery and the rebs. I started on a run, and fairly *flew* as I went; but before I could get out of range, the battery opened on the rebs with double charges of grape and canister, which came howling and tearing the ground all about me. How I escaped instant death is a wonder to me. I succeeded in getting out of the way before another round was fired, quite satisfied with my experience there.

I then moved round much further to the right, and took with me a corporal of the 20th Ohio, by the name of Wm. Grinnell, whom I found engaged in sharp-shooting. After reconnoitering a little, we discovered a rebel battery of eight guns, that kept up a harassing fire upon our lines. We succeeded in sheltering ourselves from view, in close rifle range of the guns, behind a large clump of bushes, and then commenced paying our respects to the gunners. We were doing "bully" execution, and had fired ten or twelve shots apiece, when the rebs returned our compliments with a charge of canister that mowed the bushes all about us. The charge made such a terrible whizzing and howling, and came so suddenly and unexpectedly, that I involuntarily dropped to the ground.

"Are you hurt, Bunker?" called out the corporal.

"No; are you?"

"No; but if we had stood anywhere else we should both have been killed."

The ground was literally plowed up all about us.

A few minutes later, the 8th Illinois and 32d Ohio made a charge on the battery to capture it. As the line advanced, there became a strife between the two regiments which should reach it first and take possession. The officers and men of the 32d Ohio had been smarting under the false accusation of "Harper's Ferry cowards," and had longed for an opportunity of retrieving their reputation.

"Come on, boys; we are 'Harper's Ferry cowards!'" shouted a Captain; and the words were instantly repeated by the whole regiment, and with a dash they outstripped their Illinois rivals. As they raised the hill near the battery, a round of canister was fired at them, but, fortunately, it was aimed too high to do much injury. The rebs then broke and run, leaving six of their guns to fall into the hands of the 32d Ohio. Major-General Logan complimented the regiment highly for its gallantry, and allowed Company F to retain the guns and serve them. That company was originally recruited as an artillery company.

On the 17th of May we resumed our march, and on the 18th we crossed Black River, and on the 19th our lines extended around Vicksburg, from the river above to the river below, occupying a line of about seven miles in length.

Major-General Sherman's corps occupied the right, Major-General McPherson's the center, and Major-General M'Clernand's the left. Then began the siege of Vicksburg.

Up to the commencement of the siege, the troops had marched over two hundred miles and taken part in five distinct battles, and accomplished it in twenty-five days; and a large portion of that time they had been without rations, except such as they foraged from the country.

CHAPTER XXII.

First sharp-shooting at Vicksburg—Silences two guns—The rifle-pit—Shoots a Carolinian—The Carolinian's comrad—Outshoots a squad of sixteen—The defiant rebel—Shoots for General McPherson and General Logan—Beats the Parrot rifles—Joke on the Adjutant-General—Visit to Admiral Porter—The French spy—The disclosures—Capture of a rebel dispatch—The fate of the spy.

I shall not attempt to give the reader a detailed history of the siege of Vicksburg, but shall confine myself to incidents in my own experience during the siege.

The country lying about the city of Vicksburg is of a very peculiar formation—very hilly and extremely broken. It consists of threads, or narrow ridges, with deep ravines between, running in every direction, with spurs or smaller ridges putting out from them.

The lines occupied by the two contending armies were a succession of those ridges, with a general course nearly parallel, but at unequal distances apart, forming an irregular circuit about the city from the river above to the river below.

The next day after the regiment to which I belong moved into its position at the rear of Vicksburg, two pieces of the enemy's artillery opened a very annoying fire upon it with shell. The men were under the necessity of laying flat on the ground, behind the ridge, for protection, and even then were in great danger from the explosion of the shells. I went to Colonel Force and asked him if I might go and try my hand at silencing the guns with my rifle.

He said, "Yes; but you must be very careful, for the shells are coming very low."

I started out, and made my way along under cover of the ridge on which we lay, until I came to one of the spurs mentioned, that approached much nearer to the enemy's works than did the ridge occupied by the regiment. From that I succeeded in getting a good view of the guns that were shelling us. In front of me was a dry oak log, and underneath it I dug out a hole that enabled me to shoot under it, and the log prevented the enemy from seeing me.

As soon as I had become fixed in my position, I commenced to pick off the gunners. I succeeded so well that only two shells were fired after I took my position. Several ineffectual attempts were made to load the guns, but the moment a gunner stepped up to fill the place of his fallen comrade, I picked him off, and, finally, the guns were abandoned, and the bodies of those that had fallen left where they fell.

My success seemed incredible. To put it beyond a doubt, I concluded to go back and get some officer to come and see what execution I had done. I went back to the regiment, where I found Colonel Force. I said to him, "Colonel, I have silenced those two guns that were shelling us."

"I see they have n't fired much since you left."

"How many did they fire after I went away?"

"Only two or three, I believe."

"Well, now, Colonel, for my credit, please to go over with me where I have been at work, and see what I have been doing."

"Really, I do n't know as I ought to leave here a moment, but I want to learn the lay of the ground, and I do n't care if I go."

He followed along behind me to where I had been at work, and then commenced looking with his glasses.

"See there! see—see—see that man leading that horse yonder!" "Do you see him?" said he.

"Yes."

"Well, try him a pull."

"Do n't get me excited, Colonel, but watch the man."

"Crack!" went my rifle.

"I declare!" said the Colonel, "that 's—that 's a valuable piece! Excuse me, I must go back."

Rifle-trenches were immediately dug on the ridges of ground nearest the enemy's works, and in them were stationed sharp-shooters, who kept up a constant fire, night and day, which answered as a cover for our fatigue parties engaged in digging approaches to his works, and also prevented him from doing much execution with his artillery. Our artillery was not idle but kept up a fire from some part of the line at all hours of the day and night.

A few days after the siege was fairly in operation, General Logan asked me to go out, at night, to an elevated spot of ground between our rifle-trenches and the enemy's, on which stood a large stump, and dig myself a pit behind the stump and see if I could pick off some of the rebel sharp-shooters.

As soon as it was dark, I took a spade and a canteen of water and went over. The spot was not more than fifty yards from the enemy's trenches. During the night, I dug myself a pit large enough so that I could squat down in it. When daylight came, I found that I had an excellent view of the enemy's trenches, without being seen myself. I worked out a little hole underneath one of the roots of the stump, and through that I did my shooting. Toward the middle of the day the sun shone down excessively hot, and I had nothing to shade me from its burning rays. My pit was not large enough for comfort, and, besides, I had neglected to take any rations with me. My supply of water also gave out, and by noon my position seemed almost unbearable. To leave it in daylight would be certain death. I bore my situation as well as I could, and improved it to the best advantage. During the day I had several fair shots, which I improved, and did good execution.

About 2 o'clock in the afternoon, a rebel sharp-shooter (whom, from his dress, I took to be a Carolinian) undertook to crawl up to the top of their earth-works, behind a stump that hid him from the view of our sharp-shooters, that he might be enabled to get a shot at them. He crawled along, with his gun in his right hand, till near the spot, and then took off his big-brimmed hat and turned his head up sideways to look around the side of the stump at our sharp-shooters. My position to him was such that I could see every movement that he made. He evidently did not know where I was. While his head was turned up my gun cracked, and his feet flew straight behind him.

A comrade of his then undertook to crawl up and drag him away. When he was about ready to grasp the dead man by the legs, my gun again cracked, and he rolled over on his back near his comrade. Both of them remained there until dark, without any attempt being made to remove them.

As soon as it was dark I made my way back to my quarters, well satisfied with my experience in an advanced rifle-pit.

Not many days after the foregoing incident, I was passing along the intrenchments, when I found a squad of sixteen men, part of them of the 23d Indiana Regiment, and the rest from the 45th Illinois, engaged in sharp-shooting. They saw me passing with my rifle, and, having heard of its long range and accuracy, called me, and expressed a desire to have me try it on a fellow that they had been shooting at for about two hours, but without success.

The fellow that they had been shooting at was engaged in digging a rifle-pit in advance of the enemy's intrenchments, and while digging he was exposed to full view.

I asked the boys what distance they had been shooting, and they informed me that they had been trying him at a range of nine hundred yards, and had succeeded in hitting the dirt about him. I raised the sight of my rifle to nine hundred yards, and then requested the squad to cease firing for a few minutes, and let the smoke clear away, and then to watch where my ball struck. As soon as the atmosphere was clear of smoke, and every thing quiet, I leveled my piece and fired.

"You've hit him! you've hit him!" exclaimed several.

The fellow straightened up, whirled about, as if angry, and flung his shovel from him as far as he could, and then sat down. In about a minute after he began gradually to throw up his hands, and then fell over backward on the ground, evidently dead, where he remained, as he had fallen, during the rest of the day. The next morning his body had been removed.

On another occasion, two companies of the 20th Ohio were engaged at digging in the approaches to the rebel Fort Hill, and were subjected to a very annoying fire from a squad of about fifteen rebel sharp-shooters, stationed in a ditch, not accessible, at that time, to our artillery.

I was sent for, and requested to bring my rifle and see if I could silence them. A place had been fixed for me near where the companies were at work, considerably in advance of any other sharp-shooter. I worked a long time at them, during which time I hit several. After awhile there was but one to be seen; the rest had either been disabled or so badly frightened as to have laid down in the bottom of the ditch for safety. I kept up a fire at the single individual for some time. My balls would strike the ground close to him, and then he would swing his hat in defiance or return my shot. Twice he put his balls within an inch of my head; once a sliver from the timber under which I shot was knocked off and struck me on the head, hurting me considerably. Another ball hit a bayonet that I had placed in the dirt to rest my rifle upon, and, glancing upward, just missed my head.

A Lieutenant came along, and I told him what I had been doing. He got upon the earth-works where I was, and, seeing the defiant rebel, asked me to let him try his hand at him. He fired several shots, but with no better success than I had had.

By that time it was nearly night, and I had fired at the squad forty-eight shots, so I concluded to give up the shooting of the defiant man as a bad job.

The next day the ditch was unoccupied; the experience of the day before had evidently satisfied them.

On another occasion, while I was engaged in sharpshooting, General McPherson and General Logan came into the fortifications, and were watching a party of ten or twelve rebels engaged in digging a ditch. They called me, and General McPherson said:

"Bunker, can you shoot into that ditch yonder, where those men are at work? They have been shooting at them with the Parrot rifles, and have n't thrown any shot in there yet."

"Yes, I think I can."

"Well, try it."

I raised my sight to one thousand yards, and fired at the ditch.

"There!" said McPherson, looking through his glasses, "you've hit one of them!"

"By G—d! they *are* carrying out one!" said Logan, looking with his glasses.

"Try it again," said McPherson.

I did try. I fired two more shots into the ditch, and the whole squad ran out and left it.

A few days afterward, I chanced to meet General McPherson, who asked me how my ammunition held out. I told him that it was nearly all gone.

"Well, Bunker," said he, "come over to my tent day after to-morrow, and I will try to have some on hand for you. I think that I can keep you supplied."

In the morning of the day agreed upon, I went over to General McPherson's tent. He was absent; but Colonel ———, Assistant Adjutant-General, was there, who, as soon as I entered, inquired of me what I wanted.

"I want to see General McPherson."

"What do you want of General McPherson?"

"I want to see him about some ammunition."

"Who are you?"

"I am an Arkansas school-master."

"What kind of ammunition do you want?"

"Cartridges for one of Henry's repeating rifles."

"Well, this a'n't the place to get ammunition. Go to the ordnance officer, and see if you can't get it of him."

I did as I was directed, but found no cartridges. I returned to the tent, and said to him, "Colonel, that officer did n't have any cartridges."

"Are you a soldier?"

"Yes, *sir*, I'm a soldier."

"Well, you had better go to your quarters."

"Oh, yes, I'll go to my quarters! I'd like to see General McPherson first, though; he told me to come here. Have n't you got some whisky, that you can give me two or three hundred swallows before I go?"

"Yes, I'll give you some whisky if you'll leave and go to your quarters."

"Oh, yes, I'll go to my quarters if you'll give me some whisky!"

He turned me out enough for three drinks, to spite me, I suppose, for my impudence in asking him for it, and I deliberately drank it all down. "Thank you!" said I, and went out. Before I had got out of hearing, General McPherson entered, and I heard some one tell him that there was a man just in to see him, and that he had stepped out. The General came out and called me back.

"Well, Bunker," said he, "I have n't got those cartridges yet; but you go over to General Grant's head-quarters, and tell his Chief-of-Staff that I sent you over to get some cartridges for your rifle. He has got a rifle of that kind, and I presume that he has got some cartridges."

"Well, I'll go and see. But it's a pretty warm morning, General, and I hate to come all the way up here for nothing. I think your Adjutant-General has got some pretty good whisky in there; can't you induce him to give me a drink before I go back?"

"Yes! Adjutant, give Bunker two or three hundred swallows of whisky!"

The Adjutant-General looked at me and then at General McPherson, as if about to say that I had just had some, and then, as if recollecting that it was military to obey orders without questioning them, turned me out a *large tumblerful*, which I drank, and then went out.

By the time I had reached my quarters, my physical nature was so much under the influence of the "spiritual," that I deferred my visit to General Grant's head-quarters until the next morning.

In the morning, early, I went over to General Grant's head-quarters, and told him that General McPherson had sent me there to see if I could get some ammunition for my rifle from his Chief-of-Staff. He told me that his Chief-of-Staff had gone to St. Louis, and had taken his rifle with him.

"Do you know of any body that has got any of that kind of cartridges?" I inquired.

"I think," said the General, "that Admiral Porter has got ammunition of that kind, and I will give you a request to carry to him, and you may go and see him about it.

He wrote a note for me to hand to Admiral Porter, and commenced to write me a pass, but was interrupted by some business, so he handed me the note, and told me to step over to the Provost-marshal and ask him to write me a pass.

I did so; but, being a stranger to him, he did not know that I was a soldier, and the pass that I received read as follows:

"Head-quarters Dep't of the Tennessee,
"Rear of Vicksburg, Miss., June —, 1863.

"Lorain Ruggles, a citizen of the South, has leave to visit Admiral Porter's flag-ship and return with a gun.

"—————— ——————
"*Provost-marshal.*"

I took my rifle and went to Chickasaw Landing, on the Yazoo river, where I succeeded in getting on board the steamer Diligent, a dispatch-boat, as she went down to the gun-boats with dispatches. The flag-ship, at that time, lay in the Mississippi River, a short distance above Vicksburg.

I found the Admiral, and handed him the note from General Grant, which he read; and then, giving me a searching look from head to foot, he said:

"Well, Mr. Scout, you want some ammunition for your rifle; but I do n't keep any such trifling guns about me, and, consequently, I have got none of that kind of ammunition."

"Look 'e here, Mr. Admiral," said I; "that gun a'n't so *small a trifle* as you imagine. I can kill a reb. with it at a distance of nine hundred yards, and I can outshoot the Parrot rifles!"

"Ah, you can't commence with my guns! They are better than that. Orderly, go down and bring up one of my favorites."

The orderly soon returned with a beautiful Spencer rifle. "There," said the Admiral, handing me the gun; "how do you like the looks of that?"

I took it and examined it carefully all over. It was a seven-shooter, with a bayonet, and every part of it most beautifully finished. It suited me to a charm.

"Well, inasmuch as I have got no cartridges for my gun, how will you trade guns with me?"

"I can't part with that gun; you might as well try to get my wife as that gun!"

He then told me that if General Grant wanted I should have one, he would get one like it for me. I told him that I could not carry two guns, and that I did not want one unless I could trade him mine. He promised, however, to make an effort to get me some cartridges. By this time the dispatch-boat was ready to return, and I went back to Chickasaw Landing.

On my arrival at the landing, I met a little Frenchman, whom I had frequently seen in Memphis, and at the camps about there, and I had for some time suspected that he was a Confederate spy.

I first saw him in the camps of the 20th, 78th, and 68th Ohio, and the 23d Indiana regiments, engaged in buying Confederate money of the soldiers. At that time he wore very long hair, and was dressed like a citizen; but on this occasion his hair was cut short, and he was dressed like a clerk about some head-quarters.

I saw him several times at Memphis, while I was under the assumed character of a rebel Major. He had never seen me in any other dress than that of a citizen.

I expressed delight at meeting him, shook hands with him, and inquired about his health, etc.

"Who are you to work for now?" he inquired.

"For General Johnston."

"Are you? So am I!"

"What news have you got?"

"Nothing new. Have you any news?"

"No, not at present. Come, let us go over to the steamer Arago and get something to drink before we separate. There is an old friend of ours that is commissary clerk aboard of her. He used to live in Holly Springs, Miss., and, when we were in Memphis last winter, he was there engaged in buying mules and smuggling them through the Yankee lines to sell. Let us go over and see him."

The Frenchman accompanied me on board the steamboat, and there we found the clerk I had told him about, who took us to the bar and got us something to drink. He also induced the barkeeper to sell me a canteen of whisky, as a favor to a special friend.

Having procured the whisky, I prevailed upon the Frenchman to accompany me, and we went up the bank of the river to a secluded place, where we sat down to enjoy ourselves.

My companion seemed to relish the whisky much better than I did, and its effects soon made him very communicative, so that I was enabled to draw out a great deal of information concerning his business as a spy. He told me that he was engaged in getting dispatches through the Federal lines at Vicksburg to Generals Johnston and Pemberton.

During his visits to the Federal camps at Memphis, to purchase Confederate money, he had noted down the names of the officers in the different regiments, and the companies to which they belonged.

With that knowledge, whenever he wanted to get

from Chickasaw Landing into our lines, he would go to the Provost-marshal and represent himself as belonging to Captain such-a-one's company, in such a regiment, on detached service, and get a pass to visit his regiment, and with it he could pass our lines.

The dispatches of General Johnston were brought across the country, by cavalry, to a point on the Yazoo River above Haines' Bluff. There the spy received them, and crossed over to the opposite side of the river, and then came down the river opposite to Snyder's Bluff; there he would manage to cross at night in a canoe, and land inside of our lines, without being seen. There he would get on board a dispatch-boat and come down to Chickasaw Landing, and there he would procure a pass, as I have explained. From there he would go to Mr. Smith's, who lived between the picket lines at the landing and the troops at the rear of Vicksburg.

He would give the dispatches to Mr. Smith's daughter, and she would give them to a servant of hers, a smart, intelligent colored boy, rather small of his age, who would carry them to the river above Vicksburg. He described to me the route the colored boy would take to get to the river.

At the river, the colored boy would give them to a fisherman, who staid there, and was engaged in catching fish and selling them to the gun-boatmen and the soldiers. The fisherman had lost a hand while in the rebel army, in the battle of Shiloh, and had been discharged.

He had represented to Admiral Porter that he had belonged to the Federal army, and had been wounded, as before stated, and discharged, and had succeeded in getting permission from him to fish in the river and visit his lines at all hours of the night. He had managed to make himself a favorite at the picket-post near the river, and his frequent visits to his lines near the post, at all hours of the day and night, had ceased to excite any suspicion whatever.

The fisherman would take the dispatches, and at night, while visiting his lines, pass the pickets, and carry them to the rebel pickets and then return.

In the same channel, General Pemberton's dispatches went out. How long communication had been kept up in that way I did not learn.

After having drank the most of the whisky, we returned to the landing and separated. I went to the Provost-marshal, and told him that there was one of General Johnston's spies there, and requested him to send some guards and arrest him.

"Are you a soldier?" he inquired.

"Yes!"

"Where did you come from?"

"Admiral Porter's flag-ship."

"Have you got a pass?"

"Yes!"

"Let me see it."

I handed it to him, and he commenced reading, "Lorain Ruggles, a citizen of the South "— "You go to h—l!" he exclaimed. "*You a'n't any better than the rest of them!*"

I went out and found that the Frenchman was just stepping on board the dispatch-boat Diligent,

18

and in a moment more the boat was under way for Snyder's Bluff.

I reported to General Grant the information that I had received, and then asked him if I might kill the spy wherever I found him. He told me to do with him just as I thought proper, under the circumstances, and that the military authorities should not hurt me for it.

In two days after, the colored boy was captured, and a dispatch from General Johnston found on his person. About the same time the fishing arrangement at the river was broken up. I can also assure the reader that the little Frenchman, though never arrested, will never buy any more Confederate money nor carry any more rebel dispatches.

CHAPTER XXIII.

Sent for by General Grant—Instructions—Crosses Black River—
Is captured by rebel cavalry—Sent to General DeVieu—The
interview—Passes as Johnston's spy—The attempt to escape—
The pursuit—Fired at by Federal pickets—Again fired at by
the enemy—The pursuers driven back—Again fired at by Federal
pickets—The alarm—Reports to General Osterhaus—Reports
to General Grant.

WHILE the siege was progressing, General Johnston was engaged in concentrating a large Confederate force, to attack General Grant in the rear and force him to raise the siege of Vicksburg, and thereby relieve General Pemberton and his forces.

General Grant, in the mean time, had been considerably reinforced, and had formed a line of defense from the Black River bridge north-west along Clear and Bear Creeks, across to the Yazoo River at Haines' Bluff, and a heavy force was stationed along that line to resist any attempt on the part of the enemy to raise the siege.

The difficulty of rapidly crossing Black River with a large force below the bridge, rendered it necessary to keep a force stationed on the line running from the bridge to the Mississippi River below Vicksburg; for the enemy, once across, would run a very poor chance of recrossing without destruction. A constant watch was kept up by our scouts, however, to see whether the enemy would attempt to cross there.

Some time toward the latter part of June, General Grant sent for me, and requested me to make a trip across Black River, and find out whether the enemy was making any attempt or movement indicative of crossing.

I was instructed to cross at the bridge, through General Osterhaus' lines, and take the road to Fifteeen-mile Creek, and, if I met with nothing to prevent, to go on to the creek and remain there two days, and at the end of that time return. If I discovered any movement of importance while on my way, I was to report it immediately.

The General cautioned me not to go inside of the enemy's lines, because it was a critical time, and if I did I would probably lose my life. He told me that several scouts had been sent out for the same purpose, and that none of them agreed in their reports. He told me that he was extremely anxious to know what the enemy was doing there, and what were his intentions, and charged me to be very cautious, so that I might return.

I was handed an order to General Osterhaus, to the effect that I was to be passed out of his lines, and when I returned I was to be immediately sent to General Osterhaus, under guard, and whatever I reported to him was to be immediately telegraphed to General Grant.

I carried the order to General Osterhaus, at Black River, who, when he had read it, sent me, under guard, to the picket line, with instructions to the officer in command of the pickets to pass me out. The picket line was on the east side of the river.

As I left the river, I was very particular to notice minutely the roads and fences and the features of the ground. About a mile from the bridge, on the road that leads to Edwards' Station, the Fifteen-mile Creek road turns off to the right. At the corners of the road the reserve pickets were stationed. About a quarter of a mile from the reserve, the road turns square to the left, and, at a distance of about one hundred yards further on, it turns back again square to the right. At that point the vedettes were stationed. On the left-hand side of the road, going out from the reserve to the vedettes, was a hedge fence. From the vedettes, in a straight line across to the reserve, was an open field, and the fence had been torn down or removed to allow the cavalry a chance to charge across it, if necessary.

Before leaving the pickets, I told the Lieutenant in command of the guards that I should not come back that night, unless I was driven back, and that if I came back I should come on the run, and that I would have no gun in my hands, nor any thing else that might be taken for one. I also requested him to describe to each man in person, as he took his post as vedette, my dress, so that there could be no mistake about who I was and no cause for firing into me. The Lieutenant instructed his men as I requested him; and besides, I found that several of them knew me, which very much relieved my fears about being fired at. I was on foot and dressed like a citizen.

Supposing that I had made all the necessary arrangements for my safety in case I was driven back, I started out. About half a mile from the vedettes, the road crossed a low piece of ground, and had been filled in with brush and rails, while wet, to keep wagons from miring, but the dry weather had dried up the mud and left the rails and brush bare, rendering it extremely difficult to cross without making a great deal of noise.

I had gone but a short distance after crossing it, when I heard a cracking of brush behind me, and turned to see what it was. The reader can judge my surprise when I saw, in the road behind me, fourteen rebel cavalry. I was ordered to halt, which I did, and they, at the same time, dismounted.

There I was, captured almost within sight of our own pickets. It was no time to show timidity, so I resolved upon a bold expedient.

"Who are you?" said one of the cavalry.

"I am a Confederate soldier."

"Have you got a pass?"

"No, sir."

"What are you doing here?"

"Gentlemen, I don't know as this is any of your business. I am a Confederate soldier, and I have business here, and all that you have to do is to send me, under guard, to general head-quarters."

One of the men, seemingly commander of the squad —I could not tell whether an officer or a private— ordered two of the men to take me to Gen. DeVieu.

They took me on in the same direction that I had been traveling. Not a word was exchanged between us on the way. I watched narrowly every feature of the road and the country as we went, determined, if possible, to make my way back that night.

About five miles from where I was captured, and nearly seven miles from Black River bridge, we came to General DeVieu's head-quarters. They were situated near the crossing of the roads, where the road from Baldwin's Ferry (below Black River bridge) to Edwards' Station crosses the one that I was on.

When we arrived at General DeVieu's quarters, one of the guards went in, and I heard him say to the General, "We have got a man out there that we captured close to the Yankee lines, without a pass, and he says that he is a Confederate soldier. We could not find out his business, but he told us to bring him to you, and we have done so."

"Well, have him come in," said the General.

The guard came out, and told me to go in. As I entered, I took off my hat, and, saluting him, I looked him in the face with as much composure as though I had been his commanding officer.

"Where have you been?" he inquired.

"I have been inside of the Yankee lines about Vicksburg."

"Where do you belong?"

"I belong to General Price's army."

"What were you doing here?"

"I am now under orders from General Johnston to reconnoiter thoroughly about the Yankee lines at

Vicksburg. I have done so, and I am now on my way to report to General Johnston."

"Have you got any pass, or any papers to show that?"

"No, sir, I haven't got the scratch of a pen about me; but, General, if you will go with me to General, Johnston's Adjutant-General I can show you papers in his office that will tell you who I am and what my business is."

"What is your name?"

"Lorain Ruggles, sir; I am a brother to General Ruggles."

"Ah! A brother of General Ruggles!"

"Yes, sir."

"Well, what is the news about Vicksburg?"

"General, if you insist upon it, I shall have to tell you, because you are my superior officer, but my instructions from General Johnston were to reconnoiter thoroughly, and get all the information that I could, and then to report to him and to *him only*, and I reckon that he'll not like to have me report to any body else."

"Ah! I beg your pardon, Mr. Ruggles. Excuse me! I don't want you to violate your instructions. I won't ask you any further questions about it. Do you wish to go right on to General Johnston's headquarters?"

"General, I have been considerably exposed, and a little short of rations for several days, and have traveled about on foot a great deal, and am very much fatigued; and if it would be agreeable to your good will and pleasure, I would like to remain in your brigade over night, and then go out to General Johnston's head-quarters to-morrow."

"Very well, you can stay; any of those orderlies out there will give you something to eat. I shall send two men out to head-quarters in the morning, and, if you like, you can go with them."

"Thank you, General; I shall be very glad of company!"

It was about 2 o'clock in the afternoon when I arrived there. The orderlies gave me some dinner and also some supper. I improved my time, in conversation with the officers and men, in picking up information.

The force stationed there was a brigade of Texas cavalry, about 1,200 strong. Their business was to watch the Baldwin's Ferry road for any attempt of General Grant's forces to cross and get to the rear of General Johnston.

The brigade was destitute of tents, except six at head-quarters, and the men slept at night without shelter.

About 9 o'clock in the evening, I laid down on a pile of corn in the husk, in company with a lot of soldiers, and feigned to be asleep. I reflected upon my situation, and of the best means of making my escape. I was satisfied that it would be dangerous for me to wait till morning and start with the orderlies for General Johnston's head-quarters. No suspicion had as yet been excited. The soldiers were all asleep, and the whole camp was quiet. About midnight I got up, as if to relieve the necessities of nature, and went to a piece of woods about a hundred yards distant, and returned. My movements did not seem to have disturbed any one. The moon shone brightly, and the night was very light. The moon had not yet reached its meridian, but made a long shadow on the ground. I again laid down upon the corn-pile, where I lay until 2 o'clock, when I arose. The moon was then favorable and made but a short shadow, and every thing was quiet. I again visited the woods.

As I entered, I looked back and all was quiet. As the guards brought me in, I had noticed that there was but one picket-post in the direction that I wished to return, and that one was stationed in the road about half a mile from the rebel camp. I resolved to try an escape at all hazards.

I made a detour large enough to insure safety from the pickets, moving forward as rapidly as possible through the brush, without making any noise, until I gained the road that I had come out on, and then I sped along as fast as I could run.

I had on light shoes, and made very little noise as I went, and avoided stepping upon any thing that would make any disturbance.

When I reached the place in the road filled with rails and brush, near where I had been captured, I slackened my pace, and walked carefully across it. I had become tired from running so far; my close proximity to our own pickets considerably relieved my fears, and I moved along more leisurely than I had done.

When about two hundred yards from the bad place in the road, I was startled by the sound of horses crossing it. I looked back, and there came a squad of twelve or fourteen cavalry, as fast as their horses could run.

I dashed ahead at the top of my speed, when, within about one hundred yards of our pickets, "Bang! bang! bang!" went their pieces.

"*For God's sake, don't shoot! It's me!*" I shouted.

"Bang! bang!" went the carbines of my pursuers. The vedettes ran for the reserve. I fairly flew along, and the rebs after me, gaining rapidly. I kept straight after the vedettes till I had entered the field past the hedge fence; then I turned and followed it a few steps, and then plunged through it and crawled along on my hands and knees some distance in the weeds and grass by the side of it.

My pursuers dashed on across the field, firing at the vedettes as they went. The reserve was immediately in saddle, and returned the fire of the enemy. The chase now turned the other way, and the rebs were pursued by our pickets.

I kept on making a detour around to the rear of the reserve post before coming up, lest, from the confusion and excitement, I should again be fired at. Nearly all the reserve had joined in the chase, and but three or four men remained on the post.

As I came up to the rear of them, without any challenge to halt, "Bang! bang!" went their pieces.

"*What in hell and d—nation are you doing?*" I shouted. "You are determined to shoot me!"

"That's Bunker!" said one.

"No, by G—d, it a'n't!" said another, bringing his piece to a ready.

"*For Christ's sake,*" I shouted, "*do n't shoot again! Are you determined to kill me?*"

"Do n't shoot! It *is* Bunker!" said the others. By this time they were convinced who it was, and allowed me to come up.

The alarm did not stop with the pickets, but extended across the river. An entire brigade turned out under arms, and orders were dispatched all along the lines to be in readiness to repel an attack from General Johnston.

I requested to be immediately sent to General Osterhaus, under guard, agreeable to General Grant's instructions; but the Lieutenant refused to let me go until daylight, and then sent me in without guard.

I reported to General Osterhaus, and explained to him where the rebel force was camped, and also its strength and what it was there for.

"Vare you stshay they are? On the Baldwin's Ferry road?" inquired the General.

"No; they are on the Fifteen-mile Creek road, near the crossing of the Edwards' Station and Baldwin's Ferry road."

"Vell, dat ish vot I stshay! On the Baldwin's Ferry road!"

I then marked out the position for him, and explained it, and still he insisted.

"Vell, dat ish vot I *stshay!* On the Baldwin's Ferry Road!"

He then telegraphed to General Grant as he understood it, and received, in reply, orders for me to return immediately.

I reported in person to General Grant, and told

him the difficulty that I experienced in making General Osterhaus understand me. He replied, "I thought he did not understand you, so I ordered you back.

After explaining to the General the position, strength, and object of the enemy, he asked me if I was *sure* of that fact. I told him that I was, and that time would show whether I told him the truth or not. He then said that he would rest satisfied; so I returned to my quarters. The confidence he placed in my reports amply paid me for the danger that I had encountered. General Grant always paid his scouts well whenever they had done any thing deserving of special compensation. To pay me for this trip, soon after the Vicksburg campaign ended, General Grant gave me two hundred dollars and a furlough for thirty days.

CHAPTER XXIV.

Visit to Chickasaw Landing—Surrender of Vicksburg—Visit to the city—The paroled Major—The Yankee trick—Returns to Vicksburg—Made detective—Is sent to Yazoo City—Attends a guerrilla organization—Makes them a speech—Returns to Vicksburg.

On the 3d day of July, I again went to General Grant to see if he had found out where I could get some cartridges for my rifle. He told me that the Paymaster-General (I have forgotten his name) had a rifle of the same kind and some cartridges, and that he made his head-quarters on board the steamer J. D. Perry, at Chickasaw Landing.

The General gave me a line to the Paymaster, and I went over to the Landing. When I arrived there, the steamers had nearly all gone down to Young's Point, and with them the J. D. Perry. It was nearly night, and too late to return to camp, so I remained there all night, with a Sergeant from my own regiment, who was on detached duty there, in charge of the camp and garrison equipage belonging to the regiment.

When I arose on the morning of July 4th, I found that *all* the steamers had left. A few hours later the dispatch-boat Diligent came up, and brought the news that Vicksburg had surrendered.

That accounted for the absence of the steamers. A flag of truce had been sent into our lines on the afternoon of the 3d, before I left, but I had not heard that it was to arrange for the surrender of the place.

When the dispatch-boat returned, I went on it to Vicksburg. There the whole fleet of transports and gun-boats, including the Marine Brigade, was moored, decorated with all their streamers and colors, and from the Court-house dome proudly floated the glorious emblem of our country. It was a grand and sublime spectacle. The levee and streets of the city were thronged with thousands of weather and war-worn heroes, that had heroically suffered and fought for the capture of the place.

It was a proud day for them, and their countenances beamed with such expressions of satisfaction and delight as only heroes can wear.

The magnitude of their victory was proportionate to the day on which it was achieved, and such a celebration of our national anniversary was never before had, and probably never will be again.

The sufferings and privations and hardships of long marches, and exposures and hard-fought battles and a long-continued siege, were all forgotten in the realization of the most glorious victory that had ever crowned the arms of an American hero.

Promiscuously mingled with the blue uniforms of the Federal soldiers was the dirty yellow of the Confederate prisoners, and their filthy appearance and fear-worn faces were in striking contrast with their elated victors.

The magnitude of the victory can perhaps be better understood by the following official report:

Rebel losses in Major-General Grant's Department since the landing of the army at Grand Gulf, Mississippi, May 1, 1863.

Loss in men up to May 18th..........................40,000
Prisoners taken at Vicksburg........................31,000

Total..71,000
Citizen prisoners, 1,500 of whom were women and children.. 5,000
Prisoners sick and wounded............................13,220
Prisoners fit for duty................................18,000
Tents captured.. 4,000
Mules captured.. 1,500
Horses captured....................................... 1,000
Freight cars..   200
Locomotives...   5
Large siege-guns captured.............................   188
Field-pieces captured.................................   151
Rounds of ammunition..................................   300
Stands of small arms..................................35,000
Shot-guns, etc..30,000
Value of public property captured, from ten to fifteen million dollars.
   Approved, by order of   JAMES WILSON,
                       Lieutenant-Colonel and Provost-marshal.

I found the Paymaster-General at Vicksburg, and succeeded in getting from him a box of cartridges. Not liking to remain in the place while the prisoners were there, lest some of them might, at some future time, recognize me, should I be so unfortunate as to get captured, I told General Grant how I felt about it, and he sent me to my regiment, then at Black River, to stay until the prisoners were sent away.

A few days after the surrender, the prisoners were all paroled, and then marched through our lines at Black River. While they were passing our camp, I kept out of sight by remaining in my quarters. The second day after the prisoners commenced to pass an exception occurred.

A rebel Major came along and dismounted, and sat down as if to rest, holding his horse by the halter. It was soon evident, from his numerous inquiries, that rest was not so much of an object as contraband information. His horse was a nice one, and was equipped with a fine saddle and bridle, and across his saddle was a portmanteau.

A soldier of the 30th Illinois Regiment came to my quarters, and requested me to go out and see the Major and converse with him. He also told me that the Major was trying to get information from the soldiers that he had no business with, and that if I would succeed in holding his attention, the boys would play some kind of a caper upon him for his improper inquisitiveness.

I went out, and found him engaged in trying to find out the strength of General Grant's army. As I came up I squatted right down in front of him, and commenced to ask him questions about how he liked the siege, etc.; then, fixing my eyes on his, I gave him a severe rebuke for participating in such an unjust cause, and tried to show him its utter hopelessness. I then spoke of the blessings of peace, prosperity, and happiness, as they had existed under our Government before the war, and then contrasted that state of affairs with the existing state of affairs in the rebellious States, and concluded by telling him that any man who had been guilty of raising his hand against the best Government that ever existed, ought to be satisfied with the experience that he had had, and heartily ashamed of himself.

As I began to talk, the soldiers began to gather in a crowd around us. I suspected that some of them would cut the halter-strap and lead the horse off into the woods, before the crowd would open sufficiently for the Major to see which way it went.

Whenever the Major showed any inclination to look behind him, I would become emphatic in my expressions and gesticulations, and look so earnestly at him that I kept his attention riveted upon me. While I was talking, the portmanteau was opened, and a beautiful silver-mounted ten-shooting revolver taken out and carried off.

When I had finished, the crowd dispersed, and the Major prepared to leave. In doing so, he discovered that his revolver was gone. He told me about it and described the revolver, and said that it must have been taken while I had been talking with him.

He went to Brigadier-General Force, commanding the brigade, and complained that, while he was resting, somebody stole his revolver.

The General immediately issued an order requiring all the company commanders in the brigade to search the men of their commands at once for the revolver, but it was without success.

The Major told the General that one of the men standing by was called by the name of Bunker; consequently, I was sent for.

"Do you know who got this man's revolver?" inquired the General of me, as I went in.

"No, sir. I did not see his revolver, and did not know that he had one until he told me that some one had stolen it."

"Do you know what regiment the man belonged to that took it?"

"No, sir, I do not! But I did think that the Major was asking *very improper questions* for a paroled prisoner to ask, and I expected, while I was talking to him, that the boys would take *horse and all*, and I think he may feel *thankful* if he has n't lost any thing but his revolver!"

"That will do!" said the General; "you can go to your quarters. Major, I do n't see as I can do any thing for you!"

When the prisoners had all crossed Black River, I returned to Vicksburg. On my return, I chanced to meet Major-General Logan, who wanted I should engage in the detective business, the same as I had done at Memphis. I told him that I did not like the business and did not understand it, and that I did not see any thing brave or daring in it, and that it seemed like rather a low business. He, however, insisted upon my taking hold of it, and gave me an order to go on board the steamer Swon to board, so that I might pass as a citizen without being suspicioned.

I boarded there three days, at the end of which time I was so completely disgusted with the business that I could not do any thing at it, even if I had wanted to. I then went to General Grant, and told him what General Logan had set me at, and that I did not like it, and asked him if he had a trip that he wanted made into the Confederacy. He replied that he had none of much importance, but that I might make a trip to Yazoo City, if I was a mind to, and see if any thing was going on there, and gather what information I could.

The Federal forces had, since the surrender of Vicksburg, already taken the place, and captured such public stores as were moveable, and destroyed the rest and vacated it.

I made the trip on horseback, dressed like a citizen. The route was rather a lonesome one, and nothing occurred of interest on my way out. On my arrival at Yazoo City, I found every thing quiet, and the place unoccupied by troops.

I then crossed the Yazoo River to the west, and visted the neighborhood of Silver Creek, at a point eighteen miles from Yazoo City. There I learned that a band of guerrillas, known as the Silver Creek guerrillas, were to have a meeting the next day, at a log church, about six miles distant to the southwest, to reorganize their band, so as to make themselves more efficient. Thinking that I might learn something of them that might be of service, I determined to attend the meeting.

The next morning I started in the direction of the church alone, but had gone only a short distance when I was joined by six citizens, on horseback, going to the same place. We arrived at the church about 10 o'clock, A. M., and found the meeting already commenced. I walked in with those that had accompanied me and sat down, a listener to their proceedings.

Remarks were made by several individuals, and I learned by them that the band had become disorganized and ineffectual by the slackness of the members in turning out. Many of them had failed to report for duty when ordered, and some of them had never reported at all. A great deal was said about what valuable services *might* be rendered by a *well-organized band*, and appeals were made to the patriotism of each individual present "to stand by the South in the hour of her trial, and let the world at large know that the people of the South were *determined* in their purpose, and would fight for her liberties until relieved from the thralldom of a Lincoln tyranny."

Each man present was invited to express his views on the matter, and I, in turn, was called upon. To kill all chances of suspicion that might occur from my presence, I responded to the invitation. I said to them that I was a stranger to all of them. I told them that I belonged to Daniel's guerrillas, at Somerville, Tennessee, and I knew from experience that a *well-organized band* could make itself of great service to the Government, and that I felt it was the duty of *every individual* in the Confederacy to put forth his *best efforts*, without regard to *cost* or *sacrifice*, to *sustain* the Government and *establish* our liberty. Our band, I told them, intended to live on the Lincoln army, and we kept close to it, and frequently got inside of the Yankee lines and got valuable information, and sometimes we captured prisoners, and horses, and mules; and we calculated not only to do service to the Government, but to make it *pay us*, and I hoped that the people of that neighborhood were as patriotic as they were in mine.

The meeting resulted in the reorganization of the band, with eighty members.

It has often been reported that citizens of the South who had taken the oath of allegiance to the Federal Government, were subject to abuse and cruel treatment by guerrillas and soldiers of the Confederate army; but in that meeting several of the members said that they had taken the oath, and had done it because compelled to do it, and it was not spoken of as an offense nor regarded as an obligation.

I had hoped that, in attending the meeting, I would be enabled to learn of some intended raid or campaign, but none was spoken of and probably none contemplated by the band at that time.

About 1 o'clock, P. M., the meeting closed, and I resumed my way back. Two days after, I arrived at Vicksburg, and reported to General Grant.

CHAPTER XXV.

Taken sick with the ague—Encounters his Satanic Majesty—The Devil afraid of General Grant—Expedition to Bogue Chitto Creek—Captures a rebel Colonel—Enlists as a veteran—Makes a speech to the soldiers.

FROM the time that I finished my trip to Yazoo City until the next November I had but very little to do, and nothing occurred of interest in my experience as a scout. About this time I was taken with the three-day ague, which troubled me more or less for a whole year. At times, when the "shakes" would leave me and the fever come on, I would have dreams or visions of a delirious character. I usually fancied myself engaged in some fearful and desperate encounter with the rebels. My fancies were audibly uttered, and to-day are as distinctly visible to my mind as though they were realities of yesterday. Indeed, they seemed like actual experience. In those delirious hours, officers and soldiers would visit me, to listen to my utterances of what was passing before me.

On one occasion, I fancied that I died and went to hell. There I found, in one corner of the infernal regions, an inclosure of several acres, filled with Federal soldiers. They were suffering intensely for want of sufficient water. A small rivulet made its way down a little hollow across the inclosure, but the stream was so small that its supply aggravated rather than diminished the thirst of the soldiers. Having placed me in the inclosure, the devil started back to earth after more soldiers. After a careful examination of the locality, I concluded that I could relieve very much of the suffering by damming up the stream. I set to work at once making a dam, and, by the time the devil made his appearance, I had succeeded in raising the water to a depth of four feet.

"Have you come here to interfere with my arrangements?" inquired the devil, angry at what I had done.

"No, sir; but I thought I would build a dam here and have as much water in it as there is in some parts of the Mississippi."

Whereupon the devil picked up a big cannon and punched a hole through it, which let the water out. Just then a twenty-two inch shell came into the inclosure, and exploded with a tremendous crash, completely enveloping us with the smoke. As it cleared away, two persons were seen coming through the regions of space directly toward the inclosure. The quick eye of his Satanic Majesty was the first to catch sight of them.

"Who are these?" he inquired. "A'n't one of them General Grant?"

"Yes," I replied; "that man in citizen's clothes is General Grant, and the man in uniform is General McPherson."

"I believe that *is* Grant," he said, after a more careful look.

"Yes, that's Grant."

"Then I must light out of this!" and away he went, as fast as possible.

I told my dream to General Grant. "I know," said he, "that I could run the rebels about, but I did not know that I could run the devil out of hell." He has asked me several times since if I *had had any more dreams.*

In the month of November, General McPherson made a demonstration with 14,000 men toward Canton, Miss., to draw the attention of the rebs while General Sherman, with his command, was moving from Memphis eastward to Chattanooga.

At Brownsville we came upon a small force of rebs, who undertook to check our advance, but we drove them from their position. The next day, at Bogue Chitto Creek, they made another stand, but were again driven from their position. General John A. Logan then sent me out to the front of our right to watch the movements of the enemy, and see which way they went. I was accompanied by a scout, by the name of James E. Bader. About a mile out, we left our horses under cover of the woods, and then, by ourselves, we ascended a rise of ground that enabled us to see the course the enemy had taken. While we were thus engaged in watching, we saw a man leave the rebel forces and ride toward a house that stood near by. As he neared us, we saw that he had on the uniform of a rebel Colonel. He unsaddled the horse at the house and then led it away to the stable, and then returned himself to the house. We then went to our horses, mounted, and rode to the house, dismounted and went in. We found but one man in the house, who said, "Good morning! You gave the Johnnies a good fleecing this morning!"

"Yes," said I, "we fleeced the Johnnies. But where is your uniform?"

"I ha'n't got a uniform, boys. I am no secesh. I have always been a good Union man."

We then searched the house for the saddle and uniform, which we found, hid under the floor.

"What uniform is this," said I, hauling it up from its hiding-place.

"It belongs to one of the boarders."

"It's my opinion that the boarder's clothes will just fit you. Take off the clothes you have on and put on these, and do it quick, too."

"I declare, gentlemen, that's not my uniform."

"No matter; you must put it on and see how it fits."

"Jiminy-pult!" said Bader, brandishing his revolver; "put this uniform on in a hurry, or we'll help you!"

"No more excuses," said I. "It a'n't but a few minutes since we saw you have it on."

The Colonel reluctantly changed his former dress for the uniform. "There—your military clothes fit well. Now go with us."

Bader saddled the horse and brought it to the door, when we made him mount and go back with us to General Logan. I told him the course the enemy had taken, and how we had captured the Colonel.

"Good morning, Colonel," said Logan. "Have you got any meat?"

"Yes, sir."

"Bunker, you go over and get some for our supper to-night."

I returned, accompanied by my partner, to the Colonel's house, where we found a nice flock of turkeys. Knowing that officers were fond of turkeys, I called a dog that was lying in the yard and set him to work. In a few minutes we captured six nice ones, which we carried to the General in lieu of meat.

"Here, Colonel," said Logan, showing the turkeys to the prisoner, "you shall have a nice supper in the Federal fortress. Boys, have you got any for yourselves?"

"No, sir."

"Here, take these," (handing me two of them.)

They made us an excellent supper; but whether the Colonel relished his own turkeys, and himself a prisoner, I am not so sure. The next day I was laid up with the ague, and was not able to scout any more during that expedition.

In the month of December, 1863, the re-enlisting of soldiers as veterans commenced in my regiment. I at once re-enlisted, and set about using my influence to persuade others to do so. This I did, generally by private conversation. Once, however, Bunker was called upon to make a speech, of which the following is what he had to say:

"*Fellow-soldiers and comrades in arms:* It is with feelings of pride that I attempt to address you—

pride because it is not often that an occasion offers for one to address a body of men whose deeds of valor have called forth such praise and such rejoicings as yours have done. Aye! I am proud that I have been a comrade in arms with you in such struggles as Donelson, Shiloh, Champion Hills, and Vicksburg! Such victories attest that you have done your duty well, and the glory is yours. Your country appreciates the value of such men, and, because of it, she now asks that you and I stand by that tattered flag for three years more. We know how it came by those shreds, and, as we gaze upon it, our hearts swell big with emotion in the recollection of the scenes through which we have passed. It is *our blood* that has spattered it, and our arms that have borne it and won for it glory. You know, by experience, the lot of the soldier. Your faces are bronzed in the service, and many of you bear scars from the battles that you've fought, mementoes of which your children and children's children will be proud to speak when you are laid away in the hero's grave.

"Our regiment has already taken part in nine battles and several severe skirmishes. In addition to my services as a scout and spy, I have taken part in all of them but one, and that was missed because I was sick and unable for duty. But, as much privation and hardships as I have experienced, and as much danger as I have been exposed to, I can not turn a deaf ear to the call of my country.

"Living and mingling, as I have, with the people of the South, and being with them at the time the war commenced, I was able to discern, with approximate correctness, the gigantic proportions of the rebellion. I well knew the feelings that had impelled them, and the obstinate and reckless determination with which they would hold out against the attempt of the Federal Government to bring them into subjection.

"In responding to the call of my country to sustain her noble prestige and glory, I had well counted the cost of the sacrifice that I was about to make; and, contrary to the general expectation of a large proportion of those that volunteered, I had no idea that the rebellion would be put down in a few months, but expected that *years* must elapse before our country would be restored to its former proportions, peace, and prosperity.

"Two years and a half have already passed since the first shot was fired at that star-spangled banner by the hands of traitors who had been reared under its protecting folds.

"During that period, thousands of patriotic hearts, that beat with love for their country, have ceased their pulsations in the noble effort to crush the traitorous arm that was raised against the most glorious structure of human liberty.

"Fathers and mothers, brothers and sisters, wives and sweethearts have mourned the loss of the noble fallen.

"Some of the heroes of this war have dragged out a lingering, distressing existence by disease, breathing the hero's prayer as they closed their eyes in death. Others have died amid the clash of arms and the din of battle; others, smitten down by the hand of the foe, have spent days of horrible agony, without food, water, or shelter, and then—died, glorious martyrs of liberty, on the field where they fell.

"Still the war continues, and the distant boom of cannon announces that more martyrs are being sacrificed and other hearts are being broken.

"The page of history will never reveal the anguish and suffering caused by this unholy rebellion.

"The fond father and mother, who have invoked the blessings of Heaven upon their heroic son, as he was about to leave them to encounter the hardships, privations, and sufferings of the warrior, will never know the sufferings which that loved one has endured; nor will the loved one know the intense anxiety and the agony of the broken hearts of those aged parents, until they meet in the blissful bowers of a patriot and hero.

"No pen can ever portray the sighs and anguish of the devoted wife and tender children, whose husband and father, their solace and support, has been smitten down by the hand of the foe.

"It has been my lot and pleasure to be a comrade and a sharer with those that have thus freely suffered and bled to perpetuate the blessings of liberty; and I can testify that there has been no hardship so great, no suffering so intense, no death so horrible as to efface the calm smiles of satisfaction and love from the face of the war-wrinkled hero, as he closed his eyes in death, with his last lingering look upon the flag of his country.

"Notwithstanding the many narrow escapes and

perilous adventures and sufferings that I have experienced, from long marches and from sickness, and from exposure to the weather by sleeping upon the ground, unsheltered by blanket or cover, during my travels as scout; and, notwithstanding the dangers I have experienced upon the field of battle, amid the roar of musketry and the crash of artillery, and the groans of my mangled comrades, wounded and dying, as they lay weltering in pools of blood, I prize my country *no less* than I did two years and a half ago, and my heart beats with the *same patriotism* that first prompted me to raise my arm in defense of the Union.

"So long as an armed traitor shall be found in rebellion against the Government, I shall continue my career as a soldier. I can not leave the field until this rebellion is crushed.

"The spirits of my fallen comrades are hovering about me, and beckoning me on to avenge their sufferings and our insulted flag; and their moldering bodies would turn over in disgust in the graves that inclose them, were I to leave the laurels that we have so gallantly won to the uncertainty of strange hands. Come, then, to the rescue!

"Your fathers and mothers, your wives and sweethearts, and all your loved ones at home, will cheer you on in the noble cause. Their thanksgivings and prayers are already encircling the throne of God in your behalf; and when you return to your homes, their kind hands will place garlands of flowers upon your heads as crowns of glory that you have won. Cast your eyes upon the sacred emblem of our country—to the flag which you have followed to the field of blood, and around which you have rallied in the din of battle, and beneath which your brave comrades have fallen, and remember the glorious victories that you have won, and that a nation's gratitude is yours.

"March bravely on, as you have already done, winning victory after victory, and but a few months more will elapse till you have planted the stars and stripes in every nook and corner of the rebellious states.

"Then will peace, happiness and prosperity shed their effulgent rays over all the land, and you will return to your homes, enshrouded with glory, to meet the warm embrace of friends, *knowing* that you have a country, and that a *free* country."

CHAPTER XXVI.

Frightened by a dead Colonel—Burns Confederate corn in face of the enemy—Gets into a tight place—A frightened Major—Captures information—A headstrong Captain gobbled up—Captures a rebel Provost-marshal General—Encounter with General Ross' cavalry—A strange adventure—Races with a rebel Colonel—A hard-hearted woman.

THE next service that I performed was in the month of February, 1864. It was in that month that General Sherman made what is known as the "Meridian raid." I accompanied the expedition. The second day out from Vicksburg, General McPherson sent me to watch the movements of Wirt Adams, who was hovering about our right flank with a battalion of cavalry. I found a movement in progress to attack the ordnance and supply train, which I reported in time to prevent; it was handsomely effected by the 11th Illinois Cavalry. At night the army halted at Baker's Creek.

There an incident occurred that I can never forget. I expected to go home with my regiment on veteran furlough as soon as the campaign that we were then on was completed. I had felt desirous of procuring a complete Confederate Colonel's uniform to take home with me as a trophy. I had already secured every thing except a coat. When I had completed my day's ride, and secured my horse for the night, it had got to be so late as 9 o'clock. Passing along the line to find somebody that would lend me some tobacco—which, by the way, was a scarce article then—I met a soldier, who said, "Bunker, did n't I hear you say that you wanted a rebel Colonel's coat?"

"Yes."

"There was a rebel Colonel killed on the skirmish line in front to-day."

"Was there! Where is he?"

"Go up the ditch yonder, to the left, till you come to the end of it; then take a hollow that leads away to your left. The first body that you come to is a dead private; the next is that of a Colonel."

The night was very dark, but my desires to obtain the coat were so strong that they overcame all fear, so I started out. I found the hollow described with less difficulty than I had expected. Coming to the dead private, I said, "Good evening, Johnnie! You'll get cold there, won't you?" A few steps further brought me to another body. "Good evening, Colonel!" said I. He made no reply. I continued: "You are going down below, where it is warm, and when we get back from this raid I am going up north, where it is cold; you have got a good coat and I want it. Since it is so warm down where you are going that you do n't need it, what objections can you have to my taking it?"

The Colonel made no reply.

"Well, Colonel, they say, when sparking old maids, that silence gives consent so I guess I'll take it."

He lay on his back, with his feet crossed, and one arm laying across his breast. His boots were already gone. Taking hold of his arm and raising it up, I found that it was limber. Said I, "You have n't had your furlough long, have you, Colonel?" He made no reply. I set the body up, and got down upon my knees in front of it, and commenced to take off the coat. A gasp and a convulsive spring forward brought the Colonel's open mouth suddenly against my face. Unearthly horror seized me; with one bound I was on my feet, and the next thing that I knew I was in camp. To say that I was frightened is no description of my feelings. Had a demon from the infernal regions placed his gnashing jaws against my face, I could not have been more horrified. I covered myself in my blankets, and cold tremors crept over me for hours after. Every attempt to court sleep would force through my mind a vivid recollection of every mean thing that I had ever done, followed by all the stories of ghosts and hobgoblins that I had ever heard. I have had no desire since to obtain a rebel Colonel's coat.

The next morning the march was resumed. Nothing of particular interest occurred, save the usual skirmishing, foraging, and burning consequent upon such expeditions, for several days. After we had crossed Pearl River, I was kept constantly on the flanks, scouting and foraging. I usually had a squad of men with me. At Jonesboro I was sent out on the left flank, with a squad of eight men. A few miles out from Jonesboro, the road leading to Hillsboro forks. The straight and most direct road leads through seven miles of swamp, and is known as the "lower road." The right-hand road leads to the south, around the swamp, and is called the "upper road." The latter was the one taken by the army in its route to Hillsboro. When I left the troops in the morning, I did not know that there was more than one road leading to that place. The consequence was, I kept to the left of the lower road, which carried me entirely too far from the main force of the army for safety.

After traveling about eight miles, we came to a cross-road. Our course, thus far, had not been confined to any road, but lay across the fields. As we came to the cross-road we emerged from a piece of woodland. Half a mile beyond us was a double log-house and several large rail-pens, which we had learned were filled with Confederate corn. Three hundred yards to the left of the corn we discovered a camp of two regiments of rebel cavalry. These we tried to clear, by filing to the right and keeping along in the timber to the west of the road. Less than a hundred yards brought us to a small stream of water, whose banks were lined with a dense growth of alders. The stream, after crossing the road, made its way along to within fifty yards of the corn-crib. Taking advantage of the cover afforded by the alders, one of my party waded down the shallow stream until opposite the cribs, and then, under cover of the cribs, made his way to them and set them on fire, and then retraced his steps.

Two miles further south, we came to a planter's house, where I found a table spread for eighteen persons, and fried sausage figured extensively in the meal, which was then nearly prepared.

"You've got the table set for some Johnnies, I reckon," said I to the planter.

"No, sir; for none but our own family."

"I reckon you have; I'll go out and stand picket while my men come in and eat." I went out and sent the men in to eat the sausage. As I was about to step behind an ash-house that stood in the yard, the old man, who had followed me out, stepped up to me and begged of me not to go there. Said he, "If you do, you will surely get shot."

"You want to frighten the men away from that sausage," said I, still determined to go there.

"No," said he, "I have never seen a man shot, and I don't want to see you shot in my own yard; you will certainly get shot if you go there. If you want to stand picket at all, go up into my garret and watch from the window."

The old man turned so pale and looked so much in earnest, that I concluded to take his advice. Instead of going into the front door I went round to the back door; both doors were open. In the front end of the hall sat the planter's daughter, waving a white handkerchief, and in the field beyond, not more than three hundred yards distant, I saw a line of Johnnies coming, hiding their approach as much as they could by intervening objects. I said to the boys, "Grab the sausage, kick over the table, and be off, for the rebs are on us." We took to the trees, when quite a lively skirmish ensued, which lasted for several minutes. The rebs then took to their horses, evidently bent on intercepting our retreat on the cross-road. As soon as they were out of sight, we started across the fields for the "lower Hillsboro" road, which proved to be about a mile distant. There were eighteen of the rebs, and they had evidently been watching the "lower road" for forage parties. We had been coming up in their rear until we stopped to confiscate the sausage. On reaching the road, I found that the troops had not passed that way, and consequently must have taken some other. The fact now flashed upon my mind, that we were much further from our command than we had any idea of.

There was a brick church at the corner of the road. I got the boys into that as quick as possible, and ordered them to knock out the windows. While they were preparing for defense, I stood in the road and watched. While the boys were getting ready, a Lieutenant and a private of the Federal Signal Corps came up, each armed with revolvers, and soon after several infantry soldiers, that had strayed away from their commands, came in sight. I hurried them up, and had hardly got them into the church when a party of rebs made their appearance. We opened on them lively, and killed two of their number and wounded others, which caused them to clear out and leave us. I knew it would not do to stay there long, so we "lit out" to find the army, taking the cross-road to the south. Being mounted, I rode on ahead, until I came to the upper road. The 16th Corps had just passed, and the 17th was just coming into sight. In a few minutes General

McPherson and staff came up, and wanted to know what the firing was about. I reported the situation of affairs. Just then two of my squad, who had brought up the rear at a distance of three hundred yards behind the rest, came up on the run, with information that two regiments of rebel cavalry were coming. The General ordered a brigade of infantry into position on a double-quick. They were hardly in line before the rebs commenced firing. A lively engagement ensued, which lasted about thirty minutes, and resulted in a handsome defeat of the enemy.

A march of three days more brought us to Decatur, Miss. The 16th Army Corps passed on beyond the place to encamp for the night. As the rear of their supply train was passing out of the place it was attacked, and one man and twenty-six mules were killed. The 17th Corps encamped for the night at Decatur. The next morning General Leggett sent me out on a road running south from the place, to ascertain whether there was a rebel force near. I had only gone half a mile before I discovered, a short distance ahead of me, a squad of rebs. I returned to report the fact to General Leggett, and as I was passing the first line of our troops, Major Fry, of the 20th Ohio, said to me, "Bunker, what is there out there?"

"There are rebs out there."

"How far?"

"Not more than half a mile."

"Pshaw! Bunker, you are mistaken; there can't be rebs that near."

"Perhaps you had better go and see, if you do n't believe it."

The Major mounted his black stallion and went out. The road was crooked, and lined on both sides with a heavy growth of pine underbrush, so that it was impossible to see far. He had n't been gone long enough to have rode half a mile, when he was seen coming back with his horse under full spur, and at its utmost speed, with hat in hand, shouting at the top of his voice, "Fall in! Fall in! Fall in!" From the Major's actions, we all supposed that a large force of rebs were about to attack us. The troops instantly fell in, when a company was sent out to find the cause of alarm, and discovered seven men that had given chase to the Major. Officers sometimes get frightened as well as enlisted men.

General Leggett then gave me a squad of twenty-six men and sent me out on a road to the south-east of town. Two miles out I saw a citizen fleeing from his house to the woods, as if alarmed at our approach. I gave chase and soon caught up with him. Brandishing my revolver, I said to him, "Daddy, you have got to tell me one thing or I will kill you right here; now tell me the truth."

"Well, what is it?"

"Where were you going, and what were you going for?"

"There are six hundred State militia down in the woods, about three quarters of a mile from here; I was afraid of you all, and I was going down there for protection."

"You belong to them, I suppose?"

"No, sir."

"What are the militia doing there?"

"They are going to attack your supply train."

"That's a fact, is it?"

"Yes, and they are going to do it right quick."

"It was the militia that killed the mules last night, I suppose."

"No, it was the citizens of the town."

"Did you have a hand in it?"

"No, sir; but my brother did. I'll tell you how it was done. Before the Yankee force came up, the citizens of the town met on the public square, and joined hands around the Confederate pole, with the Confederate colors flying, and swore by Almighty God that they would resist the march of the Yankees through the place, or every man would die in the attempt. As soon as the Yankee advance made its appearance, they all fled to the woods. As the rear of the train came up, they rallied and made the attack; but as soon as they saw other troops coming, they again fled."

I returned to General Leggett, to report the information that I had gained. I found him still in Decatur, superintending the departure of troops. The train was already moving out. I told him what was up. Said he, "They dare not attack it; and if they do, there a'n't enough of them to wake up one side of it."

"I guess they will try it, General."

At that instant the crack of rifles was heard, which increased in frequency until the firing was quite lively.

"They are at it, I guess," said the General. "I must see about that." So out we went to the scene of action. The guards were doing bravely, but the presence of the General inspired them with new courage, and they pitched into the militia like so many tigers, and whipped them without any reinforcements to assist them.

At Meridian, General McPherson sent me out alone to hunt up a grist-mill that was suitable to grind corn for the army. It was rendered necessary because of our having advanced into the enemy's country one hundred and fifty miles from our base of supplies, which compelled us to subsist upon the products of the country.

Two miles out from Meridian I found a mill, but it needed some repairs. The man who kept it told me that there was another, six miles further out, that was in good running order. I went out to find it, but had gone only about a mile, when I discovered rebel forces of both infantry and cavalry. From appearances, I judged them to be quite strong. I then retraced my steps toward camp. On my way, I met a Captain, with a detail of forty men, going after forage. I advised him to go back. I told him that if he undertook to go on the rebs would gobble him up. He insisted upon having his own way, and went on. Two men of company K, of the 17th Illinois Infantry, who knew me, heard what I said to the Captain, and, not liking very well to be captured, fell back a short distance to the rear of the squad, and watched the motion of things. The result was, the Captain and his men were surprised and all gobbled up without making any resistance, except the two that fell back, and they made a narrow escape.

After leaving the Captain, I hurried back and reported to General McPherson, who sent out a force of cavalry as quickly as possible to support the Captain, or release him if captured. The assistance, however, was too late. The rebs had departed with their prisoners.

We staid at Meridian two days, which time we spent in gathering supplies and devastating the country. The object of the raid was to impoverish the country as much as possible, and it was successfully accomplished. The destruction of property could not have been more complete. At the expiration of two days the army retraced its way eighteen miles, and then made another halt of two days, to rest the teams.

From that place, Colonel Potts, of the 32d Ohio Infantry, (since a Brevet Major-General,) in command of the Ohio Brigade, was sent with fifty-six wagons to the north of our line of march after supplies. I went with him. He ordered me to ride on some distance in advance, and see what I could find.

Twelve miles out, I came to a plantation that looked as if it belonged to a man in wealthy circumstances. As I came in sight of the house, I saw two men go in. The house stood in a yard inclosed by a picket-fence; behind the house was a small oak grove. Halting in front of the gate, I shouted. Two men came out, and one of them inquired what I wanted.

"I want you to come out to the gate," I replied.

"Go along to your command," he continued; "you have no business here. Your command has just passed the corner yonder, out of sight. I do n't want you straggling back and prowling around my premises. I am Provost-marshal General of this district, and I order you to go on."

"Oh, come out here. I am no straggler. I have got some news to tell you about the *Yankees, and it's good news, too.*"

At that they both came out into the road. As the Marshal closed the gate, and stepped away from it, I reined my horse between him and the gate, and, quickly presenting my revolver, told them that they were my prisoners, and if they made any attempt to get away I'd kill them both on the spot. I then marched them back till I met Colonel Potts.

"What have you got here?" he inquired.

"The Provost-marshal General."

"Is that your rank, sir?" he inquired of the prisoner.

"Yes, sir."

"What is your name?

"Davis, sir; Doctor Davis, they call me."

"What is your name?" (addressing the other.)

"My name is Davis; I am a brother of the doctor.

"What is your rank?"

"I am a private in the 35th Mississippi Regiment.

"What are you doing here?"

"I am on furlough. Here it is," said he, pulling it out and handing it to the Colonel.

I told the Colonel that it was only a few rods to the doctor's house; so he brought them along to the house, where they were turned over to my care. I now discovered, for the first time, that there were several persons chained to the trees in the little grove behind the house. Leaving my prisoners with a guard, I went to find out who they were. I found that they had iron collars around their necks, to which the chains were made fast. They said they were Union people, and lived in the country about there, and that they had fled from conscription, and Doctor Davis had hunted them down with bloodhounds, and then chained them there. I went to the doctor and asked him who he had got chained up in the grove. He said, "They are Confederate soldiers that have deserted their regiments. I captured them, and fastened them that way for safe-keeping, until I could return them to their commands."

I made him give me his keys, and then I unlocked the Union men, and put one of the iron collars on Doctor Davis' neck, and locked him to the hind end of one of the wagons. The doctor's brother cried, and said he would rather see him shot than treated that way, and begged of me to let him go. I told him that such treatment was no worse for rebs than it was for good Union men. I had hardly stepped away from the doctor when the Union men pitched into him, and I guess they would have killed him in a very few minutes if I had not interfered. I was very sorry afterward that I did n't let them do him justice.

We loaded the fifty-six wagons with oats, corn,

and bacon, from the doctor's plantation, and then burned every thing that was left. While the wagons were being loaded, some Indians that lived near by came to us, and seeing that I had the doctor chained, said: "Bad man; very bad man. Be glad he's gone."

As soon as I reached camp, I reported to General McPherson who I had captured. He said, "Doctor Davis is notorious for his cruelty to loyal people. Bring your prisoner in."

While I was gone for the prisoner, General Sherman and General Logan came over, and were there when I entered with him. General Sherman asked him a few questions, and then gave him a most severe upbraiding for his barbarous cruelty. When the Generals had all given him a piece of their minds, he was turned over to me to take care of, with permission to kill him if I wanted to.

The next morning I took him out into the woods alone, to see what I could do toward scaring him. I chained him to a tree, and then, drawing my revolver, told him that I was going to kill him. He begged of me to spare his life.

"Yes," said I, "the ox is yours now; why did n't you think of that when loyal men begged of you for mercy? You have no time to beg; you had better go to praying."

He plead and cried, and finally prayed. As much as he deserved death, I had n't the heart to kill him; so I returned him to his place behind the wagon. He was made to travel all the way to Vicksburg with the collar and chain fast to his neck.

Sometimes the driver would stop his team, and wait till the teams ahead would go three or four hundred yards. Then he would crack up his team, and make the doctor run to keep up, and, while running, he would have to hold on to the chain with both hands, to keep it from dragging him by the neck. At Vicksburg he was tried by court-martial, and sentenced to confinement on Johnson's Island.

When the army arrived at Jonesboro, on its return, General McPherson sent me, with a squad of nine men, into the country to hunt up forage. We were all mounted. When we had gone about eight miles to the north-west, we came to a small stream that flowed within deep perpendicular banks, and a few yards beyond the stream we came to a house, where we dismounted. I went to the stable in search of horses and mules. On returning to the yard, in front of the house, I found my men gathered in a circle around a young lady that had come out of the house. She was dressed extravagantly gay and rich, evidently in expectation of a visit from somebody. Her gay appearance had had something to do in gathering the men around her.

"Boys," said I, "don't you know better than to huddle together in that way for bushwhackers to shoot at? One shot would kill two or three of you."

"That's so, Bunker," said they, scattering out.

"What are you dressed up so nice for?" said I to the lady. "Who's coming to see you?"

"I a'n't dressed up; this is my every-day attire."

"You need n't lie to me in that way; there is

somebody coming to see you, and if you do n't tell me who it is, I 'll burn your house down."

"Perhaps, if you stay here long enough, you will find out who it is."

"Whereabouts is General Ross' command?"

"He is not far from here."

"Well, where is he?"

"Down in the woods yonder."

"Come on, boys, we 'll go down and see!"

We mounted and rode down into the woods; there I discovered a great many fresh horse-tracks. I ordered the boys to dismount and form a skirmish line. We had hardly got into position, when a Confederate General made his appearance on a rise of ground in our front, a hundred yards distant, coming toward us. When he had ascended fairly to the top of the hill, he halted to look. He was the richest dressed General that I ever saw. His uniform was heavily trimmed with gold lace, and his saddle, bridle, and holsters were mounted with gold. The General was straight, and well proportioned, and made a splendid appearance. I presumed that it was General Ross, on his way to visit the young lady.

"Jim," said I to the man nearest me, whom I knew to be a good shot, "why do n't you shoot that General?

Jim fired, but missed him. We gave chase, and fired twelve or fifteen shots at him, but, in the excitement of the occasion, we all missed him. We followed about forty rods, then returned to our horses, recrossed the bridge, tore it up, stationed ourselves behind trees, and waited for the approach of the enemy, who, I felt sure, would give chase. We had not waited long until the expected enemy came. We opened fire on them as they came up, which was kept up by us for several minutes, and returned with equal vigor by them. Finding they made no impression on us, they withdrew. Suspecting that they knew of some other place to cross the stream, I told the boys to "light out." We were hardly in saddle till we saw the rebels coming from another direction. They had crossed the creek, intent on our capture. Away we went, and the rebs after us. It was now nip and tuck who had the fastest horses. Fortunately for us, during our absence the 16th Corps had moved out on the road that we were on, and gone into camp, and we had only about three miles to ride before we ran into our own lines. The rebs kept up the chase until they were fired into by our pickets. I never learned whether we injured any of the rebs or not; my own men received no injury.

Two days' further marching brought the army within four miles of Pearl River Swamp, where it halted to lay a pontoon bridge across Pearl River. While the army was waiting, I was ordered by General Leggett to get a detail of eighteen men from the 32d Ohio Infantry, in addition to which I had a squad of nine that had been on detail with me for several days. With these I was to go after forage, and be ready to start at daylight the next morning. I got horses for my men, and had them all ready that night. In the morning we started for General Leggett's head-quarters for special instructions. On the way I met a Lieutenant of the 23d Indiana Infantry, with a detail of ninety men, all mounted. He said to me, "Bunker, what is your detail for?"

I told him that I was going after forage. He said, "I am ordered to take command of all forage parties to-day. You and your men fall in with me." The men, supposing it was all right, fell in, except one. I knew well enough that he had lied. He wore shoulder-straps and I wore none. I was vexed. I sat on my horse and watched his movements. He rode on to the head of his command, with more assuming dignity than a Major-General with a command of a hundred thousand men. He paid no attention to his men, and they strung out behind long enough for a good sized regiment. I told the man that had remained with me to go on, and tell the men of my detail that I wanted them to run with me, and to drop back behind till I came up. This they did, without being missed by the Lieutenant. I got them all back but one man. The Lieutenant filed to the left at the first left-hand road; I went on to the second left-hand road, and then filed left. I calculated to let the Lieutenant have the outside track, and I would forage inside his operations. After turning to the left, we went a mile, and then took a track that led to the right, down through a field, and then into a piece of woods, until we came to a creek, with a steep bank on the side that we were on that was four feet down to the water. We could only get our animals down the bank by pushing them. In this we succeeded. The opposite bank we ascended without difficulty. We were then about five miles from where the Lieutenant and I parted. Going on a few yards further, I heard the sound of voices, and motioned to the boys to stop. We listened, and could distinctly hear loud talking, and occasionally such expressions as "thar," "you all," and "gwine," which led us to conclude that we were coming upon a party of rebs. I knew that Carson's cavalry was somewhere not far distant, and readily enough suspected that the talking we heard was from his men. To retrace our steps was impossible, owing to the nature of the opposite bank of the stream. To remain long where we were was dangerous. "Boys," said I, "we must do one of two things—either fight these rebs or go to Andersonville. Which will you do?"

"Try 'em a whack, Bunker.'

"Well, then, tie your horses, and get into a line of skirmishers, and I'll ride cautiously forward and see what's there. I went so near that I saw two Confederate soldiers and a nigger, clad in Confederate uniform This confirmed my suspicions that we had run into Carson's cavalry. I concluded that our only hope lay in the trial of strategy. From the voices that I heard, the party, whoever they were, greatly outnumbered mine.

Having placed myself at the rear of my command, I shouted, at the top of my voice, "ATTENTION BATTALION! COMPANY A, ON THE RIGHT, AND B, ON THE LEFT, DEPLOY AS SKIRMISHERS! FORWARD—DOUBLE-QUICK—MARCH!" Away the boys went. Then I shouted, "BATTALION—FORWARD—DOUBLE-

QUICK—MARCH!" I was the battalion. I kept on giving commands, as we advanced, as loud as I could yell, as if I was commanding a full regiment of infantry. The strategy had its effect. The party did not wait to see who we were, but very unceremoniously "lit out." We only got sight of three persons; those were the two Confederate soldiers and nigger that I have mentioned, who remained behind for us to capture. We now found out that we had stampeded a party of Federal soldiers. They had left two yoke of oxen and a wagon, loaded with a barrel of sugar, a sack of flour, and nice hams. On top of the load was a roll of carpeting. The fleeing party had left along their line of flight great numbers of nice hams, that they had thrown away in their efforts to escape. The three persons that we had captured had hauled the stuff down into the woods that morning, to hide it from the Yankees. A party of Federal soldiers had discovered the track, and followed it up, and were in the act of appropriating the best of the hams to their own use, when we surprised them. We took possession of the property, and started on, keeping a plantation road that wound its way round to the main road, on which the army was encamped.

Shortly before coming out on the main road, I halted my party to give the oxen a chance to rest. While there, the 11th Illinois Cavalry and a brigade of infantry were seen coming out on the road that we were on, with battle-flags flying. Coming up to us, they halted. At the head of the command, with the Colonel of the 11th Illinois Cavalry, was the

Lieutenant of the forage party and a private of the 23d Indiana Infantry. Said the private to me:

"Bunker, was there a carpet on that wagon?"

"Yes; but we threw it away."

"Was there a barrel of sugar?"

"Yes."

"And a sack of flour?"

"Yes."

Turning to the Lieutenant, "Here is your wagon."

"Do you claim that wagon, Lieutenant?" I inquired.

"I don't know as it is my wagon."

"If it is, just say so; I don't know as one soldier is better than another. These supplies are for this noble army. If they are yours, just say so; then I'll tell how I came by them."

"I don't know as I care who has them; only I would like to have had one of those hams for my dinner."

"Well, why didn't you save one of the hams that you threw away, if you wanted one so bad?"

"I declare!" said the Colonel, "if this a'n't a pretty flirt! A brigade of infantry and a battalion of cavalry sent out to attack *Bunker and his squad!*"

The Colonel then moved with his command back to camp, and I reported with my forage to General Leggett.

The next day I took out a squad of six men on a road leading to the north-west. Two miles out I came to a cross-road leading down to Pearl River. Near the corners stood a dwelling-house, and in the yard lay a dead horse, which, from appearances, had been killed only a few minutes before. Riding into the yard, and reining up to the door of the house, I called the occupants out, who proved to be a widow lady and two daughters. I inquired how the horse came to be killed in her yard. At first she refused to tell. By threatening to burn her house, I succeeded in drawing out the information that a Federal soldier had been there but a few minutes, when a Confederate Colonel, an Adjutant, and a servant rode into the yard; the servant was mounted on a mule. The Federal soldier, seeing them, rushed out of the house and fired his piece at the Adjutant, and then rushed at the Colonel with his bayonet. The shot missed the Adjutant and killed his horse. The Colonel shot the soldier in the right arm and disabled him. The Adjutant left the servant to shift for himself, mounted the mule, and rode off with the Colonel toward Pearl River. They hurried their prisoner off as fast as he could go, without giving him time to tie up his wound. Having learned this, I said, "Come on, boys! we can outrun a mule, and perhaps we can catch them." Away we went, under full spur. A chase of a little over two miles brought us in sight of a dwelling-house, where, by the roadside, was hitched a horse and a mule, and sitting upon the porch was a Federal soldier.

The Colonel and Adjutant had entered the house and called for a snack. The man of the house replied, "Really, Colonel, I should like to get you something to eat, but I am afraid the Yankees will be upon you before my servants can get it ready."

SURRENDER, OR I'LL KILL YOU RIGHT HERE.

"No they won't; they are afraid of me. The cowardly sons of b——s das n't follow me! I've got one of them now; if they come I'll get some more."

The soldier, seeing us coming, and having heard the conversation, said: "The Colonel is a brave man, indeed; but, by the looks of things out here, he is gone up. Hearing that, they made a rush for their animals, and we fired a volley from our revolvers, which killed the Adjutant instantly. We emptied our revolvers at the Colonel; but in the excitement of the occasion every shot missed, and he succeeded in mounting his horse and starting off toward the river. By the time he was in his saddle, I was within twenty feet of him. The chase was a desperate one. The Colonel, at intervals of a few rods, would let drive a back-handed shot toward me, until he had emptied his piece. My horse would lay back his ears and open his mouth, and spring forward with all his force, as if to catch hold of the Colonel's horse with his teeth. A mile and a half brought us to the river. I had gained at least ten feet. The Colonel's horse splashed into the water, and mine gave a leap and came nearly up, and then outswam his, till I came near enough to strike the Colonel on the back of the head with the butt of my revolver, which considerably stunned him, and enabled me get his horse by the bridle.

"Surrender," said I, "or I'll kill you!"

"I'm your prisoner," said the Colonel.

"Bring him out," shouted the boys, who, by this time, had come up.

We conducted the prisoner back to the house,

where we found the soldier, still bleeding and very weak from the loss of blood. He belonged to the 32d Ohio Infantry. He said that he had asked the woman of the house for a rag with which to tie up his wound, which she refused to give him, adding, " I hope you will bleed to death." We dressed the wound as well as we could, and then took care of the woman's rags by setting fire to the house and outbuildings. We then carried the soldier to his regiment, and the Colonel to General McPherson's headquarters.

After crossing Pearl River, very little occurred of interest in my individual experience during the march back to Vicksburg. A great many forage parties and straggling soldiers were gobbled up by the enemy during the raid; but, though I was out with men under my charge nearly every day, I never lost a man during the entire campaign, which lasted thirty days. On the march from Canton to Vicksburg the troops were not allowed to destroy property. The raid was a demonstration of the feasibility of the plan of campaigning, which was afterward inaugurated by General Sherman in the state of Georgia.

CHAPTER XXVII.

Starts home on veteran furlough—Trouble at the table—Bluffs the Captain—Suspected of being a rebel spy—Commissioned officer serves him at the table—Kind attentions at home—Silences an old maid—Returns to the front—Shot at twenty-one times—The remedy—A Union lady—The dwarf weaver—The weaver beheaded—Goes into Marietta as a spy—Confederate side of the lines—Escape from the rebs—General McPherson's death—Hard fighting.

EARLY in March, 1864, my regiment went home from Vicksburg on veteran furlough, and I accompanied it. Every thing passed off pleasantly on our homeward trip, save that, now and then, it became difficult for a man like myself, without shoulder-straps, to get admitted to the table for meals. We were embarked on board the steamer Continental. She had on board, besides our own, a New York regiment, going home from New Orleans. I was a stranger to them, and was frequently halted by them when they were on guard. This I might have prevented by procuring an order, or pass, entitling me to the full privilege of the boat; but I chose to keep my real character disguised, except to such as personally knew me.

On one occasion, after having imbibed rather

freely at the bar—nothing unusual for some soldiers on veteran furlough to do—I sat down to dinner without having procured a ticket, and placed a five-dollar bill by the side of my plate for the clerk of the boat to take his pay from. The Captain's son came round for tickets, in place of the clerk, and, seeing my bill lying there, and supposing that I was in too happy a frame of mind to take notice of so slight a mistake, picked it up and walked off.

That aroused my anger—or rather my liquor—and I called out, "Stop! you d—d thieving son of a b—h! Bring back that money." Finding that he was caught in the act, he came back and gave me the change. While he was making the change, I gave him a regular cursing. The chaplain of the New York regiment was sitting at the table opposite to me. The loud talking brought crowds of officers and others to see what was up, and with them the boy's father, who took me to task for such disrespect to his boat in presence of the chaplain.

"Chaplain, h—l!" said I. "Do you think that I would sit here and see your son steal my money without saying any thing? He deserves something worse than curses. He ought to have his neck stretched. As for chaplains, they are no better than other folks. Some will steal, or hire soldiers to do it for them. We had a chaplain in our regiment, who said to me once, 'Bunker, can't you bring me in a good horse?' 'Yes, I can bring you in a good horse.' 'Well, I wish you would. I can't pay you the full value of the horse, but I'll pay you for your trouble.' 'Oh, never mind the trouble, chaplain,' said I; 'you preach the boys a good sermon some Sunday morning, and *I'll steal you a horse!*'"

When I had finished my reply, the Captain disappeared in one direction and the chaplain in another, in a midst of a roar of laughter from those gathered around. I heard no more from the Captain about disgracing his boat in the presence of chaplains.

At Memphis, we changed from the steamer Continental to a Memphis and Cincinnati packet. General Breman took passage with us as far as Cairo, Ill., and, being the senior officer in rank on board, was in command of the troops. It is customary, when troops are on board transports, to have a guard and an officer of the day, whose duty it is to preserve order, subject to the instructions of the commanding officer.

The next morning after we left Memphis, Captain Ayres, of the 20th Ohio Infantry, was the officer of the day. On reporting to General Breman for instructions, he was informed that there was a "suspicious character" on board. He pointed me out to the Captain, and told him that I came on board at Memphis, and that, in all probability, I was either a rebel spy or an incendiary, watching an opportunity to burn up the boat. He instructed the Captain to watch me, and if my actions confirmed his suspicions, to arrest me and place me under guard. The Captain was personally acquainted with me, but kept the fact to himself. As soon as an opportunity offered, the Captain told me what the General had said; so I resolved to see how he would act when he found out who I was. Walking back to the after-cabin, I found General Force and General Breman engaged in reading. Said I to the latter, saluting him, "General Breman, you don't know me, do you?"

"Not that I know of."

"You don't remember of having me arrested in Tennessee as a rebel spy? I am a 'suspicious character;' you had better watch me."

"That's Mr. Ruggles, General," said General Force; "he's a useful man. He's a valuable scout."

"Ah!" said Breman, remembering his instructions to the officer of the day, and coloring slightly, "I didn't know *what* to make of you. *I did suspect your loyalty.*"

"I'm *loyal* enough, but I am among the rebs *so much* that I sometimes *act* like one." The officer of the day was saved the necessity of placing me under arrest.

Before reaching Cincinnati, the boat supplies became so nearly exhausted that it became necessary to issue an order forbidding any but commissioned officers and their *attachés* being furnished with meals by the boat. There were so many to eat that it generally required the table to be set three times before all would be supplied. The first time the table was set after the order was issued, I called at the clerk's office to buy a ticket for dinner for myself and a friend, and was refused on the plea that the order forbid furnishing meals to *enlisted men*. My friend and I then seated ourselves at the table, but were ordered away by the steward. On our refusing to go, he reported us to the clerk, who came and ordered us away. I told him that we were *entitled* to get our meals there, and if he could n't furnish us a waiter, I 'd get a commissioned officer to wait on us. I then ordered a waiter to serve us, but the clerk countermanded it. Just then Captain Bostwick, of the 20th Ohio Infantry, was passing by us.

"Here, Captain," said I; "these men have got above their business. They won't wait on us because we ha'n't got on shoulder-straps. Can't you wait on a poor soldier?"

"Certainly, gentlemen; what will you have, roast beef or boiled ham?"

"Some of the beef, if you please, Captain."

Away went the Captain with our plates. General Force, having heard our words, now made his appearance. "General," said I, "this man and I fare rather slim; they wo n't give us any thing to eat on this boat unless we have a man with shoulder-straps to wait upon us."

"Clerk," said the General, "let these men have what they want to eat. That man there (pointing to my friend) is a commissioned officer, and the other man is a great deal more deserving of his meals than I am."

"I beg your pardon, gentlemen," said the clerk. "Waiter, serve these men."

"Never mind the waiter, clerk. We do n't want any of your *trash* around us; we have *commissioned officers to serve us.*" The Captain served us till we had finished our meal, very much to the amusement of those looking on.

On my arrival in Ohio, I found that my reputation as a scout and spy had preceded me, and wherever I went I could scarcely make my appearance on the street without having a crowd gather around me, eager to hear my experience in Dixie. I was pressed with invitations to call upon people whom I had never seen or heard of before. Circumstances, beyond my control, rendered my position an embarrassing one. We were to have been paid our bounty, back pay, and veteran bounty at Columbus, O., but, by the carelessness of the commissary of musters that mustered me, my veteran papers were lost, so that I drew no pay, and, consequently, my clothes were ragged and my pocket empty. Embarrassing as this was to me, it seemed to have very little influence with others, and ladies in silk would listen with intense interest to the narratives of the ragged soldier.

I am proud that I live in a country where patriotism, valor, and services rendered to the Government, are more highly appreciated than dress or a lavish expenditure of money. My war-worn clothes did not diminish the number of my friends and admirers, otherwise my veteran visit would have been an unhappy one.

In the course of my visiting, I spent an evening at a farm-house, where was boarding the schoolmistress of the district school. She was a lady aged forty-two years—my age exactly—and would usually be called an "old maid." Her tongue was as flexible as mine; indeed, I found it hard to get the start of her. At first, we were shy of each other; she was afraid of soiling her silk, and I was afraid to show my rags. Our seats were at opposite sides of the room. Gradually, however, our interest in each other's stories increased, and our distance apart as gradually diminished, until, finally, we were sitting side by side, and became the center of attraction for the evening by our narratives, alternately told—hers of school-teaching experience and mine of army experience. At last she said: "Mr. Ruggles, I should like to know how you learned to practice the art of deception, as you did, among the Southern people. They are not all fools, are they?"

"No, ma'am, they are not all fools."

"Really, then, I should like to know how you learned it."

"I'll tell you, if you will permit me to do so."

"I *should* like to know."

"I learned it in paying my respects to *old maids*."

"*There! there! that will do!*" and away she went to the opposite side of the room, much to the amusement of the company present. For the remainder of the evening I had to keep at a respectable distance from her.

Our veteran furloughs having expired, we reported to General Leggett, at Cairo, Illinois, who sent me to Clifton, Tennessee, to report to General M. F. Force for duty. He sent me to Pulaski, a distance of sixty-two miles, with dispatches. A squad of twenty men, under command of a Lieutenant from a battalion of Tennessee cavalry, was sent with me as an escort. The entire battalion of cavalry—in all, four hundred men—had been in the Confederate service. They were captured at the taking of Fort Donelson, and had been released by the Federal authorities, and had enlisted in the Federal service. They had been running the courier line to Pulaski, but had never got through with their dispatches. The men of the battalion lived in the country lying between Clifton and Pulaski.

Soon after starting out from Clifton, my cavalry escort began to drop off, one at a time, to visit their homes, and when I arrived at Pulaski I had but two of my escort with me—one was the Lieutenant and the other a Sergeant. I went through without being molested, but I came to the conclusion that *"Confederate-Federal cavalry"* was of but little service to the Government. *I never could trust a Union-secesh!* It is too much like serving God and Mammon. *The Government has placed entirely too much confidence in that class of men.* I would as soon trust a dog with my dinner. My life has many times been placed in jeopardy by such characters, and my convictions are the result of experience.

I returned to Clifton with dispatches alone, and without being molested. Two days after I was sent back again alone. I always passed over the most dangerous part of the route in the night. I went through undisturbed, but on my return I was shot at twenty-one times. At Lawrenceburg I was fired at from the dwelling-houses, as I passed through the place, without any challenge to halt. One man was standing on his porch, with his gun in his hand, evidently watching for me to come, and fired at me as I passed. Four miles from Lawrence I came to several cotton-factories; the locality bore the reputation of being loyal. There I was fired at, both from the factories and dwelling-houses. I went through both of these places under full spur. The last shot that was fired at me was by a man standing in the middle of the road, who challenged me to halt, and at the same time brought his piece to an aim. Instead of halting, I put spurs to my horse and dashed by. I was not more than six feet from him when he fired, but, in the excitement of the moment, his shot missed me, and I passed on unharmed. I can assure the reader, from actual experience, that it is no very pleasant thing to be a mark for people to shoot at. I am fully convinced that it was citizens that fired at me, and that they had found out, through the cavalry, that I have mentioned, that I was a bearer of dispatches, and were watching for me.

I delivered my dispatches to General Force, and told him that I was afraid to run the line alone. He gave me an order for twenty-one men, with the privilege of selecting men of my choice. Two days after, I again started to Pulaski, with my escort, who were infantry soldiers, mounted. Previous to starting, I told the General my plan of operation, to which he said, "Very well." I called at every house along the entire route. If the people were in bed, I made them get up, and said to them, "*I am running a courier line from Clifton to Pulaski, and you good, loyal people have fired at me twenty-one times. If I am ever fired at again, whether I am killed or not, every man, woman, and child within four miles of this road, on either side, shall be shot, and your houses burned.*"

All of them claimed to be innocent, and said they were quiet, peaceably-disposed citizens. I went through and back with my escort without being molested, and for three weeks after, I ran the line alone, without being disturbed.

The disposition of the Southern people is very much like that of a butcher's Irish bull-dog. The more you try to coax and pet them, the more they will try to bite you; but take a fire-brand and run at them, and they will sneak off as cowardly as can be. The more the Government coaxed and petted the Southern people, the worse they acted. If a favor was extended to them, they would snap and snarl at the hand that held it; but go right at them, with a sword in one hand and a fire-brand in the other, and they cower down directly. So my barbarous threat proved a wholesome remedy.

At the expiration of three weeks, General Leggett arrived at Clifton with the 3d Division of the 17th Army Corps, bringing with his command twenty-two hundred head of cattle for beef. The troops now prepared to march across to Georgia, to increase the force operating under General Sherman for the capture of Atlanta.

Preparatory to the marching of the troops, General Force sent me out on the road to Florence, to ascertain the locality of Roddy's cavalry—which was known to be hovering around—to prevent any attempt it might make to stampede the cattle. I found out that the cavalry, 4,000 strong, was at Florence, and that Bill Johnson commanded 900 of Roddy's choicest men, and that he—Roddy—

had heard of the arrival of the cattle, and had ordered Johnson to be on the alert for an opportunity to stampede them. This I learned from citizens who seemed to be well informed of the intended movements of both forces. Having satisfied myself that the information was reliable, I did not go into Florence, but crossed over to the Nashville and Florence military road, which I came to seven miles from the latter place. I then went toward Lawrenceburg, on my return to my command. Twelve miles from where I came into the road, I halted at a dwelling-house, and said to the man of the house, "Can I get my horse fed, and some supper here?"

"Where do you belong?"

"I belong to Bill Johnson's cavalry, and I'm going down to look up the Yankee beef-cattle."

"Yes, yes; come in. The servant will feed your horse. I hope you'll succeed in finding the cattle."

The servants were already engaged in preparing supper for the family. Just before supper was announced, a daughter of the planter came in. I should judge that she was about sixteen years old.

"Mother," said she, "what are you doing with that man here?"

"He's one of Johnson's men, and he's going down to hunt up the Yankee beef-cattle," was the reply.

"Well, you had better watch him, or he'll steal something before he leaves."

"Behave yourself, and not insult the man in that way," said the mother.

"I do behave. He ought to be insulted. You

are going down to hunt up the Yankees, are you?" she continued, addressing me. "You are a *pretty* object to be engaged in hunting up *Yankees*. The sight of *one pair of blue breeches* would make *six such spared monuments of God's mercy as you are get up and leave.*"

At the table the impudent thing would watch me, and whenever she could get my eye, she would make faces at me, which she carried to such an extreme that her mother slapped her ears to make her be still.

Whether the whole family were loyal, or only the daughter, or whether the daughter was secesh, and tried only to draw out my true character, the reader alone must judge; my duties were such that I dare not trust any of them.

I reached Clifton without being disturbed.

On the arrival of the troops to within two miles of Lawrenceburg, I was sent ahead to that place, with instructions to go out on the military road toward Florence, and see if Johnson was coming. I had an escort of fourteen men from the 11th Illinois Cavalry. When we had gone three miles on the military road, we came suddenly upon a dwarfish looking man, mounted on a horse, who was wonderfully frightened at our unexpected meeting.

"How far have you come on this military road?" I inquired of him.

"I have come from Florence."

"Did you see any of Bill Johnson's cavalry on the road?"

"No, sir; there is no cavalry on the road. Roddy's

cavalry is at Florence; there is none this side of there."

"Look here, you are lying to me," I said, eying him closely. A'n't there any cavalry camped at Shoal Creek?"

"No, sir; if there is I did not see them."

"*You are lying to me sure.* Johnson's cavalry is at Shoal Creek, not more than a mile and a half from here, and you could not pass without seeing it. You belong to the cavalry, and have been sent out to see if the Yankees are coming with the cattle."

"No, indeed, I do n't belong to them," he persisted; "I am no soldier, and did not see any soldiers along the road. I am a weaver by trade, and do not belong to the army."

"Well, go with us; we'll find out whether you are a soldier or not." His fright now turned into terror. We went about a mile, when we met Johnson's cavalry coming up, and were obliged to turn back. As we turned, one of the cavalry, with a single stroke of his saber, severed the weaver's head from his body, and left him for his comrades to take care of. I have no doubt whatever but that he was a scout for Johnson, and that he calculated his being a dwarf would clear all suspicion of his belonging to the army.

I reported the approach of Johnson to General Leggett, who threw out a brigade of infantry in line of battle, and prevented an attack upon the cattle.

At Huntsville, Alabama, the ague came on me so bad that I was unable for duty. Leaving my horse with a scout that had run with me considerable, I went to the hospital. I did not like the looks of things there, so I got sent on to Chattanooga, where I remained four days, at the end of which time I felt a little better, and resolved to go back to the front. Hospital discipline and I could not agree very well. I went to a member of General McPherson's staff and told him what I wanted, and he gave me a pass to report to General Sherman, wherever I could find him. I came up with him just at the opening of the Buzzard's Roost fight, in which I took a part. From there I was with the advanced guards until we came to Resaca, at which place I assisted, on the right flank, in fighting Wheeler's cavalry. I kept along with the advance of the army until we arrived at Kingston, where General Leggett's command formed a junction with us. There I found my horse. From there I had nothing of particular interest to do until the rebs were driven to the Kenesaw Mountain.

At that place General McPherson sent for me, and asked me if I thought I could go into Marietta and get back again. I told him I could, if allowed to take my own plans to accomplish it, which he said I might do. He told me to go in and find out whether the battery that commands the approach along the railroad is a masked one, and count the guns; see whether any State militia were there, and whether any part of the line was held by them, and whether they were mixed in with other troops. I was to examine the enemy's first line of works, and see how far they extended; and how deep the ditches were, and whether I thought it practicable to carry them by assault. He gave me fifty dollars in greenbacks to defray my expenses, and sent me to Major-General Logan for a Confederate uniform and some Confederate money. Thus equipped, I started out the next day on horseback. I passed along our lines to the extreme left, to General Garrard's head-quarters, where I left my papers, and procured a pass through the lines. I passed the vedettes about noon, and proceeded on in an easterly direction until I reached Canton, sixteen miles from General McPherson's head-quarters. There I staid all night. In the morning I resumed my journey, on a road leading south, and halted for the night at a small village on the Chattahoochee River, called Roswell Factories, twenty-eight miles from Canton. The next morning a division of South Carolina cavalry came along from the east, just as I was ready to start out. I fell in and attached myself to company A, of the 1st South Carolina, and represented myself as belonging to the 11th Texas Cavalry—which I knew was in our front when I started out—going to join my command. The explanation proved satisfactory, and I kept along with them till we reached Marietta, a distance from Roswell Factories of eighteen miles. Then I left them, under pretense of going to my own regiment, and went north along the railroad, until I came to the battery that I was directed to visit. It contained twelve large guns well masked. I then turned to the right and rode along the first line of intrenchments. About eighty rods from the masked battery I found a six-gun battery of small guns, and about eighty rods further on was another six-gun battery of small guns.

About midway between the two six-gun batteries, I came upon a small squad of militia that had been digging a spur from the main ditch for a rifle-pit. One of the party stepped out of a pit that he had just completed, and for a moment contemplated the result of his labor, and then said: "Nary a Yankee is gwine to *come* up thar; *thar* is whar I'll *stay*, and *thar* is whar I'll *die!*" When we came in possession of the place, however, we found no dead bodies "*thar*."

Down under the hill from the six-gun batteries, toward Marietta, I found a large force of State militia, who were holding the right of the rebel lines by themselves. There was nothing military in their appearance. Their camp was without regularity, and filthy in the extreme. Many of them had their families with them, and some of them had cows tied to their wagons. The dog and cat were not left behind. The tongues of their wagons usually pointed outward, and boards laid across from one wagon-tongue to another served them as tables. Decrepit old men and little boys, women and babies, white and black, were there. The various kinds and calibers of small arms were as numerous and different as the individuals that carried them. I thought to myself that it would be a fine place to throw a few big shells. It would have created a panic, at a trifling expense, that would have eclipsed any thing in the history of the rebellion.

The ditches of the first line I found to be four feet deep and six feet wide. A little to the right and front of the militia, I found a brigade of Texas cavalry, composed, in part, of the 11th and 3d Texas Regiments; two other Texas regiments made up the brigade. I went to the Orderly Sergeant of company A, of the 11th Texas, and told him that I belonged to company A of the 1st South Carolina Cavalry, and that my regiment had just come in that day, and that I had got separated from my command, and would like to stay with him over night, and then hunt up my regiment in the morning. He went to the Colonel and asked permission to keep me, which was granted. The Colonel of the 11th Texas was in command of the brigade.

In the morning the brigade prepared to make a demonstration upon General Wilder's command; so I told the orderly that I would go along and see the fun. The command moved out a short distance and then halted. Just then an orderly rode up and handed the Colonel a dispatch, which, when he had read, he sent the whole command back to camp except the company I was with; with that he said he would go out and capture a Yankee vedette. We rode on until we came to a narrow ridge of ground. As we were rising this, and just as we had reached its summit, we unexpectedly received five shots from Federal vedettes, which killed the Colonel and two privates. The command immediately broke to the rear and fled toward camp. I broke back with them until we reached the foot of the hill, when I turned to my right, and went up the hollow, I should judge about three hundred yards, and again ascended the ridge, and crossed to a little brook that flowed along the base of the hill, and crossed the road between the vedettes and where the Colonel was killed. A little below me, in the brook, was a Federal soldier, engaged in washing his face. His hat and gun were lying upon the bank. He was but a mere boy. Seeing me approach, he seized his gun, cocked it, and raised it to his face, when I called to him, "Hold on, my little man, I am a Federal soldier; don't shoot me!"

"Well, then, come in out of the wet! Don't you try to get away; if you do I'll *bore* you!"

The little fellow kept his piece leveled at me until I came up, and then marched me away to the reserve. He was so elated with his capture that he forgot his hat, and marched me in without it.

From the reserve I was taken to General Wilder's head-quarters, and then to Colonel Miller's, where my horse was taken from me. From there I was taken to the corral of rebel prisoners, near General Garrard's head-quarters, and turned in. I sat down upon a block of wood, near the entrance to the inclosure, and leaned my head upon my hands. I had been there but a moment, when a prisoner, discovering that I was a fresh arrival, stepped up and said, "To what command do you belong?"

"Clear out, and don't bother me," I replied; "I'm mad now."

The prisoners, seeing that I was not in a talking mood, left me to myself. Shortly after, the Adjutant-General came out and discovered me sitting there. I heard him call the sergeant of the guard, who shortly came to the entrance and said, "Halloa, there, you long-haired fellow! you are wanted here." He took me into the head-quarters, where I received the papers that I had left there, and an order for my horse and a pass to General McPherson's head-quarters, where I arrived after an absence of three days and a half.

The information that I gathered showed that the enemy's right was the most advantageous point for us to attack; so much so, that it was thought by good judges that a single army corps could easily have entered Marietta. General Sherman, however, was not left to choose his place of attack, for the next morning the enemy made a furious assault upon our right, against General Hooker's command. The onslaught was impetuous and the pressure tremendous, but was heroically resisted. For a time it seemed as if Hooker's entire command would be swept away by the masses that were hurled against it. It was enough, however, that "Fighting Joe" was there to animate his troops by his noble bearing.

The action was sustained in all its fury, and gradually spread from right to left, until the whole line was engaged, and lasted until, overpowered by the boys in blue, the enemy broke and fled, resulting in a complete victory to the Federal arms, with the possession of Kenesaw Mountain and Marietta.

The next day, at my request, General McPherson and staff, accompanied by General Leggett, went with me to see the places that I had described in my report. After we had visited them, General McPherson said that he was convinced that I had reported correctly. I mention this because it is not uncommon for spies to go out, and, on their return, report that which they knew nothing about. It was a satisfaction for me to know that he was satisfied that I had visited the places that I had described.

General Sherman continued to press the enemy toward Atlanta, and his victory at Kenesaw Mountain was followed by an advance of his lines to within two miles of that place, and extending around three sides of it.

The 20th day of July, General Hood's supersedure of General Johnston in the command of the Confederate army was inaugurated by a furious attack upon the 4th and 14th Corps, comprising General Sherman's center. Very much to our satisfaction, General Johnston's slow-retreating process of campaign was changed to one of rapid evolutions, and bold, desperate dashes. Our greatest difficulty had been to get the enemy to fight. This we now had an opportunity of doing. The hardy veterans of the North-west received the attack with coolness and determination, and, though the enemy came in massed columns, they stood their ground, dealing out death and destruction, until Hood was glad to withdraw, leaving his dead and wounded in our hands.

On the morning of July 22d, General McPherson was informed, by a member of his staff, that he had heard, during the night, a noise like the moving of artillery, which he surmised to be the enemy evacuating Atlanta. General McPherson thought the officer was mistaken about the evacuation of the place. The noise of moving troops, he thought, was probably a body of rebel cavalry that had moved out on our left flank, which lay stretched along on the east side of the place.

To clear up the matter, General McPherson told me to take my horse and ride out to Decatur, which was four miles distant, and from there out on the Stone Mountain road, and find out whether the enemy was there. He instructed me to go as far as I could, and not get captured. If I found the enemy, I was to drop back toward our lines, and feel along, at intervals, for the enemy toward our left. This was on the supposition that the enemy might have a line extending around our left flank and along its rear.

Three-quarters of a mile out from Decatur, I came upon five rebel soldiers on picket. They challenged me to halt, but I had no intention of halting there; so I wheeled about and "lit out." The rebs might have shot me as well as not. I returned to our lines, and went out on another road, and had proceeded but about half a mile, when I came upon more rebel pickets. They did not fire at me. I tried to get out, in all, at thirteen different places, and every time encountered pickets, none of whom tried to shoot me. I was well satisfied that the noise of moving troops, heard in the night, were infantry and artillery moving round to our rear, intending to surprise us, and for that reason their pickets were forbidden to fire upon individuals or small parties.

I then hastened back and reported to General McPherson what I had seen. He wanted to know if I was sure the pickets were infantry, and I told him that I was. He seemed to doubt the possibility of their being infantry. He and his staff then rode out to our rear picket-line, on a road that I had not been out on, and, waiting there, he sent me out to see if I could find any pickets. I went about sixty rods, when I came to a dwelling-house, standing in a little opening in the woods that lined either side of the road. It was then about 11 o'clock, A. M., I had become very thirsty from constant riding in the hot sun since early in the morning; so I rode up to the door of the house, and inquired of a lady there if she would have the kindness to give me a drink of water. Said she, "I have just drawn a bucket of fresh water at the well, back there, and you can have some in welcome; but I reckon you are a Federal soldier, and if you stop to get it, you will get killed, for a Colonel and two of *our* soldiers have just this minute stepped away from the well." Without stopping to drink, I rode back into the road, and there, about two hundred yards further on, stood the Colonel and two soldiers. They did not fire at me, but the Colonel, who had his sword in his hand, gave it a defiant flourish, as if to say, "You'll catch it directly." I went back to General McPherson, and reported what I had found, who then rode out with me and saw for himself. He said it was about noon, and he would go back to dinner and send out a reconnoitering party.

While we were eating our dinner, a firing commenced on the picket-line to the rear, and in less than five minutes an entire division was engaged. Brigades of troops had been stationed near the rear pickets as a reserve. It was these troops that were attacked. The troops known as the "Iowa Brigade" of the 17th Army Corps, were among the reserves. Against this brigade were massed such overwhelming numbers, that it was compelled to give way and fall back. General McPherson immediately rode to the scene of action, and ordered up a brigade to its support. Anticipating that when the first shock of the onset was over the enemy would ease up, and swing round in mass against the rear of his left, he immediately dispatched his staff with orders to the different commanders to counteract such a move. He watched the progress of the action until satisfied that his presence was no longer needed there, and then started for the left.

The falling back and changing of position of the Iowa brigade had left a gap in our lines to the rear. Through this a part of the rebel line advanced. As we were making our way along, we met the rebel skirmish-line, whose direction of advance had become changed by the broken character of the country. A volley was fired at us, which instantly killed General McPherson, the ball passing in at one side and out at the other, piercing his heart and lungs; another wounding his horse across the breast, and another wounding his horse across the neck, and another passed through the lower part of one of the forefeet of my horse, tearing off a shoe and leaving a groove across the entire foot. Seizing the General's horse by the bridle, I led him away out of danger.

Two orderlies and a Captain of the Signal Corps were the only persons, besides myself, that were near the General when he fell. As soon as it was known that McPherson had fallen, Major-General

Logan took command of the Army of the Tennessee. "I turned the horse over to the Captain of the Signal Corps, to take care of, who despatched an orderly to Colonel Clark, Assistant Adjutant-General of McPherson's staff, with the intelligence of his death. My horse was so lamed by his wound that I could not ride him, so I took him to General Leggett's head-quarters and left him, took my gun and went to the front.

By this time the action had become general along the Army of the Tennessee, and raged furiously in front and in rear. Attaching myself to the first regiment that I came to, the 18th Missouri Infantry, I fought with my rifle until the action was over.

The contest was a desperate one, and the slaughter on both sides dreadful. Five times we jumped our works, fighting sometimes to the front and sometimes to the rear. The action did not extend beyond the Army of the Tennessee. When the action had ceased, we were ordered to fall back a short distance and throw up intrenchments. The Colonel of the regiment I was with now saw me for the first time, and, from my dress, supposing that I was a reb. trying to evade capture, said to me: "Look 'e here, mister, where do you belong?"

"I am a member of the 20th Ohio Infantry, but I belong to Gen. McPherson's head-quarters."

"What are you doing here?"

"I have been in the fight. I had my horse disabled in the beginning of the action, so I took my gun and went to fighting with your regiment, and I have been with it for two hours." I then handed him an order that General McPherson had given me, which said, "Guards, pickets, and patrols will pass Corporal Lorain Ruggles, of the 20th Ohio Veteran Volunteer Infantry, who is on special duty, at all places and at all hours, without the countersign."

When he had read it, he said, "May be General McPherson gave you that and may be you stole it from the pocket of a dead soldier. You look to me more like a *reb*. than any thing else."

I then showed him an order that General Leggett had given me to draw fresh beef for myself and scouts that messed with me. Having read it, he said, "It may all be right, but I do n't want such a looking man in my regiment; if you have got a hole you had better hunt it."

We won a victory, but at a fearful cost of life, of both officers and men. Among the fallen heroes of this war, there has been none more amiable in character, none whose services were of more value to the Government, and none whose loss was more regretted by the men of his command than the brave, gallant McPherson. He was loved and highly esteemed by all that knew him. I can scarcely describe my sorrow at his loss. My attachment had become intimate, and I felt that I had not only lost my commanding officer, but my most valued friend. Such feelings of sorrow and loneliness came over me that I was well-nigh incapacitated for duty. I had felt lonely when General Grant left the Army of the Tennessee, but now I scarcely knew what to do.

Shortly after the battle of the 22d of July, General Sherman changed his position by ordering the Army of the Tennessee to take its position on the right of the army, leaving the armies of the Ohio and the Cumberland where they were. This movement enabled General Sherman to extend his right toward the junction of the railroad to the south of Atlanta. The movement having been effected, General Logan, on the 28th of July, ordered the 16th Army Corps to advance its lines, and the 14th Corps, at the same time, to swing round its left, and the 15th Corps to swing round its right, so that the 14th and 15th Corps formed converging lines toward the intrenchments from which the 16th Corps had advanced. General Hood ordered an attack on the advancing Corps, which, when it had fairly drawn on the engagement, as had been previously arranged, fell back as if beaten, until it reached its place of starting behind its intrenchments, closely followed by the enemy. The 16th Corps then poured a tremendous fire into Hood's front, and the 14th and 15th Corps an oblique fire into his flanks. He kept pressing his men up in masses to the contest, until it seemed as if the entire Confederate army would be swept away by the terrible cross-fire to which it was exposed. The action lasted from 9 o'clock, A. M., until 5 o'clock, P. M., when the enemy withdrew, leaving his dead and wounded in our hands. The loss of the enemy was five thousand killed, besides wounded and prisoners. Our loss was very light in comparison to that of the enemy. I had no hand in this fight, but had an excellent opportunity of witnessing it. The next day I went over the battle-ground. The rebel dead lay so thick upon the ground that I could not ride along without stepping on them, and was compelled to leave my horse and proceed on foot. The destruction of life to the enemy, compared with our own loss, was greater than in any other action that I have ever witnessed.

CHAPTER XXVIII.

Goes to Ohio to recruit—Raises twenty-one men—Difficulty with the Governor—Visits Lieutenant-General Grant—Order from the War Department—Again in difficulty—Runs away from the Governor—Reports to General Sherman—Georgia raid—An amusing coincident—Reports to General Granger, at Mobile—Reports to General Grierson, in Texas—Makes a trip to the Upper Colorado—Incident at General Grant's head-quarters—The war over.

WHEN General Grant left the Western Department to take command of the armies of the United States, I felt very lonely and depressed in spirit, on account of being parted from one to whom I had become strongly attached. I might have accompanied the General to the Army of the Potomac, but I had no acquaintance with that part of the country, and I preferred to operate where I had some knowledge of army movements, as well as of the country and people. The death of General McPherson made me feel gloomy and discouraged, and in the absence from the department of my two most valued friends, I determined to seek relief for my depressed state of mind by attempting to raise an independent command of my own, for secret service purposes.

I visited Major-General Logan—then in command of the 15th Army Corps—and told him my state of mind, and that I felt as if I had rendered service valuable enough to the Government to entitle me to a command of my own, and if he thought I was worthy of it, I wanted him to assist me. He immediately drew up and gave me the following letter:

"HEAD-QUARTERS 15TH ARMY CORPS,
"BEFORE ATLANTA, GA., Aug. 15, 1864.

" *Captain L. M. Dayton, Aid-de-camp Military Division of the Mississippi:*

"CAPTAIN—The bearer, L. Ruggles, of the 20th Ohio Volunteers, has been for two years in the secret service of the Government, and has, during that time, made it his study to become efficient in all its branches. Now, feeling confident in his ability, he wishes to raise a company of scouts, and wants authority to do so. I respectfully recommend that necessary authority be given him, believing him to be eminently fit to direct the movements of such a body of men.

Under my directions, in the Mississippi campaign, through Holly Springs, Miss., and again in the Vicksburg campaign, he rendered the most signal service in obtaining information. He once entered the city of Vicksburg, during its investment, and returned with valuable and reliable information. If such authority can be, under any circumstances, granted, I respectfully recommend that it be granted him.

"Very respectfully, JOHN A. LOGAN,
" *Major-General Volunteers.*"

I carried the letter to General Leggett, who placed on it the following indorsement:

"HEAD-QUARTERS 3D DIVISION, 17TH ARMY CORPS,
"BEFORE ATLANTA, GA., Aug. 15, 1864.

"I am well acquainted with said Lorain Ruggles, and have been familiar with his career since he entered the secret service, and I can fully susberibe to all that is said for him by Major-General Logan.

" During the most of his time he has been in the secret service he has been under my direction. He has often had under his direction from six to thirty men, as scouts, and has always handled them with great skill, collecting valuable information and yet saved his men. " M. D. LEGGETT,
"*Brigadier-General.*"

From head-quarters 17th Army Corps, I received the following indorsement:

"HEAD-QUARTERS 17TH ARMY CORPS,
"NEAR ATLANTA, GA., Aug. 15, 1864.

"Respectfully forwarded. Approved.
"FRANK P. BLAIR, *Major-General.*"

At Department of Army of the Tennessee, it was indorsed as follows:

"HEAD-QUARTERS DEP'T. ARMY TENN.,
"August 15, 1864.

"Respectfully forwarded. "O. O. HOWARD,
"*Major-General.*"

The reader will bear in mind that I was a stranger to both Generals Blair and Howard. I then carried it to General Sherman, who disapproved it, as follows:

"HEAD-QUARTERS MILITARY DIVISION MISSISSIPPI,
"IN THE FIELD, NEAR ATLANTA, Aug. 15, 1864.

"Respectfully returned. There is no general law for such organization as the within. General officers, when they have secret service funds, can employ men for such secret service.
"States have had authority for raising independent companies of any kind that might be converted.
"By order of Major-General W. T. Sherman.
"L. M. DAYTON, *Aid-de-camp.*"

I was disappointed with General Sherman's decision. I felt confident that there was some way by which I could get such a command as I wanted. I went to General Leggett for advice, who, after having read General Sherman's reasons for disapproval, wrote and handed me the following letter to Governor Brough:

"HEAD-QUARTERS 3D DIV. 17TH ARMY CORPS,
"BEFORE ATLANTA, GA., August 17, 1864.

"*To his Excellency John Brough, Governor of Ohio:*

"GOVERNOR—The bearer of this communication—Corporal Ruggles, Co. H., 20th O. V. V. I.—has been in the secret service in the Army of the Tennessee for more than two years past, and has been eminently successful in that department. He has frequently had charge of considerable numbers of men employed as scouts and has always managed them with great discretion and skill.

"I would respectfully recommend that authority be obtained, if possible, for him to recruit in Ohio from among non-veteran soldiers, who have been discharged from service by reason of expiration of term of enlistment, an independent company, to be armed with Spencer rifles, and used as sharp-shooters, scouts, secret service men, etc.

"It is believed that such a company can be raised of men skilled in such service, and that the service will be greatly benefitted thereby.

"Very respectfully, your obedient servant,
"W. D. LEGGETT,
"*Brigadier-General.*"

The foregoing letter was indorsed as follows:

"HEAD-QUARTERS 15TH ARMY CORPS,
"BEFORE ATLANTA, August 17, 1864.

"Approved and recommended.   JOHN A. LOGAN,
"*Major-General Commanding.*"
"By R. R. TOWNES, *Lieutenant-Colonel and A A G.*"

"HEAD-QUARTERS 17TH ARMY CORPS,
"BEFORE ATLANTA, GA., AUGUST 17, 1864.

"Approved and strongly recommended. This man has proved himself a trusty scout, and has been of great service.

"[Signed for Major-General Blair.]

"A. J. ALEXANDER, *A. A. G.*"

"HEAD-QUARTERS ARMY AND DEP'T OF TENNESSEE,
"August 17, 1864.

"Respectfully forwarded.

"I could make good use of a *good* company, skilled as within described. I have no personal knowledge of Corporal Ruggles.

"O. O. HOWARD, *Major-General.*"

The foregoing letters and indorsements, and General Grant's indorsement—which is yet to follow—were furnished me for these pages, accompanied by the following letter by the War Department:

"WAR DEP'T, ADJUTANT-GENERAL'S OFFICE,
"WASHINGTON, August 13, 1866.

"*Mr. Lorain Ruggles, (Care of Major E. C. Downs, late of the 20th Ohio Vols., Henrie House,) Cincinnati, Ohio:*

"SIR—I have respectfully to acknowledge the receipt of your letter of the 2d inst., requesting to be furnished with copies of letters asking authority for you to raise a command of scouts, etc., with the indorsements thereon recommending the same, for publication in a work detailing your experience as a scout.

"In reply, I have to transmit herewith copies of the letters referred to, with the indorsements thereon, as requested.

"I am, sir, very respectfully, your obedient servant,

"THOMAS H. VINCENT,
"*Assistant Adjutant-General.*"

With the two letters of recommendation and their indorsements, I proceeded to Ohio, and presented them to Governor Brough, who read them over very carefully, then returned them to me, and ordered that I be furnished with the necessary recruiting papers and set to work immediately.

Having received the necessary documents, I set to work at once, and in a very short time had procured twenty-one men. With these, I went to Columbus, and reported in person to the Adjutant-General. He read over my order from the Governor, and then said, "Did you raise your men under that order as scouts?"

"Yes, sir."

"Well, there a'n't such an organization known in the United States Army Regulations as a *company of scouts*. I can't do any thing with such men."

"I can't help that," I replied; "I have acted under authority of the Governor of Ohio."

"Well, let us go and see the Governor."

We carried the order to the Governor, and the Adjutant-General explained to him that there was no such organization known in the Army Regulations.

"Well, Mr. Ruggles," said the Governor, "you go on and raise the men, and assign them to a regiment, and then have them detailed out for scouting purposes."

"That won't do at all, Governor," said I. "I have commanded detailed men long enough; I want a command of my own."

"Well, put your men into the 197th Ohio Infantry, and I will extend your time to recruit and give you a commission as Captain."

"I do n't want such a commission, Governor. I do n't want to be in the infantry service."

"Very well; I have got to fill that regiment up, because it is needed immediately at Nashville, and the men will have to go into it."

"Then take them and put them there, and I'll go to Washington," said I, and walked out.

I still held the letters of recommendation, with their indorsements. With these I proceeded to Baltimore, where I found Major-General Lewis Wallace, and obtained a pass from him to General Grant's head-quarters, at City Point, Va. I showed General Grant my papers, and told him of my difficulty. He took my papers and addressed them to the War Department, with the following indorsement:

"HEAD-QUARTERS ARMIES OF THE UNITED STATES,
"CITY POINT, VA., October 13, 1864.

"I know Private Ruggles well, and the services he rendered in Mississippi as a scout. With an independent company of such men as himself, he would be worth more in the Shenandoah Valley, and over the district of country over which Mosby roams, than a regiment of cavalry.

"I would recommend that he be authorized to raise a battalion of men, and be put in the Department of West Virginia.

"U S. GRANT, *Lieutenant-General.*"

Thus approved, General Grant sent me with them to the Secretary of War; but, as I was about to leave his quarters, he said, "Perhaps you had better show these papers to the President." Thus prepared, I bent my way toward Washington, with a somewhat lighter heart than I left the Governor's office, at Columbus, Ohio.

Finding several army officers of my acquaintance at Washington, I showed them my papers, and told them that General Grant advised me to show them to the President. My friends said that it was not necessary, so I proceeded at once to the War Department, and handed my papers, in person, to Secretary Stanton. I felt happy when I entered the office, and, though I had no conversation with the Secretary, when I came out I had lowered considerable in my own estimation. The way of doing business at the War Department seemed to me cold and repulsive. I have since been sorry that I did not carry my papers to the President. From the Secretary of War, I went to the Adjutant-General's office, and from there to the Provost-marshal General's office. There I was told to call in a week, and my papers would be ready.

Though I was somewhat crest-fallen when I left Secretary Stanton's office, I am quite sure I was not as much so as many Brigadier-Generals that I have seen making their egress since. It was so general a thing for an officer to enter that office spruced up and dignified, with hopes elated, and then to return chop-fallen and disappointed, that I could not help laughing at those I saw enter so expectant and return so downcast. It is an excellent place to cool a man's military ardor.

At the expiration of seven days, I again called at the office of the Provost-marshal General, and was handed an order of which the following is a copy:

"WAR DEP'T PROVOST-MARSHAL GENERAL'S OFFICE,
"WASHINGTON, D C., October 21, 1863.

"*To his Excellency the Governor of Ohio:*

"SIR—Subject to your approval, it is hereby ordered that Corporal Lorain Ruggles, Company H, 20th Ohio Veteran Volunteer Infantry, has authority to proceed to Ohio and raise a company of cavalry, for certain special services, whereas ordered by these head-quarters.

"Should the Corporal's success warrant it, authority will be given him to raise three additional companies—not more than one company, however, to be under recruitment at one time.

"As soon as a company is raised, he will report with it at once to these head-quarters. The men must be enrolled under the present existing regulations, for the period of one, two, or three years, as the men may choose to enlist. The company must be raised within twenty days from the time the Corporal commences to recruit.

"By order of the Secretary of War.
"JAMES B. FRY, *Provost-marshal General.*"

With this I again reported to the Governor of Ohio. He opened the order and commenced to read aloud. When he came to the date, which was 1863, when it should have been 1864, he inquired: "Where have you been for a year past?"

"You know where I have been, Governor," I replied. "You know that that paper is dated wrong."

"Well, do n't you know that when a military order is dated wrong it is *all* wrong."

"Yes; but what shall I do about it?"

"Go back to Washington and get it made right."

"I do n't want to spend so much time running about. I would like to raise a company and get back to the front *before the war closes.*" He then finished reading the order. When he had done, I asked him what he thought of it.

"Well," said he, "I would advise you not to do any thing with it as it is."

"That's my mind, exactly. *It a'n't what I wanted at all.* It looks like making a recruiting officer of me to fill up some fancy regiment. All I wanted was authority to raise a *company.* I am subject to your orders. What shall I do—go to recruiting, or go back to the front?"

"I don't know, Corporal, what you had better do."

"Well, if you don't know, I don't; so, I guess I'll leave."

I waited a few days, and then called on him again for orders, and still he did not know what I had better do. I felt as if I had rendered service to the Government that was worthy of some notice from the Chief Executive of my State, and to be treated with such indifference was to me provoking. He might have done one thing or the other: got my papers made right and set me to raising a company, or have had me ordered back to the front; but he did neither.

At length, being disgusted with making any further effort to raise a company, I went back to the front without orders, and reported to the commanding officer of my regiment. Finding that I had no order returning me to duty in the regiment, he refused to have me in his command. I then reported to Major-General Howard, who said that I was subject to order from the War Department, and that he had no authority over me. I remarked, "I guess, then, that I must be out of the service altogether. I'll go and see what General Sherman can do for me." I went to him and told him what I had done, and he said to me, "You may remain at my head-quarters until further orders."

I must say that I felt sadly disappointed and disheartened at my failure in raising a command of my own. If I had humored the Governor in the first attempt to raise a company, I would, undoubtedly have been a Captain, but I was determined to have such a command as I wanted or none. The reader must judge for himself whether I have merited it or not.

In about five days after my arrival at the front, General Sherman started on his grand campaign through Georgia. Not a doubt was entertained by the troops of their ability to march triumphant across to the Atlantic coast. Very few there were but who anticipated correctly the point of destination at the outset of the march, and at the prospect before them were highly elated. Never were men in better spirits than when the march commenced.

It was the most decisive and glorious campaign of the war, and yet fraught with the least of personal adventure of any campaign that I have taken part in. My duty was one in common with the other scouts, and the soldiers of the *entire army were all scouts*. My individual experience was not different from that of the great mass of soldiers.

Our duty was to subsist ourselves and devastate the country as completely as possible, taking good care not to get captured. This we accomplished successfully. The army never lived better and the men never enjoyed better health; and when we reached the Atlantic coast we were in better condition physically than when we started from Atlanta. The march occupied a period of seventy-seven days, every day of which we were on the move.

During our progress, though we were cut off from all communication with home, we were not altogether ignorant of General Thomas' glorious victory, and route of the Confederate army under Hood. We learned, by way of the Southern people, of "Hood's disaster," and could plainly comprehend the strategy that had drawn him unwittingly to the defenses at Nashville, and it added not a little to our courage. We plainly saw that the enemy was utterly powerless to resist our advance.

On our arrival at the coast, near Savannah, we were visited by Mr. Stanton, Secretary of War. General Leggett gave me an introduction to him, as "a very efficient and worthy scout and spy," to which he replied, "Yes, I know him."

"Does the *President* know you, Mr. Ruggles?" inquired General Leggett, surprised that the Secretary knew me.

"Yes, I expect so; I know him."

The Secretary asked me if I was acquainted about Mobile and New Orleans. I told him that I was not much acquainted about Mobile, but had been there twice, and that I was pretty well acquainted about New Orleans and Lake Pontchartrain. He asked me if I was willing to make a trip across the country and report to General Granger, and I answered, "Yes, any where."

The next morning I received an order from the War Department to proceed across the country on horseback, and report for special service to General Granger, at Mobile, Alabama. I was not limited in time to make the trip.

It was some time in the month of January, 1865, that I set out on my journey. I traveled very leisurely, and visited every place of any importance that lay near my route. I had been instructed by the Secretary of War to gather as much information as I could while passing through the country. To accomplish this, I made frequent stops to converse with the people, and I frequently rode many miles, to one side or the other of my route, to find people that were influential and leading members of society, so that I might learn the sentiments of those who wielded a controlling influence. I traveled in the disguise of a citizen carrying my order from the War Department with me. It was not often that I ventured to carry such papers with me.

I found that most of the people were willing to give up to the Federal authorities—not because they had been wrong, but because by the force of war they had become overpowered and exhausted. While there was a desire for peace, there was also a hatred of the Federal Government. A few were satisfied with the old Government as it was, and had reluctantly been drawn into rebellion by the force of the elements around them Such people hailed the overthrow of the Confederate Government with joy.

"Hood's disaster" and "Sherman's raid" had revealed to the Southern people their weakness in a more alarming view than they had ever before seen it. It seemed, in their case, that the last straw had been laid upon the camel's back, and the overloaded beast was unable to rise.

The most of the way I enjoyed my journey finely. Sometimes I would lay over several days, on account of rain and bad roads. Wherever I stopped I found something to interest me. I made it a point to make myself as interesting and agreeable to the people that entertained me as possible.

I spent three weeks in Florida. There I found the people more disheartened than anywhere else in my route; in fact, resistance to the Federal army had been given up. During my stay there I spent several days with a planter by the name of Fanshaw, who lives near the coast, at St. Marks. He was formerly from the State of New York. I passed myself while there by my real name, and as a brother of General Ruggles, and represented that I was on my way home to Bolivar County, Mississippi, from Savannah, Georgia, where I had been on business pertaining to the Confederate Government. I gave him such an account of the general state of affairs all over the Confederate States that he did not doubt, in the least, the statements that I made. When I called at his house I had no intentions of remaining there long, but his hospitality was so strongly urged upon me that I accepted it to enable my horse to rest.

While staying there I was much amused by reading a story in the Natchez (Miss.) Courier concerning myself. How the paper had made its way there I can not tell. Miss Ella, a daughter of Mr. F.'s, handed me the piece to read, remarking that it was one of the curious incidents of the war. Little did she think that in presenting it to me she was making it doubly so.

The story was written by Mr. James Dugan, a friend of mine in the 14th Illinois Infantry. Sergeant Downs, of the 20th Ohio, had related to Mr. Dugan several of the incidents in my experience as scout; and from one of those he wrote a romance, in which I figured as the hero, giving instead of my full name only the initial letter to my surname, together with the name of my company and regiment. It was given to the public as a narrative of facts, and the announcement made that an extended history of my services would be forthcoming from the able pen of Captain Downs. It was first published in 1863, in the paper I have before mentioned.

Coming to me as it did, under such peculiar circumstances, it amused me exceedingly. I took good care, however, that my lady friend did not find out that I was the hero of the story. My feelings at the time can be better imagined by perusing it. It ran as follows:

"On board the magnificent steamer 'Imperial,' on her passage from St. Louis to New Orleans, in the month of October, A. D. 1860, reclining upon one of those elegantly-furnished sofas in her sumptuous cabin, might have been seen the hero of our story wrapped in a 'brown study.'

"His form was attractive and commanding; something over a medium size, and well proportioned. His features were pleasant, and his hair brown and wavy, extending in a rich profusion of glossy curls down over his shoulders. His eyes were of a deep blue, and as sharp and piercing as those of an eagle. His forehead was broad and high, imparting a look of more than usual intelligence; indeed, he was what might be called a handsome fellow, and though he has passed the age of five and twenty, he looked as fair and fresh as though but just of age. Lorain R——s (the subject of our sketch) was a resident of Ohio, but was then on his way to New Orleans on business.

"It is said that Lorain once loved a beautiful and accomplished young lady of an amiable disposition, and, withal, of no inconsiderable wealth; but upon the very day upon which they were to have been married he followed her remains to their long home. Three years had passed since then, and he had found no fair one to fill the heart thus made vacant.

"As he sits reclined upon that sofa, he is meditating upon the strange vicissitudes of life. Recollections of scenes in his own experience pass vividly before him, and, as if but yesterday, he strolls for the last time in the green meadow. Just as the declining sun is shedding his last lingering rays across the landscape, accompanied by his own angelic Belinda, and as they are about to pass the gate to her father's house, they pause for a moment, and with her soft fingers playfully twirling his glossy curls, she presses her lips to his and whispers, '*My own dear Lorain!*'

"Since then three summers have passed without obliterating the blank in his heart caused by the transfer of his fair one to the spirit land, and he wonders whether, indeed, there was but one heart born whose emotions of love can soften his. Again and again he recalls the scenes of his love until his eyes are suffused with tears. Dashing them away, he starts from his seat and mingles with the gay crowd that are passengers with him.

"Among those passengers was a young man by the name of Charles Rollins, who had just finished a course of education at one of our northern colleges, and was then on his way home. He was a young man of an ardent temperament, of fine appearance and accomplished manners. His parents resided at Natchez, Mississippi.

"Lorain sought relief from the recollections that had passed him by seeking to make the acquaintance of those around him. The fine manly bearing of Charles attracted his attention, and he at once sought an interview, which proved to be agreeable. Frequent interviews were had, and their acquaintance soon ripened into friendship.

"Charles had a sister—an only one—by the name of Annie. She was then entering upon her twenty-fourth year; and though not in the strict sense of the word handsome, she was, nevertheless, good looking, and possessed of what is of more consequence than beauty—all the graces that adorn the life of a devoted, exemplary Christian. She had early embraced the Christian religion, and her pure devotion, genial nature, and agreeable manners won for her the love and respect of all who knew her.

"Annie had received the attentions of several young men of unexceptionable character and reputation, possessed, withal, of that worldly competence and business tact that would have placed her, beyond doubt, above want for means to administer to her worldly comforts; and yet, strange to say, she saw reason to decline their offers. Why she had failed to love was known, if at all, only to herself. Her parents would have been pleased to have seen their daughter united in holy wedlock to a worthy young man that she loved; nevertheless, they had too much respect for her judgment to question the propriety of her decisions and the reasons for them, and the only reason, perhaps, that they could assign was that old and common one, 'matches are made in heaven.'

"The entire passage from St. Louis passed off agreeably to our new-made friends, and, sooner than they could have wished it, the signal was sounded to land at the beautiful town of Natchez. There Lorain was unable to refuse the pressing invitation from Charles to stop and spend a few days, or at least a night, with him at his father's house.

"It is not necessary to describe the introduction that followed, nor the welcome that was extended. Suffice it to say, the journey was not renewed the next day, nor the next. A week rolled around, and then another, and another, until three months had passed, and still Lorain was a welcome guest at the home of the Rollinses. At the end of that time Lorain and Annie were engaged to be married.

"At last business became so urgent that Lorain was obliged to resume his journey to New Orleans. The hour came for departure, and he sought a last interview with Annie, to give her the parting farewell.

"During the winter of 1860 and '61, the country, North and South, had become agitated with political excitement, which ran so high that the two sections seemed in imminent danger of becoming involved in a civil war. The South claimed that the North had encroached upon her rights, and even went so far as to threaten to withdraw from the Federal compact and take up the sword in vindication of her rights.

"As Lorain was about to leave, Annie still clung to his hand, and said: 'My dear Lorain, before you leave me, I want you to make me one promise.'

"'Well, Annie, what is it?'

"'You know, Lorain, that our nation is being shaken to its center by political excitement, and it is more than probable that before I shall see you again the Southern States will secede from the Union, and the country become involved in war. Promise me that in case the South becomes engaged in war with the North, you will not take up arms against her.'

"'My dear Annie, as much as I love you, I can not make you that promise. The North is my birthplace and home. I love and respect the flag under which I was cradled, and if the country needs my services to preserve her glorious nationality, I am under sacred obligations to render assistance.'

"She pressed his hand warmly and drew him closer; her eyes filled with tears and her bosom heaved with emotion as she said, 'Make me, then, at least this promise—if the country does become involved in war, with you upon one side and Charles upon the other, and you should chance to meet him as your enemy, you will, dearest Lorain, *spare my brother.*'

"'Yes,' he uttered, as he imprinted a farewell kiss upon her nectar lips.

"Time rolled on, and, as had been anticipated, one after another of the Southern States seceded and took up arms against the North, and involved the country in a civil war. Charles Rollins, as his sister had feared, identified himself with the interest of his own State, and enlisted in a Mississippi regiment of infantry. Lorain R——s, true to his country and his country's flag, rallied at the first call of the President to save his country from destruction.

"His devoted patriotism and noble bearing, and his obstinate bravery in the hour of battle, won for him the confidence of his commanding officers, who often sent him on missions of danger. General Grant, having learned of his reliability, address, and daring, frequently sent him to obtain information of the enemy's movements.

"In November, 1861, preparatory to moving the grand army south into Mississippi, and while the troops were being concentrated in the vicinity of Lagrange, Tenn., General Grant sent Mr. R——s out, on horseback, to find the enemy's advanced pickets. It was in the night, and extremely dark, which rendered the undertaking a hazardous one. He felt his way along with utmost caution, and had made a distance of twenty miles, when, in the midnight darkness, not six feet in advance of him, he was confronted by a single sentry, standing in the middle of the road, who challenged him with 'Halt! who comes there?'

"It was a desperate situation, and Mr. R——s determined to make the best of it. 'Friend, with the countersign,' he answered, drawing his revolver.

"'Advance and give the countersign,' was the reply.

Mr. R——s did advance, and, thrusting his revolver to the breast of the sentry, fired. The flash of his piece revealed to him the face of Charles Rollins! *'Oh heavens!'* he cried, and sprang from his horse and embraced the fallen form. 'Charles! Charles! speak! if but once; for God's sake, speak!'

"It was too late; the ball had penetrated his heart, and Charles was dead. The sharp report aroused his sleeping companions, who were lying by the roadside, a little distance from him, and the noise they made as they sprang for their guns warned Mr. R——s of his danger, who quickly sprang to his saddle and dashed away unharmed, but not without being fired at by the remaining pickets. He made a safe return, and reported to General Grant, but since that time his acquaintances have noticed that he has become a changed man."

I arrived at General Granger's head-quarters in Mobile, Alabama, April 9, 1865, the next day after the capture of Blakely. I had traveled in all, since leaving Savannah, a distance of nine hundred miles, and that without molestation.

During my journey, two of the most important events of the war had transpired. General Lee had surrendered his command to General Grant, and

General Johnston had surrendered his command to General Sherman. Kirby Smith's command, west of the Mississippi, was the only armed force that had not surrendered.

The returned Confederate soldiers, wherever I met them in my route, had expressed themselves as satisfied with their attempt to sustain the Confederacy, and gave it up as a lost cause. Experience is said to be the "best school-master." The Confederate soldiers evidently thought so.

A few days after my arrival, the intelligence was received that President Lincoln had been murdered. It was too sad intelligence for the soldiers to believe, nor would they believe it until officially confirmed. Then their anger knew no bounds, and it was with the utmost difficulty that commanding officers restrained their men from committing retaliatory depredations.

In the midst of a nation's rejoicing, she was called to mourn the death of the man who had steered the Ship of State clear of the shoals that threatened her destruction, was to be swept from the helm as the ship was entering the haven of peace, and within sight of her desired moorings. While it was hard to deprive him thus of the sweet anticipations in prospect before him, it was nevertheless necessary, in the wise directions of a beneficent Providence. The murder of Abraham Lincoln was necessary as the closing act of the great rebellion. The picture of the scene, revolting as it had been, was not complete until the finishing shades of blackness had been added by the hand of an assassin.

The war was now virtually closed, and during our stay at Mobile General Granger had nothing for me to do. In July he moved to New Orleans, taking most of his troops with him. It was generally supposed that we were going there to take transports home to our respective States, to be mustered out; but in this we were disappointed. At that place General Granger ordered me to report to the Provost-marshal for duty as a detective. Why I was so often selected for such duty is more than I can tell. If I had all other necessary qualifications for that business, my dislike for it was so great as to overcome them. I went to the Provost-marshal with my order, and told him that I was at his disposal for duty, but that I had objections to engaging in that kind of service—not that I was unwilling to obey my superior officers, but simply because I had a dislike for the business that it was impossible for me to overcome. I told him that I had twice tried to operate as a detective and had failed, and the more I tried it the less I liked it. It was a kind of duty that was not congenial to my nature, and it seemed to me like low business. I was satisfied that there were those who were better adapted to such business than I, but if he insisted upon it I would go to work and do the best that I knew how.

He told me that he had but very little detective business to do, and that he did not wish to have me engaged in business that was not agreeable to my feelings. He told me to return to General Granger's head-quarters, and that if he found occasion to need my services he would send for me.

I have since had reason to suspect that setting me to work as a detective was simply a show of something for me to do, on the part of commanding officers, that I might be retained in the service longer, lest, in the future, something might turn up that would give them occasion to need me. At that time there was great clamoring among the soldiers to be mustered out, and orders had been issued to muster out all detached men who were not actively engaged.

We remained in New Orleans until the latter part of July, when we embarked on board the transports and went to Galveston, Texas. At that place there was as little for me to do as there had been in New Orleans. Having no use for me, General Granger sent me to Columbus, Texas, a distance of one hundred and sixty miles inland, to report to General Grierson.

I made the journey alone and on horseback, dressed as a citizen. For the last year and a half of my service, I very rarely wore any thing but a citizen's dress. I occupied five days in making the journey, and got through to General Grierson's headquarters without having experienced a single incident of interest. That kind of scouting was dry business to me. It is excitement that makes the life of a scout interesting.

I made several trips of from twenty to sixty miles inland for General Grierson, but none of them was attended with any incident. The fact was, the war was over, and there was nothing for a scout to do. General Kirby Smith had before this surrendered his command, and there was no regularly organized Confederate force to contend with. The only disturbance was from lawless, evil-disposed persons, who roamed over the country, robbing both loyal and disloyal alike, their sole object being plunder.

In September General Grierson sent me alone to the Upper Colorado, a distance of four hundred miles, with instructions to see whether the rebs were concentrating a force or fortifying at any point along the river. I made the trip on horseback, in my usual citizen's dress. Very much of the distance was sparsely settled, which rendered my journey at least a lonesome one. A naturalist, no doubt, would have found in that route enough to have made a volume interesting, but to me nothing was of so much interest as the end of my journey. During the entire route it was the same dull monotony day after day.

On my return, and when within four days' ride of Columbus, I fell in with a party of outlaws numbering forty men. They wore uniforms exactly like General Grierson's cavalry, and had United States saddles and carbines. At first I supposed that they were a detachment of his command, but fortunately I discovered my mistake before having told who I was. They plundered indiscriminately, but left the impression, wherever they went, that they were a detachment of United States troops, acting under General Grierson's orders. I traveled with them three days.

As soon as I found out what they were I proposed to join their organization. This I did for my own safety. I represented myself as having been a planter in Mississippi, and that I had lost all my property by the war—a part of it by the Confederate army and a part of it by the Lincoln army; and I also told them that I was determined to get my property back in some way, and did not care a d—n how nor who I got it from. My proposition was accepted, and it was arranged that I should go on to Columbus and transact some business that I had there, and, if possible, secure by some means, fair or foul, a uniform, saddle, and carbine, and then return to a certain plantation that they would show me in our route.

The last day that I was with them, we passed the plantation to which I was to return when I had completed my business at Columbus. Toward night they plundered a rich planter who had never been at heart really disloyal. He had acted with the Confederate Government simply because compelled to, but at his earliest opportunity had taken the required oath. As the outlaws were taking his property, he remonstrated, and told them that he was a Union man, and that General Grierson had promised to protect him. They told him that he was no Union man, but a d—d lying secesh. They insulted him shamefully, and then, having secured what plunder they wanted, made their way off, leaving him to suppose that the outrage had been committed by Federal cavalry.

During my ride with them I became quite familiar with their countenances, and also learned where several of them resided. I also found out that they did not, except when on a plundering expedition, remain in a body, but separated to their homes, meeting occasionally, however, to arrange for new expeditions, but never twice in the same place, lest their haunts might be discovered. Shortly after plundering the planter that I have mentioned, they turned off on another road and left me to pursue my journey alone.

After repeating to General Grierson the result of my trip, I mentioned the incident about the outlaws, and their having plundered the planter, but did not tell him that I had agreed to return to them. The day following my report, the planter came in with complaint to General Grierson that his cavalry had plundered him of his horses and mules, and other property, and also had shamefully insulted him.

General Grierson was surprised to hear such complaints, and told the man that he must be mistaken; but he insisted that he knew they were his men; they had United States uniforms, saddles, and carbines exactly like his men. The General then called the Adjutant, to know whether he had sent a detachment out, but none had been sent. The planter still insisted that it was United States cavalry that committed the outrage. Recalling to mind what I had reported to him the day before, the General mistrusted who had done it and sent for me. I at once recognized the planter as the one whom I had seen plundered by the outlaws.

The next day I accompanied a detachment of cavalry, in disguise, to hunt up the outlaws. We proceeded at once to the residences of those that I had learned, and were so fortunate as to find them at home, all of whom we captured. I took good care to be seen by them as little as possible. I do not think I was recognized by any of the number that we captured. Every one of them were loud in their declarations of good behavior, and expressed astonishment that they should be so treated. The arrest of a part of the band put a damper upon the rest, and they cleared out, or ceased their operations. I heard of no more complaints during the time I remained there.

From what experience I have had in the secret service, I am of the opinion that the Government has been entirely too lenient with that class of men. Nothing but the severest penalty of the law will ever stop them from their depredations. They will continue to give trouble in the South so long as they are allowed to run at large. They are possessed of none of the finer feelings of humanity that can be reached by moral persuasion, and nothing but physical restraint can control them.

Sympathy for those that have erred is a fine and commendable element in the human heart, but when carried to extremes is productive of disastrous results. I think the entire secession element of the South has received, and is now receiving, more favor at the hands of the Government than is consistent for the safety of our republican institutions. People who have committed crime should be made to feel that they have done so by inflicting upon them the proper penalty. Let rebels prove themselves "prodigal sons" before being embraced in the arms of our good Uncle Samuel.

On the 2d day of December, 1865, I received an order from General Grant to proceed to Columbus, Ohio, for discharge. On my arrival there, I reported to the Provost-marshal, who refused to discharge me, because I had no copy of the orders under which I had reported from one commanding officer to another. My business had been such that it was not safe for me to carry them, and, for the same reason, my orders were generally given orally. I went to General Leggett and told him my difficulty, who at once wrote me a statement to Captain Barber, Provost-marshal, setting forth his knowledge of my services, and why I had not preserved my orders of detail. General Wiles also gave me a similar statement, of which the following are copies:

"ZANESVILLE, O., February 15, 1866.
"*Captain Barber, Provost-marshal:*
"DEAR SIR—Corporal Lorain Ruggles, Co. H, 20th O. V. V. I., reports to me that he has difficulty in obtaining a discharge from the service. Corporal Ruggles was used, during the whole war, as a scout and spy. I first assigned him to that service early in the summer of 1862. His great success made him a favorite with all general officers having charge of secret service. He was, at different times, under the immediate direction of Generals Force, Ross, Logan, McPherson, Blair, Grant, and others, generally remaining, when not on active duty, at my head-quarters. The nature of his services were such that he could not carry details, passes, or orders, and, details could not be waited for by officers when he was needed, and, in fact, were very seldom made in such cases.

"Corporal Ruggles was regarded as one of the most successful and reliable spies in the United States service, and was always called upon for desperate service where others would fail, and was equal to the undertaking.

"I hope you will secure him such a discharge as will enable

him to draw his pay. He has been a most worthy soldier. I doubt whether any man of his rank has done more for his country.

"Very respectfully, "M. D. LEGGETT,
"*Late Major-General of Volunteers.*"

"ZANESVILLE, O., February 17, 1866.
"*Captain Barber, Provost-marshal, Columbus, Ohio:*

"DEAR SIR—I certify that I have long known Corporal Lorain Ruggles, of the 20th O. V. V. I. (Said regiment was one of the regiments comprising the brigade of which I had the honor to command.) I further certify that I have known Corporal Ruggles as a scout and spy since about the mouth of June or July, 1862. He was in the secret service, under orders from Generals Grant, Sherman, McPherson, Leggett, Force, Ross, and others. He was regarded as one of the best and most reliable scouts connected with our army, and, in my judgment, has performed as much valuable service as any man in it, and I have no doubt but he is entitled to an honorable discharge, although he may be unable to account for his absence from his regiment and company by exhibiting the necessary documents. The most of his details were oral, being ordered by one officer to report to another officer for special duty. I have used him myself for scouting, by permission of the commanding General. It is with pleasure that I add this my testimony in favor of a gallant and trustworthy soldier.

"I am, Captain, respectfully, your obedient servant,
"G. F. WILES,
"*Late Colonel 78th O. V. V. I., Brevet Brig.-Gen.*"

Generals Leggett and Wiles have my thanks for the kind interest thus, and upon all other occasions, manifested in my behalf. With those letters, I was enabled to get a discharge from the service that I am proud of, and which I value more than all the gold that I might have made in dishonest traffic with outlaws. I have never been sorry that I followed General Grant's advice.

After having received my discharge, I experienced trouble in getting my pay. I could scarcely get the Paymaster to look at me, let alone paying me. Finding that I could prevail nothing upon the Paymaster at Columbus, I reported at once, in person, to Lieutenant-General Grant, at Washington, D. C., and told him my troubles. He caused my papers to be fixed so that I not only received all my pay proper, clothing account, etc., but my special service pay. Here I would express to General Grant my gratitude for the pains he has taken to instruct me in the class of duties that I have had to perform, and for his personal interest in my welfare. I am indebted to all the Generals for whom I have served for their kindness, and the instructions they have given me, and especially so to Generals Grant, Logan, McPherson, Leggett, Force, Ross, Potts, and Wiles. I always found a welcome at their headquarters.

As I was about to leave General Grant's apartment, the door opened from the Adjutant-General's office, and in stepped the South Carolina General who had taken my field-glasses from me at the Confederate House, in Jackson, Mississippi. I knew him in a moment. "General," said I, addressing Grant, "that's the son of a b—h that took my field-glasses from me at Jackson, Miss.

"Tut, tut, tut!" said General Grant. "Remember that the war is over now; you should not talk so." (Addressing the South Carolina General,) "Do you know that man?"

"No, sir, I have no recollection of him."

"Do n't you remember," said I, addressing him, "of taking a pair of field-glasses from a citizen at the Confederate House, in Jackson, Miss., at the time President Davis was there, and saying that 'citizens have no use for such things and Generals have?'"

"Yes, I remember the circumstances. Are you the gentleman?"

"No, G—d d—m you! *you* are the *gentleman.*"

"Hut, tut, tut! do n't talk that way now, Mr. Ruggles," said General Grant, with a suppressed smile on his countenance.

"I reckon I can pay you for your glasses," said the South Carolinian, running his hand in his pocket.

"No you can't," said I; "the whole stinking Confederacy would not pay for them."

If the glasses had been worth thousands of dollars, I would not have taken a cent for them in the presence of General Grant. A recollection of the incident, as occurring in the character that I was in, is all the compensation that I want. Had that character been known at that time and place, my life would have been of less value than the glasses.

CHAPTER XXIX.

Ludicrous effect of fear—A Corporal outflanks a Captain—A good Union man—A touching appeal—A scene among the wounded—An old Secesh discovers his mistake—Suggestions from experience—Concluding thoughts.

In looking back over my experience, I can recall to mind many little incidents not included in the preceding narratives. It is sometimes amusing to witness the effect of fear upon persons of different habits and constitutions. I often think of my own ludicrous sensations in my first engagement—that of Fort Donelson.

Being naturally a hearty eater, and not overly brave, I have a peculiar regard for all that concerns my appetite, and I fancied that if I was to be hit at all it would be in my "bread-basket."

When our Colonel had formed us in line of battle and brought us to an "order arms," he said: "My brave soldiers, I am pleased with the coolness and courage that I see depicted upon every face. [I was glad he did n't see mine, for my knees were smiting each other, and I was pressing my 'bread-basket' with both hands.] We are not going to have a *skirmish*, nor an *engagement*, nor a *fight*, but a BATTLE! [I was done for then, sure, and my hands pressed the "bread-basket" harder than before.] Draw your cartridge-boxes well to the front, [I tell you, the command suited me, and I got mine round in a hurry!] and act yourselves like MEN!" I can't say that I acted like a man, but I would have given considerable to have got my "bread-basket" away from there! I am happy to add that when the battle was over the "bread-basket" was all right, and has given me but very little trouble since.

I once came near getting into difficulty by not properly doing my duty while on picket. It was at Shiloh Church, a few weeks after the battle, and while the main part of the army was engaged in besieging Corinth. The entire regiment was more or less troubled with that terrible scourge of the army, camp diarrhea, and the men were constantly contriving some way to get through the picket line in search of chickens and fresh vegetables.

One morning, soon after I had taken my post on picket duty, for the first time in my life—I was a corporal of the guard—a squad of men from my own company came down to my post, without passes, and said that they wanted to go out and get some vegetables, and, if I would pass them, they would divide with me when they came in, to which I assented.

Toward night they came back to my post, and left, as my share of the proceeds of the trip, two very fat chickens, and a nice lot of onions, lettuce, and radishes. It so happened that just after the men left the post for camp, Captain R———s, of my regiment, who was in command of the guard, made his appearance to inspect the condition of his men, and, discovering the party who had just left, mistrusted that I had passed them in, and, of course, took me to task about it.

"Did those men come through the lines here?" inquired the Captain.

"Yes, sir," I answered.

"Did they have passes?"

"I do n't know whether they did or not. I did not ask them."

"Did they go out here this morning?"

"Yes, sir."

"Did you allow them to go out without passes?"

"I did n't ask them for passes. I did n't know they needed them. They said that they were going after vegetables, and I know that they needed them bad enough, so I supposed it was all right."

"What were you placed here for?"

"To watch the enemy, I suppose. I did not know that I had to watch my friends."

"Well, sir, if you do n't know your duty better than that, you are not fit to be a Corporal. I'll report you to the Colonel, sir, and have you reduced."

The Captain then went on and left me to my own reflections. I cared very little about being an eighth Corporal, and yet I disliked the idea of becoming disgraced by being reduced. I dressed my chickens nicely, and laid them away where they would be safe until morning. As soon as the relief came out, I started across the woods to camp. Taking my nicest chicken and some of my nicest vegetables in my hands, I repaired to the Colonel's tent. I knew that he had been unwell, and unable to procure what vegetables he needed. On entering, I saluted him as politely as I knew how, and then said: "Colonel, I knew that you was not very well, and I thought you would relish some chicken and fresh vegetables. Will you accept them?"

"Thank you, thank you, Corporal," said he, taking them, and looking very much pleased. "They are just what I wanted exactly. Were you on picket yesterday."

"Yes, sir, and I expect that I have incurred your displeasure."

"Why so?"

"Well, Colonel, I'll tell you. It's the first time that I was ever on picket, and I did not know what the duty of a Corporal was. There were some men from the regiment came down and wanted to go out, and I let them go without passes, and the Captain says that he is going to report me for it. I am very sorry, Colonel, that I did it, and if you will forgive me this time I won't do so again."

"Picket duty, Corporal, is one of the most responsible duties of the soldier. It should always be faithfully discharged. Since this is the first offense, I'll overlook it, if you will do better in the future."

"Thank you, Colonel; I will certainly do better the next time."

Just as I came out the Captain entered; so I remained where I could hear the conversation that followed. After the usual salutation, he said: "I am sorry, Colonel, that I am under the necessity of re-reporting to you one of the Corporals under my command yesterday for a non-performance of duty."

"Was it Corporal Ruggles," inquired the Colonel.

"Yes, sir; he—"

"Never mind, Captain; he reported himself this morning and promised to do better, and I forgave him this offense."

When the Captain came out, I noticed that he felt considerably worked up at being outflanked by a Corporal.

While encamped at Shiloh, I became acquainted with an old man, whose age was nearly three-score and ten, then a refugee from home on account of his loyalty to the Government. He had spent several weeks secreted in a swamp, to keep out of the hands of his neighbors, and on the arrival of the Union army had come into our lines for protection.

The old man was plain and outspoken in his views, and when the subject of secession was being agitated in that part of Tennessee where he lived, he boldly declared his determination to adhere to the Union. The neighbors, unwilling to give the old man up, appointed a secession meeting on a certain evening, and procured one of their ablest speakers to discuss the question at issue, and invited him over. The time appointed came, and with it the speaker. The house was crowded with anxious listeners, but the old man was not among them. Before proceeding with the exercises, a delegation was appointed to wait upon the old man and get him out to the meeting. He at first refused to attend, but at last yielded to their importunities and went over. A chair was brought in and a seat given him close by the speaker's stand, and the speaker commenced. The old man listened very attentively to the entire harangue, and his friends felt sure that the arguments were having the desired effect.

When the speaker had finished and sat down, one of the delegates arose and asked the old man if he had learned any thing new.

"Yes, I think I have," he replied.

"Well, what is it?"

"I have learned that you are a d—d sight bigger fools than I had thought you were. Your arguments amount to nothing. As for me, I was *born* a Union man, I have *lived* a Union man, and I mean to *die* a Union man!"

It was then hinted that he might get hung if he continued to give utterance to such language. He replied:

"Gentlemen, you may hang and be d—d! I want you to understand that I am a *Union man. Every thing about me is Union.* You may hang me on a gallows higher than Haman, and then cut me down and make mince-meat of my body and feed it to the dogs, and the *dogs will be good Union dogs!*"

Having thus pointedly expressed himself, he left the house and returned home, leaving his neighbors in an angry mood over his obstinacy. Half an hour later a son-in-law informed him that the meeting had determined that he should either renounce his sentiments or be hung. A rapid flight to the swamp saved his life.

Thus you see that treason has neither respect for the silver hairs of old age nor the strongest ties of blood.

It is oftentimes affecting to witness the heroic manner in which soldiers endure their sufferings, whether from sickness or wounds.

There was in my company a man by the name of Frank R——d, who, for several months, had been careless about writing to his mother, who was a widow. At last the poor widow's heart could stand the suspense no longer, and she wrote to a daughter, then living in the State of Indiana, to assist her in her efforts to find out what had become of Frank. The sister immediately wrote to the Captain of the company to learn the fate of her brother. The neglect on the part of Frank to write was not for lack of affection, but simply because of a careless habit. At last Frank was taken sick with a fever, and rapidly grew worse. The regiment was preparing to move from Paducah, Ky., up the Tennessee River, and it became necessary to leave Frank in the hospital. Just a few moments before he was to be carried off from the boat, his Captain received the letter from his sister, inquiring what had become of Frank. The Captain carried the letter to him and read it, and then said, "Frank, what shall I write to your sister?"

He thought a moment, and then, his eyes filling with tears, he said: "Oh, for God's sake, Captain, *do n't tell sister how sick I am!*"

It was affecting indeed to see the heroism with which that dear boy suffered, and his affectionate and tender regard for his sister; was unwilling that she should know the extent of his sufferings lest she should worry about him.

"Brave boy! he has gone at his country's call."

The first mail after we left him brought the sad intelligence that Frank was dead.

Wounded soldiers generally manifest a cheerful resignation to their lot that is astonishing to those who have never witnessed it. Sometimes, however, exceptions occur. I often think of an incident that I witnessed in which two extremes met.

After the battle of Matamora, where General Hurlbut's command routed General Price's army, on its retreat after having been repulsed in its assault upon Corinth, I assisted in taking care of the wounded as they were brought in. Among the sufferers on that day was a Captain, with a flesh wound in the arm, and a private, with a leg dreadfully shattered below the knee. The Captain—though his wound was not of a serious nature—gave way to his feelings, and took on dreadfully, and frequently called upon the doctor to come and dress his wound or he should die. The private, then on the table, preparatory to an amputation of his limb, was heroically cool, and scarce a groan escaped his lips. At length his nerves could no longer stand the ridiculous clamor of the Captain, and he called out, "Captain, if you do n't hush your gab until the doctor gets my leg off I'll throw it at you."

The soldier endured the operation manfully, and the Captain took the hint and "dried up" his noise. It is not hard to tell which of the two was the bravest man.

I was once very much amused by the mistake of a very old man. It happened in this way. I had been sent out on a scout, and was returning to camp, when I called at a plantation-house to get breakfast for myself and squad. Sitting upon the porch in front of the house was a very old man—a secesh—engaged in twisting up tobacco. He had a large pile of it before him already twisted. He had never seen any soldiers from either army. As we came up to the porch he kept on at his work, without being in the least alarmed at our appearance. We procured what breakfast we wanted, and was about to leave, when, addressing the old man, I said: "How do you do, daddy?"

"Speak a little louder," said the old man; "I'm hard of hearing."

"*How do you do, daddy?*" said I again, louder than before.

"Oh, I'm pretty well, I thank you. I'm a little tired now. I've got five or six little grandsons down in General Villipigue's army, and I heard that they were out of tobacco, and I thought I'd twist up some and take down to 'em."

"Boys," said I to the squad, "if you had rather the rebs would have that tobacco than to have it yourselves, let it alone."

At that the boys made a spring for the tobacco.

"Hut, tut, tut!" said the old man, looking wonderfully surprised; "I guess I was mistaken. I thought you were *our soldiers;* but I guess, from your *actions,* you are *Yankees.*"

On leaving a service that has been fraught with as much danger as that of mine has been, it is not improper, perhaps, for me to leave on record the conclusions suggested by that experience.

Few, if any, of my cotemporaries who started in the business as early as I did are now living. I know of none that are living who operated in the departments where I did, and who commenced when I did and continued as late as I did. Of eighteen (including myself) that commenced when I did, I am the only one that continued through the war. Fifteen of that number were killed in less than two years, and two were disgraced for bad conduct.

When I look back upon what I have experienced, it seems a wonder to me that my life has been spared. Others, whom I thought were my superiors in all the necessary qualifications, have sacrificed their lives in their line of duty.

It may be thought by some that a scout is of necessity of that hardened, reckless character that is insensible to the dangers that surround him; but that is a mistake. It is true that war is hardening to the finer sensibilities, but, nevertheless, if a man is unconscious of the danger of his undertaking, he is not apt to exercise the necessary precautionary measures to insure his safety, and, consequently, fails in his mission.

I can now look back and see how I might have done better. I commenced the business without having had experience, and, consequently, I had all to learn as I went along. At first I only ventured a short distance out, and thought I had done extremely well if I reached camp unharmed. I increased gradually the extent of my expeditions, until

I succeeded in making trips of several hundred miles in length.

An adaptation of means to the end to be accomplished is of as much importance in scouting and spying, as in any other branch of business. The very business itself is an evasion of what you really are, or assuming to be what you are not; consequently, an evasion of the truth is often necessary to accomplish the purpose. To be successful as a spy, it is absolutely necessary to be able to act an assumed character.

The disguise of the individual and his plan of operations must be adapted to the particular time and place, and his success must depend greatly upon his address. Generals have frequently told me, before going out, how to address myself to the undertaking; but, as it is impossible to know beforehand the circumstances under which one will be placed, it is necessary that a man be of ready address, in order to adapt himself to any unexpected state of affairs that he might find.

Presence of mind, when suddenly and unexpectedly confronted, is very essential. When a man in that situation is thrown off his guard, his condition can rarely be retrieved.

A man should never lose confidence in his own case, nor despair of escape if captured; if he does, his case becomes hopeless. Never but once was I in a situation where hope entirely left me, and that was when I was about to be shot as a spy by a Colonel of Bragg's cavalry; and even then I did not despair until the deadly weapon was being leveled at my heart.

A spy should have as little superfluous or unnecessary conversation as possible. His information should mainly be derived by observation. I once came across a spy that General Grant had sent out, who was an inveterate talker. I was alarmed for his safety, and, as soon as an opportunity occurred, I said to him, "You talk too much. General Grant pays me for *seeing*, and not for *talking*." The fellow made fun of my advice. What became of him I do not know; he never returned to our lines.

Scouts sometimes get frightened; I have been. So do commanding officers and enlisted men. I have known a Major-General to dodge at the whiz of a bullet, and a whole regiment to become stampeded by a runaway mule! The best of men are sometimes the victims of fear. It should, however, be guarded against.

I made a practice of getting all the information that I could, without exposing myself to a danger of recognition, concerning the different regiments in the Confederate service. It was often of great service to me to know where such regiments were raised, and who commanded them, and also what brigades, divisions, and departments they were in. The names and residence of prominent individuals were also of great service to me. A knowledge of the language and habits of the people, anywhere a spy travels, is of great advantage. I have no idea that I would have succeeded as I did if I had not lived in the South before the war commenced.

I have been very successful in managing scouting and forage parties. I attribute it to the fact that I always watched for myself and my men. I have known several officers and their details to get captured because of depending entirely on the men to do the watching. Men become careless in such duties, and a surprise is often the consequence.

In my travels in the enemy's country, I was very particular to observe the features of the country through which I passed—whether wooded, cultivated, level, or hilly; the condition of the roads—whether hard, sandy, or wet; the condition of the streams and their location—whether fordable or not, and the manner of crossing and the nature of their banks. Also, the location of springs and wells, and the supply of water that they afford. Such information is of great value to a commanding officer.

There is great responsibility resting upon a scout and spy. If his reports are reliable, the commanding officer knows how to execute his movements successfully; but if his reports are false, and the commanding officer relies upon them as truth, his movements will, as likely as not, end in disaster, with a sacrifice of hundreds, and perhaps thousands, of lives.

It is far better for a scout, if he fails to accomplish his mission, to report it a failure, for, sooner or later, it will be found out. It is mortifying to fail in one's mission, but that is of little consequence compared with jeopardizing a whole army. I have several times failed to accomplish my missions, but my reporting of such failures has always tended to increase the confidence of my employers in my reliability.

Having finished my services for the Government,

I am once more a citizen, engaged in the pursuits of civil life. I have "beaten my sword into a plowshare, and my bayonet into a pruning-hook," and have become a resident of the "far West;" and though I "became a changed man," and did not take for a better-half "Miss Annie," nevertheless I am married and settled in life, and can look back with proud satisfaction upon the result of my labors.

Now, reader, you have followed me in my humble career from the commencement of the war to its close, and you are able to judge whether the part that I have played is of consequence or not. I do not claim that I have always acted wisely; and if I have erred, remember the surrounding circumstances, and then judge indulgently. If I have assisted the return of peace, by bearing faithfully my part in the burden of the war, I have accomplished the purpose for which I enlisted.

The war is now over. The flag of our country again proudly floats over the entire domain. Peace, prosperity, and the pursuit of happiness have taken the place of deadly strife. In place of cultivating the art of war, we are now cultivating commerce and friendly intercourse. In a few years the blackened track of contending armies will smile with luxuriant harvests.

We have the satisfaction of knowing that American liberty still exists; that the institutions inaugurated by the hardships and sufferings of our fathers, baptized with their blood, and consecrated by their prayers, are renewed and perpetuated. The principles that they struggled to maintain still live.

The fires of patriotism that were kindled in the bosoms and burned in flames of heroic valor at Lexington, Bunker Hill, Saratoga, and Yorktown still burn in the bosoms of their children's children, and have burst forth in glorious illuminations of valor upon such fields as Donelson, Vicksburg, Antietam, Atlanta, and Richmond.

The heroes of this war have proved themselves worthy of their ancestry, and have baptized and consecrated anew their precious inheritance by giving of their best blood for its maintenance.

Never were prayers more devoutly and fervently uttered, never was blood more freely spilled, never was treasure more extensively lavished, or individual sacrifice more cheerfully borne, than in the war from which we have just emerged.

Our children's children will look back upon our deeds of valor and sacrifice with the same feelings of respect that we cherish for the fathers of the Revolution, and the institutions which we have perpetuated will be doubly dear to them for the second sacrifice that they have cost.

Let us then watch carefully the treasures of liberty, and so use them as to invoke the smiles of Almighty God upon our sacred trust. Let us acknowledge his directing hand, and, by strict integrity and adherence to the principles of truth, prove ourselves worthy of the trust that we have received. Then will millions yet unborn rise up and thank the God of their fathers that by us our country has been saved.

www.ingramcontent.com/pod-product-compliance
Lightning Source LLC
Chambersburg PA
CBHW050849300426
44111CB00010B/1192